FRENCH LITERATURE SERIES

Since 1974 the French Literature Series has been published in conjunction with the annual French Literature Conference, sponsored by the Department of Languages, Literatures, and Cultures of the University of South Carolina, Columbia, South Carolina, USA. In addition to the scholarly papers selected for publication by the Editorial Board, it also accepts notes on the conference topic.

The conference, which is scheduled for the end of March or beginning of April each year, focuses on a pre-announced topic. The deadline for submitting conference papers is November 1; for scholarly notes, the following May 1. Submissions should be prepared according to the MLA Handbook and should not exceed fifteen pages (25 lines per page, double-spacing, with ample margins). Reading time at the Conference is limited to twenty minutes. Scholarly notes should not exceed eight pages. Authors should submit two copies of their contribution, accompanied by return postage if they wish their paper to be returned.

The essays appearing in the *French Literature Series* are drawn primarily from the Conference papers. Authors are informed of the inclusion of their papers in the volume when their papers are accepted for the Conference. Exceptionally, *FLS* does publish outstanding contributions from authors not participating in the Conference. To be considered for inclusion in the volume, such essays should not exceed twenty typed pages. A style sheet is available upon request or online at <http://www.cas.sc.edu/dllc/fren/Events.Activities/flc/Style%20guide.pdf>.

All communications concerning the Conference should be addressed to the Conference Director, and those concerning the *French Literature Series* to the Editor, Department of Languages, Literatures, and Cultures, University of South Carolina, Columbia, SC, 29208, USA.

The *French Literature Series* is published by Editions Rodopi. Communications concerning standing orders or purchase of individual volumes or back volumes should be addressed to:

Editions Rodopi B.V.
Tijnmuiden 7
1046 AK Amsterdam-Holland
The Netherlands
Tel.: 31 (0) 20 611 48 21
Fax: 31 (0) 20 447 29 79
Internet: <http://www.rodopi.nl>
info@rodopi.nl

USA/Canada:
248 East 44th Street
2nd floor
New York, NY 10017
USA
Tel: 1-800-225-3998
Fax: 1-800-853-3881

Future Volumes and Conference Topics
French Psychoanalysis and Psychoanalysis in French:
Language, Literature, Culture (FLS Vol. XXXVIII, 2011)
March 17-19, 2011: The Environment in French and Francophone Literature
and Film — 39th Annual French Literature Conference
<http://www.cas.sc.edu/dllc/fren/Events.Activities/flc/index.html>

FRENCH LITERATURE SERIES

Editor
James Day

Editorial Board
University of South Carolina

William Edmiston
Freeman G. Henry
Paul Allen Miller
Marja Warehime

Daniela DiCecco
Jeanne Garane
Nancy E. Lane
Jeffery C. Persels

Advisory Board

Michael T. Cartwright
McGill University

Ross Chambers
University of Michigan

Roland Desné
Université de Reims

Ralph Heyndels
University of Miami

Norris J. Lacy
Pennsylvania State University

Gerald Prince
University of Pennsylvania

Pierre Ronzeaud
Université de Provence

Franc Schuerewegen
Univ. d'Anvers / Univ. de Nimègue

Albert Sonnenfeld
University of Southern California

Marie-Odile Sweetser
University of Illinois at Chicago

Ronald W. Tobin
University of California, Santa Barbara

Dirk Van der Cruysse
Universiteit Antwerpen

Le papier sur lequel le présent ouvrage est imprimé remplit les prescriptions de 'ISO 9706: 1994, Information et documentation - Papier pour documents - Prescriptions pour la permanence'.

The paper on which this book is printed meets the requirements of 'ISO 9706: 1994, Information and documentation - Paper for documents - Requirements for permanence'.

An electronic version of this volume is included in print subscriptions. See www.rodopi.nl for details and conditions.

ISBN: 978-90-420-3164-7
E-Book ISBN: 978-90-420-3165-4
©Editions Rodopi B.V., Amsterdam - New York, NY 2010
Printed in The Netherlands

(French Literature Series, Volume XXXVII, 2010)

STEALING THE FIRE
Adaptation, Appropriation, Plagiarism, Hoax

in French and
Francophone Literature
and Film

Edited by
James Day

Amsterdam – New York, NY 2010

From the Editor

This volume of *FLS* originated with the peer-reviewed submissions selected for our thirty-seventh French Literature Conference. The studies were multifarious: parody in Flaubert, the complexities of the Afro-French literature market, theatrical and cinematic adaptations, allegations of plagiarism, Heidegger's influence on Senghor, parodic invention in a twelfth-century courtly tale, Olivier Cadiot's readings of Daniel Defoe and Gilles Deleuze, mystifications involving names such as Émile Ajar, Paul Pavlowitch, and Romain Gary. The volume is anchored by the substantial essay contributed by Hélène Maurel-Indart, "Literary Plagiarism."

Acknowledgment goes also to the editorial board, which determined final rankings after providing at least two blind evaluations of each submission. In cases where special expertise was required, our international advisory board stood ready to provide counsel. Both the annual conference and *FLS* are indebted to the Department of Languages, Literatures, and Cultures, to the program in Comparative Literature, and to the College of Arts and Sciences of the University of South Carolina for their generous support.

Erratum: The name of Jeanne Garane should have appeared as coeditor of the 2009 volume of *FLS* devoted to translation.

James Day

Contents

Literary Plagiarism
Hélène Maurel-Indart   1

Plagiat, négriat littéraire et institution littéraire
Awa C. Sarr   17

Senghor and Heidegger:
Negritude's Appropriation of German Phenomenology
Roxanna Curto   27

Sentimental *Invraisemblance* and Post-revolutionary
French Identity: Three Parodies of *Misanthropie et repentir*
Patrick D. Murphree   43

L'originalité du plagiat
Fayçal Falaky   59

Purloined Property: A Study of Madame Reybaud's *Les Épaves*
and Its Theatrical Adaptation, *Le Marché de Saint-Pierre*
Barbara T. Cooper   73

Call Me Clara: Prosper Mérimée's Hoax Ethos
Corry Cropper   89

Le Muséum de Bouvard et Pécuchet:
Parodie, kitsch et ruine du musée moderne
Bertrand Bourgeois   99

Quand les *topoi* ne sont plus les mêmes:
d'*Ipomédon* de Hue de Rotelande
Paola Scarpini   113

Un texte en cache-t-il un autre?
Le palimpseste chez Marie Darrieussecq
Nora Cottille-Foley 129

Copycat, Copycat: The Anxiety of Influence in *Irma Vep*
Trae DeLellis 141

Le goût des autres d'Agnès Jaoui: de l'adaptation
de P. Bourdieu au cinéma à sa subversion
Patricia Reynaud 157

Non-readings, Misreadings, Unreadings:
Deleuze and Cadiot on *Robinson Crusoe* and Capitalism
Nathalie Wourm 177

L'homme qui racontait des histoires: Paul Pavlowitch
Corinne François-Denève 191

Erratum... Errata... Erasum...: The Selection of Sources
for Raymond Queneau's *Le Chiendent*
Alexander Hertich 205

"Cette nouvelle réalité": at the *Mouviez* with Raymond Queneau
Peter Sorrell 215

Hélène Maurel-Indart

Université de Tours

Literary Plagiarism

> The notion of literary plagiarism is at the heart of the process of writing, even if the meaning of the term "plagiarism" varies according to the period. First, we must specify the meaning and the context of this notion from ancient times to the present, choosing examples from among the most famous writers. For the contemporary period, it is necessary to highlight the reasons why plagiarism has not disappeared, in spite of copyright law. Economic and cultural elements can explain this phenomenon. The Paul Celan-Yvan Goll case is a perfect yet tragic illustration of all the crucial questions that literary creation, originality, and plagiarism can raise.

Is the notion of literary plagiarism not a contradiction in terms? Usually, plagiarism is taken to be writing without literary value, mere copying that is devoid of personality and style. The plagiarist is a usurper who steals someone else's work and signs it with his own name. From this point of view, it is distinguished from a forgery, which is its opposite: the forger produces a new work by faithfully imitating the stylistic characteristics of the work of an author whose signature he is stealing. The forger's purpose is to give his work a value that his own signature would not have guaranteed. The plagiarist's purpose is to give himself value by pretending to be the author of a work he has stolen. A further element to characterise plagiarism: the writer of pastiches has something in common with the forger inasmuch as the signature of the writer he has pastiched comes through into his work, which is pure imitation. But he also has points in common with the plagiarist through the distance he attempts to maintain from his model. Nevertheless, the intention is different in the case of pastiche and plagiarism: while the plagiarist cleverly disguises the original text by seeking to hide his misdemeanour and make us forget his source, the author of pastiches signals to the reader, through over-wrought stylistic devices, that a game is being played. He does not intend to steal the work, as does the plagiarist, or steal the author's signature, as does the forger. The author of pastiches is not a cheat but a prankster.

Such comparisons with these more or less genuine literary prac-tises show that plagiarism cannot be excluded from reflection on literary creation. Plagiarism remains a point of interest or even an ob-session for some authors, including the most traditional. Giraudoux's famous quotation springs to mind: "Plagiarism is the basis of all liter-ary expression, except the first, which is in fact unknown" (*Siegfried* I, 6). More seriously, Proust was fully aware that the influence or even the hold some writers had over his work could lead to plagiarism, to servile replication. He recommended that one should consciously practise pastiche in order to "purge oneself of the natural vice of idolatry and imitation" in order to avoid it.[1] The idea of plagiarism cannot therefore be put aside when considering the process of literary creation. Literature is made of borrowings, whether servile or creative. From this standpoint, the dream of absolute originality is pure illusion and stems from an idealistic but oversimplified concept of literature. But what is the limit between servile and creative borrowing? What criterion will assess the originality of a text, which necessarily draws its substance from a common wealth of ideas and is subjected to the influence of its predecessors? The systematic reproduction of a text hijacked by a plagiarist is very uncommon. Demarcation, for the pur-pose of hiding the crime, already makes use of literary transformation processes: synonyms, additions, deletions, changes in rhythm or syn-tax. Is this plagiarism or is it already another text? The criteria of appreciation have evolved through history. A tradition of imitation dominated until the seventeenth century. The concept of literary prop-erty does not occur before the eighteenth century, and the concept of a unique and original creative persona only occurs with the Romantics. Nowadays, studies on intertextuality show that works are like palimp-sests, on which texts are superimposed *ad infinitum*. Plagiarism is now part of the aesthetics of rewriting, which as a result is freed of all moral connotation to become a real literary question.

---

[1] Proust, vol. XVIII, août 1919 (À Ramon Fernandez), 380; my translation.

It will first be shown that the term *plagiarism* has different meanings according to the period. It varies according to the concept of the creative process that existed at this or that period. Attention will then be drawn to a few contemporary examples of plagiarism, in order to establish what is meant nowadays by literary creation. To what extent do literary institutions and laws concerning intellectual property entitle the author to use the work of other writers? What criteria make it possible to distinguish between the authentic author and the usurper? After this attempt to clarify the concept of plagiarism, I will take a look into those abysses where writers, caught between the difficulty of telling and the temptation of retelling, often mislead their readers. The case study of Yvan Goll and Paul Celan will illustrate the differences between truth and lies.

The meaning of *plagiarism* varies according to the period

The term *plagiarism* itself was misconstrued until the eighteenth century. It was long believed that word thieves were sentenced to whipping in Roman times in accordance with the law *Fabia de plagiariis*. Even Voltaire affirms this in his *Dictionnaire philosophique*. This mistake is due to an etymological misinterpretation: *plagiarism* is derived from the Greek *plagios*, meaning oblique, cunning, and not from the Latin *plaga*, meaning a blow. In Rome, the *Fabia de plagiariis* law was applied to those who, by their cunning (*plagios*), kidnapped children, free men, or slaves, but the law was not applied to thieves of words... Martial, the Roman poet, was probably the first to use the term *plagiarius* in its figurative sense. Considering his verses as his children, stolen by a certain Fidentinus, he called the thief a plagiarist. Martial's metaphor led to the belief that the term *plagiarist* already existed in Rome in its modern meaning. Indeed, the Ancients had no laws covering literary property. Victims could only resort to satire or epigrams... Well before La Fontaine's "Le Geai paré des plumes du paon,"[2] Horace used Aesop's fable to denounce the borrowings made by a certain Celsus Albinovanus. He issued a warning to the writers of his century, urging them to make do with their own property and to avoid the humilation of being found to have appropriated the ideas of others.

---

[2] *Fables*, IV, 9.

In the Middle Ages, book manufacturing and trade were mainly carried on by the monasteries. "Monks were in effect in turn scribes, learned men and authors" (Dock 57). The critic Michel Schneider warns against misinterpreting the idea of copying at that period: "it would be quite anachronistic to assimilate copying with plagiarism" (40). Imitation had a spiritual role, and Christian faith had no authors, only prophets.

A great change occurred with the invention of printing in 1436 and that of paper in 1440. Printing put books within every man's reach and made it as easy to plagiarise as to denounce plagiarism. In defence of the plunderers, it must be said that the sixteenth century's rediscovery of Antiquity conveniently provided rich booty for writers. The works of the Ancients were even considered as references: a writer in the sixteenth or seventeenth century wrote under the authority of Homer, Virgil, or Seneca. It was inconceivable to write a new work that did not pay tribute to the Greeks and the Romans.

In that light, Rabelais and Montaigne's well-known borrowings belong more to what could be termed creative plundering. Indeed, one example of Rabelais's flagrant copying from a contemporary source should be mentioned, no matter how incriminating, and all the more so as it concerns a saucy passage in *Pantagruel* of schoolboyish dog-Latin:

Rabelais, *Pantagruel*, chapitre VI (1532)	Geoffroy Tory,[3] *Le Champfleury*, chapitre VI (1529)
Nous transfretons la Sequane au dilucule et crepuscule: nous deambulons par les compites et quadrivies de l'urbe, nous despumons la verbocination latiale, et, comme verisimiles amorabonds, captons la benevolence de l'omnijuge, omniforme, et omnigene sexe feminin.	Despumons la verbocination latiale et transfretons la Sequane au dilucule et crepuscule puis deambulons par les quadrives et platées de Lutece, et, comme verisimiles amorabondes, captivons la benivolence de l'omnigene et uniforme sexe feminin.

But perhaps it was not so original — just a very common usage at this period between students. Montaigne, on the other hand, was the perfect humanist, blending the most diverse sources into his work. A quotation more or less disguised or admitted was an homage paid to

---

[3] Printer to François Ier, editor, engraver and author of the renowned *Livre d'heures*.

the Ancients, a reference to authority, or a decorative motif, but nothing was to be a substitute for his own words:

> Certes, j'ay donné à l'opinion publique que ces parements empruntez m'accompaignent. Mais je n'entends pas qu'ils me couvrent et qu'ils me cachent [...].
>
> (*I have given the public to think that these borrowed words accompany me. But I do not intend that they cover or hide me* [...].)

The seventeenth century continued in the same vein as the sixteenth. The great writers of the *Grand Siècle* plagiarised in abundance. Should they be exposed? Yes, but prudently, for the plagiarist is not always the person suspected. It is said, for instance, that Cyrano de Bergerac's *Le Pédant joué* supplied Molière with one of his best scenes for the *Fourberies de Scapin*: his *"Que diable aller faire dans la galère d'un Turc!"* hammered out three times is said to have become Molière's *"Que diable allait-il faire dans cette galère?"*. But this borrowing, which is Molière's best known, is in fact not one! Roland de Chaudenay revealed this in his *Dictionnaire des plagiaires*:

> Molière and Cyrano studied together at Gassendi's. Molière already had his *'que diable allait-il faire dans cette galère?'* in mind and all the dramatic intrigue to spice it up. He spoke of it. Cyrano, who had a nose for such things, took note and Molière went off on tour. The *Pédant joué* was staged in 1654. The Turk and his galley appeared in Act II, scene 4.

And so Molière was only quoting himself in *Les Fourberies de Scapin,* act II, scene 11.

With the French Revolution came the notion of individual property, and so unpunished borrowing disappeared. The eighteenth century saw the rise of the individual, who claimed his right to the ownership of his work. A fine example of this period is Rousseau, who dreamt of an individuality that would assert itself in an original, unique fashion: "I have entered upon a performance which is without example, whose accomplishment will have no imitator" (Rousseau 1). The beginning of the *Confessions* expresses his aspiration to write "a text devoid of any intertextuality, before or after" (Lejeune 13, my trans.).

However, the French Enlightenment was not exempt from plagiarism. Fréron, with true crusading zeal, published a summary of Diderot's *Fils naturel* that was a verbatim copy of Goldoni's *Vero Amico*. Diderot was racked with guilt. Moral censure intensified, prefiguring the constitution of literary property to be established by the *Convention*. Paradoxically, in the nineteenth century plagiarism increased. Literature had become a trade, a means to social and commercial success. One only has to turn to Balzac's complaints about Belgian forgeries and his claims to literary property. The writer stresses that printing, newspapers, and advertising have put books within the means of everyone. "From then on, book sales became a lucrative business" (my trans.).[4] Until the early twentieth century, plagiarism was a literary phenomenon present in each period. The eighteenth century laws on literary property failed to eradicate it. How do matters stand nowadays in a regulated state where all are supposed to be cognizant of the law?

Current literary plagiarism affairs

Plagiarism affairs today are part of the literary news. There are three main reasons for this: the first is legal, because the current French code on intellectual property states that plagiarism is a crime, equivalent to forgery. The second is economic: books are a mass-consumption product, subject to the usual constraints of free enterprise, and plagiarism is no doubt encouraged by escalating demands for cost-effective publishing; writing hurriedly for a target audience, certain authors, seeking quick and easy success, find it difficult to resist financial opportunity. In using researchers, ghostwriters, and all kinds of other subcontractors, the author signs a work over whose contents he does not have complete control. Temptation is all the stronger as plagiarism is increasingly difficult to detect. This leads to the third, cultural, aspect. Which reader today can claim to have a universal knowledge of everything published? One gets lost in the immense overproduction of books whose quality is as varied as their subject matter — essays, novels, all manner of documents. Petty theft is easy. The plagiarist, despite his awareness of the risks he is taking in a soci-

---

[4] *Notes* given to the MPs of the commission on the *Propriété littéraire* law (3 mars 1841), in *Œuvres complètes de Honoré de Balzac, Œuvres diverses III,* (1836-1848), Paris, Louis Conard, 1940, p. 423; my trans.

ety where intellectual property is protected by law, banks on the fragmentation of readers' cultural references in order to abuse them.

Such cultural and commercial reasons explain the growing number of plagiarism court cases since the 1980s. A new phenomenon is that authors who feel they have been plagiarised no longer hesitate to litigate. Since the year 2000, the authors of several novels have been charged with forgery on account of plagiarism. Alain Minc's romanced biography, *Spinoza, un roman juif*, and Michel Le Bris's narrative, *D'or, de rêves et de sang, l'épopée de la flibuste*, have both been considered as partial plagiarisms by the judges. On the other hand, complaints concerning Marc Lévy's novel, *Et si c'était vrai...* and Chimo's *Lila dit ça*, were thrown out by the courts. The latter case leads us to the crucial matter of documentary sources. On February 21, 2001, the Paris court of appeals judged that Chimo's *Lila dit ça* legally used "the materials and the cultural elements" collected by Michel Decugis and Aziz Zemouri in their 1995 study entitled *Paroles de banlieues*. The judge established a precise distinction between "information they had collected and then 'rewritten' or set out using a personal method" — this being protected by the law on intellectual property — and "the words uttered by interviewees and reproduced with quotation marks [...], without demonstrating that they had, in a personal or creative manner, rewritten them" (trans. mine). Any such raw material could be freely used in Chimo's novel.

The decision of the Paris court of appeal, which dismissed the accusation of forgery, reasonably favours the free use of documentary elements collected by researchers. Consequently, a novelist who wishes to create an effect of authentic local colour, to enhance the background of his or her novel, may use material from specialised works without authorisation, unless they are analyses or reconstructions that bear the author's personal stamp. The judge has to distinguish between protecting the researcher's intellectual investment and the writer's freedom to use pre-existing documentation.

More generally, great care must be taken when judging influence in literary matters. Rivalry, inevitable susceptibilities, and fashion phenomena — the flavour of the month, so to speak — must not be overlooked before making humiliating accusations. Judges are aware of this and take into account the random way in which ideas flow and are set down. Each period has its specific culture, its shared readings, and the unavoidable convergence of certain literary references. Since the twentieth century, the concepts of collage, play in writing, and intertextuality have required that the concept of "originality" be revised.

But one fact is known to all and contributes not a little to the mistrust and derision that the general public feels when confronted with so many affairs of plagiarism: financial considerations often take precedence over the more "worthy" ethical ones. In this age of productivity in the book industry, the consequences on the writer's "creative" work can well be imagined. A new publishing strategy intended to enhance commercial success was established in the 1920s; the initiative inevitably raised questions of literary legitimacy. Bernard Grasset, a publisher, was no doubt the first to realize the extent to which a publisher's immense powers could be used. All options were considered in marketing an author: reliance on personal relations, overstating the print run and sales, and, above all, pressure exerted on critics who could make or break the literary stars, such as members of the Académie and writers who determined literary prizes. It is in this light that the new forms of plagiarism and the plagiarists' motivations should be read.

Aware of these market factors, some authors succumb to the temptation of plagiarism and churn out quickly written "profitable" books. The public's taste for historical biographies, for instance, has been thoroughly tapped since the 1980s. Reputed writers have been solicited by publishing houses to meet this demand. Paul Guth's grotesque plagiarism, the narrative *Moi, Ninon de Lenclos, courtisane*, published by Albin Michel in 1991, is a case in point. The work by this renowned contemporary author had, of course, many more readers than the biography of the same *Ninon de Lenclos*, published in 1984 by Fayard and written by Roger Duchêne, a seventeenth-century specialist and professor at the University of Provence. Professor Duchêne, no stranger to archives or manuscripts, carried out extensive research for his book. Paul Guth merely went to the nearest corner bookstore and purchased Duchêne's book, after which he not only imitated the way the whole narrative unfolds — which might be excusable for the inevitable chronology of a biography — but also relied on quotations, references, and chunks of text (see the issue of *Lire* n° 196). The first chapters attempt a somewhat less servile adaptation, but then the writer quickly lapses into a mode that never quotes its source. Henri Troyat was equally culpable with his biography, *Juliette Drouet*, which was excessively inspired by Gérard Pouchain and Robert Sabourin's biography, entitled *Juliette Drouet ou la Dépaysée*.

A clear position must be adopted: in an era where everybody is ready to claim his or her right of property, in any field, why should anyone be offended that an author be compelled to recognise another's contribution? How does that impede creative freedom? Indeed, the interest of the literary community resides in mutual respect and paying homage to one's peers. Most writers know this and resist temptation, but for a certain number, inspiration, painstaking development, the rewriting process, and the pursuit of originality are just so many obstacles from a commercial point of view. The idea of authorship has become so assimilated with a brand name that it has completely blotted out the idea of what a work of art is. It's not the author that matters, but his works! And the more self-effacing the author is as a person, the more his works are held in esteem. The copyright system aims to protect creative works in order to prevent plundering, whatever the fame of the author may be or the commercial success of his or her writings.

Literary works are protected by the intellectual property code

First of all, plagiarism is legally likened to forgery. According to the *Code de la propriété intellectuelle* — a series of laws dating from March 11, 1957 to July 3, 1985 — literary property is defined as any of the prerogatives, whether intellectual or financial, ascribed to the authors of intellectual works. The writing of the *Code* took quite a long time. Judges found it extremely difficult to ascribe the idea of property to something that was not physically tangible and to be able to sell books while remaining the owner of the work. Usually, property rights "suppose an *extraneous link* between the possessor of an object and the object possessed" (Edelman 35; trans. mine). But in the case of intellectual works, a new category of non-material and intellectual property had to be invented so the work could become a possession without being a "thing."

Intellectual property is now recognised more or less worldwide. But there are two very different concepts of it: Anglo-Saxon *copyright*, mainly in the United States and in Great Britain on the one hand, and the *droit d'auteur* (author's rights) on the other, as enforced in France or in Germany and most other European countries. This is not just a difference in terminology. The respective expressions point to different underlying philosophies: *copyright* is the right to copy, an investment right, which favours the publisher. The link between the work and the author is therefore weakened. The *droit d'auteur* is the right of the author who exerts over his property both a pecuniary and an intellectual right. It is the author who decides if and how his work is published; "he may oppose any deformation or prejudice to his work," says a German law dating from September 9, 1965, and amended by the law of September 1, 2000. The *droit d'auteur* is perceived as being very protective. But certain free-market principles seriously impede the extent of the protection. First, law distinguishes between form and content, and excludes ideas from protection. Henri Desbois further states that

> whatever the ingenuity, even bearing the stamp of true genius, the propagation and exploitation of ideas expressed by others cannot be contradicted by the servitudes inherent to the *droits d'auteur*. They are by essence and by destination of a free nature. (*Le Droit d'auteur en France* 11)

It is only the organisation of ideas and their expression that are protected. Take the following example from the fine arts. The "Christo" case illustrates the frontier between the idea, which cannot be protected, and its individual expression, which can. Several court decisions have recognised that the *Pont-Neuf* as wrapped by Christo is a protected work; on the other hand, the Paris District Court decided that the artist could not have the monopoly of "artistic wrapping" as an author's right, and thereby prevent an advertising agency from printing posters that showed objects wrapped "in the Christo manner."

In practise, it is often difficult to distinguish between the non-protectable idea and its expression, which is protectable. The protection of expression is not just a matter of the literal reproduction of expression. Legal scholars have pointed out that it would take relatively few alterations for someone to lose possession of his or her intellectual work. Consequently, a distinction must be made between significant differences, which distinguish a copy from the original, and trivial differences, whose purpose is more to cheat and cover up plagiarism.

Maurel-Indart

Expression and order of ideas are two of the main criteria that enable one to appreciate a work of art. But with regard to the law, what is originality? "What is original is the result of a creation of the mind, which bears the 'stamp of its author's personality'" (Gautier 44). Nevertheless, how can "the stamp of an author's personality" be recognized? By examining the work's form, its composition and expression. The question of forgery is central to aesthetic judgement and literary criticism.

It was for this reason that I classified forms of borrowing in *Du Plagiat*. Different forms of rewriting make up this typology: quotation, memory, passing reference, allusion, adaptation, parody, or pastiche, to cite only those that are the most subject to debate and confusion. In addition to quantitative criteria (i.e., total or partial borrowings) and qualitative criteria (i.e., direct borrowing or transformation), I also took into account a psychological criterion whose purpose is to determine the intentional quality of the borrowing. Was it deliberate or unconscious? Forgery is presumed to be intentional. But might the plagiarist not claim it was a quirk of memory and present his borrowing as involuntary? The extent of the memory would have to be limited in order for the claim to be credible. The plagiarist, in bad faith, might also turn to another alibi: he forgot to use quotation marks. A fourth criterion gives the analysis greater reliability: the second work should be checked to see whether the borrowing is hidden or explicitly signalled as such by the author. For example, consider the difference between an authorised pastiche and an alibi-pastiche. The former displays a reference model in a more or less amusing fashion, using humorous phrases such as "a carbon copy of [...]," or "written in close collaboration with [...]." The latter, on the contrary, makes covert use of someone else's stylistic characteristics.

Thus, Régine Deforges, while making a supposedly humorous passing reference to Margaret Mitchell, in fact lifts entire, scarcely modified, passages from her work. For instance, in *Gone with the Wind*, one reads: "she walked out of the room with such dignity as she could summon and banged the heavy door behind her" (120). Here is what it becomes in *La Bicyclette bleue*: "Summoning up all the dignity she could, Léa went out, banging the door behind her" (trans. mine). The demarcation she makes from the original is all too easy.

Originality in literature is a fragile and volatile concept. The enunciator, as centre and origin of his own discourse, must not forget this: he is at the centre of other works, at the crossroads of an organised field, the

> cultural field in which I must find my words and my syntax, a historical field in which I must read while writing. The structure of theft is already embedded in the relationship between speech and language. The word is stolen. (Derrida 265, trans. mine)

According to Derrida, inspiration, the guarantee of originality, is a "drama of theft." Hence, "what one calls the talking subject is not the same or the only one who is talking. He discovers himself in an irreducible secondariness, an origin always already stolen from the field of speech" (265, trans. mine). The sad case of plagiarism between Paul Celan and Yvan Goll's widow is an unusual illustration of this "drama of theft."

The Goll-Celan case

In *Paul Celan-Die Goll-Affäre*, Barbara Wiedemann explores in minute detail the stages in this drama, which may well have driven Paul Celan to suicide. Already in 1949, Yvan Goll was very close to his young admirer and disciple, a Jew of Romanian origin. A poet from Lorraine, Goll first wrote in German, then in French. He therefore asked Celan to translate his *Chansons malaises* into German. But on his death in 1950, his wife Claire wished to do the translation work herself and have exclusivity for Goll's work. She opposed the publication of Celan's translation of the *Chansons malaises*. She claimed his translation was only an approximation. Celan suspected Claire Goll of wanting to use his work to her own ends. A sordid affair of plagiarism then burst out, used in turn by each of the two rival translators to take revenge on the other. To definitively discredit Celan, who had voiced his suspicions to Claire, she had an article published in the German press, with false comparisons between Goll's and Celan's poems: "All the verse [from Celan's book *Mohn und Gedächtnis*] was taken from Yvan's French works, which remain unknown in Germany" (Wiedemann 187, my trans. from the German).

Barbara Wiedemann unravels the accusation of plagiarism. The resemblance between certain metaphors, such as "flowers of ash" and

Maurel-Indart

"mask of ash" or "necklace of hands" and "necklace of larks" can be explained, according to her, by the fact that these images come from the hermetic register of expressionist poetry. In this case, should there be talk of plagiarism, or of poetic inspiration, or even of paying a tribute? Fault can also be found with dates quoted by Claire Goll. She accuses Celan of having "almost literally" transcribed a whole line from the poem "The Mill of Death" in the collection of poems *Magic Circles*. But it is most likely, after investigation, that the book came after Celan's. Claire Goll simply wished to discredit Celan completely. As final proof of her bad faith, Barbara Wiedemann published an article by Richard Exner, a young German poet, on whose word Claire Goll's accusation was based. However, the article, written after the publication of the press release, tried to minimise the plagiarism: "[Celan] has the greater heritage and a great talent for composition. Unveiling influences does not mean lessening" (Wiedemann 203; my trans. from the German). Claire Goll refused to publish the letter in the press, judging it too indulgent. And the falsehood continued: once the rift between Celan and her was definitive, Claire Goll never stopped altering Yvan's text. This is what Francis Carmody denounced in an anthology of Goll's poems published in Paris, *The Poetry of Yvan Goll*, in 1956. In April of 1955, this is what he wrote:

> Dear Claire,
> I suspect you of fraud, the variations between the different copies of the unpublished "Jean sans terre" poems are not due to typing errors! If there are any deletions or changes made in Yvan's hand, I strongly maintain that they must be indicated in the notes; I see you have yet again deleted a quatrain from a poem. (*idem*, 712; original text in French)

Claire's answer gives an idea of her delirious state of mind:

> Dear Francis,
> Fraud? Yvan always asked my opinion before giving out a definitive version of his poems. You know how Memnon's bust sang. Well, before I modify a poem, I always consult Yvan's bust, which stands on my chest of drawers, and he talks to me, inspires me, and allows me to make the necessary changes to strophes, or to delete a less good line. (*idem*, 713)

It even seems that she made alterations to Goll's text so that it was identical to Celan's. Her appetite for falsification enabled her to

14 **FLS, Vol. XXXVII, 2010**

later attack Celan for his so-called plagiarism. A letter from the young Romanian dated the 27th of June, 1956, testifies to this manoeuvring:

> I nevertheless know, for having seen it with my own eyes, that Claire Goll does not hesitate to "change" what does not suit her taste; and the probability that her own taste weighs a lot since she invented the plagiarism lie has considerably increased (*idem*, 232).

As the case study established by Barbara Wiedemann shows, if there is indeed a "Goll-Celan case," it is in fact a case of falsifying manuscripts and of libel against Paul Celan. Literature became prey to a would-be writer, hungry for recognition, and yet unable to assert herself as the equal of her husband, Yvan Goll. Lies, falsifications, and plagiarism are signs of her pathological delirium, which only served to disfigure two equally original works, those of Goll, the master, and of Celan, the disciple.

What, then, defines an authentic work? The myth of creation that is supposed to emanate from a unique and well-identified author falls to pieces when confronted with a text's reality, repeated *ad infinitum* by writers who inevitably draw from their own readings, but are nevertheless haunted by their striving for originality and literary recognition. The drama of writing is enacted in either a playful or a tragic mode. The Oulipiens treat plagiarists humorously by inventing the concept of anticipated plagiarism. Others, such as Malcolm Lowry, who was obsessed by the fear of plagiarism, sacrifice their lives on the altar of originality:

> Crawling on hands and sinews to the grave
> I found certain pamphlets on the way.
> Said they were mine.

Works Cited

Birney, Earle, ed. *Selected Poems of Malcolm Lowry*. San Francisco: City Lights Books, 1985.

Carmody, Francis J. *The Poetry of Yvan Goll*. Paris: Caractères, 1956.

Chaudenay, Roland de. *Dictionnaire des plagiaires*. Paris: Perrin, 1990.

Chimo. *Lila dit ça*. Paris: Plon, 1996.

Decugis, Michel, and Aziz Zemouri. *Paroles de banlieues*. Paris: Éditions Plon, 1995.

Deforges, Régine. *La Bicyclette bleue*. Paris: Ramsey, 1981.

Derrida, Jacques. *L'écriture et la différence*. Paris: Seuil, 1967. Points.

Desbois, Henri. *Le Droit d'auteur en France*. Paris: Dalloz, 1978.

Dock, M.-C. *Contribution historique à l'étude du droit d'auteur*. Paris: Librairie générale de droit et de jurisprudence, 1962.

Edelman, Bernard. *La Propriété littéraire et artistique*. Paris: P.U.F., 1989. Que sais-je?

Gautier, Pierre-Yves. *Propriété littéraire et artistique*. Paris: PUF, 1991.

Giraudoux, Jean. *Siegfried*. Paris: Grasset, 1928.

Le Bris, Michel. *D'or, de rêves et de sang, l'épopée de la flibuste*. Paris: Hachette, 2001. Littératures.

Lejeune, Philippe. *Les Brouillons de soi*. Paris: Seuil, 1998.

Lévy, Marc. *Et si c'était vrai...* Paris: Robert Laffon, 2000.

Maurel-Indart, Hélène. *Du Plagiat*. Paris: P.U.F., 1999.

Minc, Alain. *Spinoza, un roman juif*. Paris: Gallimard, 1999.

Mitchell, Margaret. *Gone with the Wind*. 1936. New York: Macmillan, 1942.

Pouchain, Gérard, and Robert Sabourin. *Juliette Drouet ou La dépaysée*. Paris: Fayard, 1992.

Proust, Marcel. *Correspondance*. Ed. Philip Kolb. 21 vols. Paris: Plon, 1970-1993.

Rousseau, Jean-Jacques. *Les Confessions*. 1782-89. Trans. S. W. Orson. London: Privately Printed for the Members of the Aldus Society, 1903.

Scherf, Kathleen. *The Collected Poetry of Malcolm Lowery*. Vancouver: University of British Columbia Press, 1992.

Schneider, Michel. *Voleurs de mots, essai sur le plagiat, la psychanalyse et la pensée*. Paris: Gallimard, 1985. Connaissance de l'inconscient.

Troyat, Henri. *Juliette Drouet, la prisonnière sur parole*. Paris: Flammarion, 1997.

Wiedemann, Barbara. *Paul Celan — Die Goll-Affäre*. Frankfurt: Suhrkamp, 2000.

Awa C. Sarr

University of Illinois at Urbana-Champaign

Plagiat, négriat littéraire et institution littéraire

> Des affaires de plagiat et de négriat littéraire, la littérature africaine en langue française en a connues un bon nombre. À travers les exemples de Yambo Ouologuem, de Calixthe Béyala, de Bakary Diallo et de Tony Labou Tansi, nous examinons les liens intrinsèques qui existent dans cette littérature entre pratiques littéraires frauduleuses, couronnements et dépendance littéraire.

"L'affaire Ouologuem" et "l'affaire Calixthe Béyala" sont deux affaires de plagiat très discutées dans la littérature en français de l'Afrique subsaharienne. Le roman du malien Yambo Ouologuem, *Le Devoir de violence,* publié en 1968, fut reçu par la critique africaniste comme une révolution, certains le considérant même comme le premier roman africain digne de ce nom.[1] Le succès d'Ouologuem fut à son comble quand les jurés du deuxième prix le plus prestigieux de France lui décernèrent le Prix Renaudot, qui n'avait alors encore jamais été attribué à un écrivain originaire d'Afrique noire.

Cependant, après cette apothéose, on ne tarda pas à crier au scandale quand il fut découvert, comme le dit Jean-Claude Blachère, qu'Ouologuem avait oublié qu' "à l'instar de l'école, on ne copie pas sur ses petits camarades" (25). L'accusation qu'il avait plagié le *Dernier des justes* d'André Schwarz-Bart, Prix Goncourt en 1959 et *It's a Battlefield* de Graham Greene, mirent fin à sa carrière littéraire.

---

[1] Voir Kasongo Mulenda Kapanga pour plus de détails entre les différences de la critique africaniste et celle africaine de ce roman.

Blachère et d'autres critiques soutinrent que le plagiat d'Ouologuem était partie intégrante de son projet d'écriture puisqu'il s'était donné comme objectif dans son roman de remettre en cause toute idée d'authenticité. La preuve, nous dit Blachère, "il a recopi[é] un prix Goncourt! Plagi[é] un monument mondial de la littérature!", avant de conclure que "cette attitude de transgression est une des composantes du 'devoir' de violence" (205), l'expression faisant écho au titre du roman d'Ouologuem. De même, selon Marilyn Randall, "regardless of the theoretical, historical or social criteria by which one chooses to define 'plagiarism' it is inextricably bound up with the transgression of notions of artistic originality, authenticity, and propriety" (532).

Cependant, Ouologuem n'a cessé de clamer son innocence, affirmant que son éditeur a opéré des transformations non autorisées de son manuscrit, parmi lesquelles la suppression des guillemets qui signalaient la reproduction des passages empruntés. Donc, loin d'avoir envisagé une quelconque subversion de l'institution littéraire, Ouologuem met sur le dos de son éditeur la responsabilité des accusations de plagiat qui lui sont adressées. Ce qui, s'il se trouvait avéré, dévoile les conséquences désastreuses qui peuvent découler du pouvoir d'un éditeur qui se permet de manipuler un texte sans l'autorisation de son auteur. Comme l'a souligné Christopher Wise dans son article "In Search of Yambo Ouologuem" — texte qui détaille les péripéties du voyage que Wise a effectué du Burkina Faso au Mali pour interviewer l'auteur malien pour mieux comprendre les raisons qui l'avaient poussé à abandonner la littérature — la rancœur contre l'institution littéraire française ne saurait seule justifier la démission littéraire d'Ouologuem.

Pourrait-on aussi dire que c'est par devoir de violence que plus d'un quart de siècle après le discrédit de l'auteur malien Calixthe Béyala plagie un roman d'un Chevalier des Arts et Lettres (*Burt* de Howard Buten dans *le Petit Prince de Belleville*) et celui d'un récipiendaire du Booker Prize (*The Famished Road* de Ben Okri)? "L'affaire Béyala" est sans doute l'affaire de plagiat la plus célèbre, la plus tonitruante, la plus discutée et la plus intrigante de toute l'histoire littéraire africaine. Béyala avait été accusée de plagiat à deux reprises et si la deuxième accusation n'a pas atterri au tribunal, la première, par contre, avait été jugée par La Haute cour de justice de Paris, qui avait reconnu Béyala coupable et condamné à payer des dommages et inté-

Awa C. Sarr 19

rêts à Buten et à son éditeur. Cependant, contrairement à Ouologuem, sa carrière ne semble pas avoir souffert de ces épisodes de plagiat. Et si le Prix Renaudot a été décerné à Ouologuem avant la polémique du plagiat, c'est après sa condamnation que l'Académie française lui décerne son prestigieux prix pour *Les Honneurs perdus*, qui ne tarda pas à faire l'objet d'autres accusations de plagiat. Ce qui, comme l'écrit Nicki Hitchcott, "undermines [the] authority [of the institution], throwing into question the very nature of the institution — in this case the French Academy and the book industry in France" (102). S'il faut en croire le jugement de Pascale Casanova, "les rares prix littéraires nationaux qui ont été décernés à des écrivains issus de l'ex-Empire français ou des marges de l'aire linguistique ont bénéficié de considérations néo-coloniales évidentes" (174). Jugement qui semble être corroboré par une partie de la critique africaine qui pense que les consécrations de Paris relèvent souvent de la condescendance.

Ainsi Mongo Béti se demandait si les consécrations d'Ouologuem et de Béyala n'étaient pas pour "conforter la littérature africaine dans la médiocrité et s'abstenir de récompenser d'autres capables d'offrir une image digne de l'Afrique". Ceci pour souligner la complicité de l'institution littéraire parisienne dans le déboire de certains écrivains africains. Béti n'a pas aussi manqué de souligner son indignation quand Albin Michel a renouvelé son contrat avec Béyala après le scandale du plagiat et de soutenir sous un autre angle que si l'auteur du *Devoir de violence* a été primé, c'est parce que "les Français aiment comme le fait Ouologuem qu'on dise qu'en fait, l'esclavage, la traite des Noirs, c'est la faute des Arabes et pas celle des Blancs" (Kom 83). Il nie ainsi que le couronnement soit basé sur des aspects formels comme veulent le faire croire les agents consacrants. Pour notre part, nous disons tout d'abord qu'Ouologuem eut effectivement l'intention de plagier Schwarz-Bart et Greene ou que ce fut la faute de son éditeur; le fait qu'il ait reproduit des œuvres pratiquement connues de tous et donc très probablement des jurés du prix Renaudot, devrait écarter l'alibi de l'ignorance. D'autre part, Hitchcott affirme que l'Académie française savait avant la publication de leur choix que Béyala avait été auparavant condamnée pour plagiat. "According to Assouline", nous dit-elle, "the members of the Academy were, in fact, made aware of the judgement against Beyala in a fax sent to them by a rival publisher before they announced their decision" (103). Il est donc légitime de s'interroger sur les raisons qui ont poussé l'Académie à passer outre cet avertissement. Ne se doutait-elle pas que ceux qui la prévenaient soulèveraient sûrement ce problème si l'auteur d'origine camerounaise venait à être primée? En dehors de l'argument du politiquement-correct — la volonté et le désir de couronner une minorité pour répondre au principe d'universalité que l'institution littéraire française fait sienne — il semble difficile d'en trouver un autre. Cependant, le fait que le représentant de cette minorité soit une plagiaire qui n'a pas recopié le premier ouvrage trouvé mais des œuvres déjà institutionnalisées, révèle ce que Randall appelle "the circularity of the self-invested authority of institutional legitimation" (530) et en quelque sorte, remet en cause la sincérité de la volonté d'inclusion que le politiquement-correct suggère. On voit ainsi à travers ces deux exemples, les liens intrinsèques qui existent dans la littérature en français des écrivains de l'Afrique noire entre plagiat (ou supposé plagiat), couronnement et dépendance littéraires.

Nous voulons maintenant discuter d'une autre forme de fraude littéraire présente dans la littérature africaine depuis ses débuts et jusqu'à nos jours, moins évoquée que le plagiat et pourtant beaucoup plus répandue: la pratique de l'écriture assistée. Contrairement au plagiat — que Randall définit comme "une offense morale et légale" qui met surtout en cause l'originalité, l'authenticité et l'honnêteté du plagiaire et qui rend victime celui ou celle qui est plagié(é) (526) — l'écriture assistée est un cas délicat. Il y a toujours offense morale, mais presque jamais d'offense légale, et on ne sait pas toujours qui est la victime et qui est le bourreau.

L'écriture assistée a une longue tradition en Afrique noire francophone. Elle peut être définie comme la participation dans l'écriture d'une œuvre de fiction d'une personne autre que celle dont le nom figure dans l'ouvrage publié. Alain Ricard soutient que l'un des premiers livres publiés sous le nom d'un Africain de l'Afrique noire, *Force-Bonté* de Bakary Diallo, "représente, à n'en pas douter, la littérature mise sous tutelle, dans laquelle l'auteur est surtout un prête-nom" (229). Mouhamadou Kane a montré dans la préface du livre qui accompagne l'édition de 1987 que Diallo n'a pu en aucun cas écrire l'ouvrage qui porte son nom pour la bonne et simple raison qu'avant de se rendre en France pendant la première guerre mondiale en tant que tirailleur, il était analphabète et n'a pas pu apprendre et maîtriser la langue de Molière pendant la guerre au point d'y composer un ouvrage. Il a donc "dû donner la matière première" du livre, nous dit Alain Ricard, et quelqu'un d'autre l'a écrit. Autrement dit, le contenu de l'ouvrage et les idées qui y sont exprimées lui appartiennent, mais la manière de l'exprimer en français est l'œuvre d'une autre personne, sa marraine française et/ou le directeur de la maison d'édition, l'écrivain Jean-Richard Bloch.

Sur le plan économique, une chose similaire se passait (et se passe encore) en Afrique noire pendant ces années de colonisation où les Africains fournissaient la matière première qui étaient transformée dans l'Hexagone en produits finis. Et de la même manière que l'agriculteur africain producteur d'arachide ou de cacao n'était pas manufacturier, Bakary Diallo, fournisseur de matière première littéraire, n'était pas écrivain. On peut dès lors s'interroger sur le choix d'attribuer la paternité du livre au seul Bakary Diallo. Pour répondre à cette question il faut se tourner vers le contenu du livre, puisque *Force-bonté* est souvent présenté comme un "naïf panégyrique du colonialisme" (Kestloot 21). En effet, un indigène qui fait l'éloge du colonialisme est plus convaincant qu'un colonisateur qui le fait. Guy Ossito Midiohouan rapporte même que les colons donnaient en exemple des écrivains comme Bakary Diallo, Ousmane Socé ou Paul Hazoumé aux *évolués*[2] pour contrecarrer l'influence d'un écrivain engagé tel que Lamine Senghor.

Ainsi, en se positionnant tout simplement en tant que traducteur implicite qu'on devine et non en tant que co-auteur explicite, l'écrivain fantôme de *Force-bonté*, et de manière générale les écrivains fantômes de la période coloniale qui ne pouvaient que traduire, transcrire et faire publier des récits en accord avec l'idéologie coloniale, donnaient à cette dernière les moyens de se légitimer. En ce sens, tout en pouvant théoriquement être considéré comme un nègre littéraire, l'écrivain fantôme n'en était pas moins un agent actif au service de la politique coloniale de son pays. De même, si Bakary Diallo n'est pas seulement entré dans l'histoire littéraire africaine comme l'un des premiers écrivains africains — ce qui pourrait être un honneur — mais aussi classé parmi ceux que Midiohouan appelle les écrivains collaborateurs, il sut, opportunément, bénéficier de sa "collaboration". De

---

[2] L'élite au sein de laquelle se recrutaient les tout premiers écrivains africains.

simple berger peul, puis tirailleur, il devint chef de canton à Podor après la publication de son ouvrage. Plus tard, il fut décoré de la Légion d'honneur. Traître pour les uns et modèle à suivre pour les autres, Bakary Diallo problématise la notion d'auteur et d'écrivain et illustre quelques enjeux de l'écriture assistée durant la période coloniale. Pourtant cette pratique n'a pas disparu avec les indépendances des pays africains.

Un écrivain comme Sony Labou Tansi a été salué, célébré, "adulé" même, selon l'expression de Jean Michel Devésa, parce qu'on croyait et qu'on croit toujours qu'il a contribué au renouvellement de la littérature africaine en faisant du travail de la forme une priorité. Pour Justin Kalulu Bisanswa, c'est avec Labou Tansi que "s'instaure le primat de la forme sur le sens. L'écrivain qui se profile en creux de ses personnages se reconnaît dans un travail formel à la limite de la gratuité" (95). Mahougnon Kakpo nous dit, quant à lui, que

> l'écriture de Sony Labou Tansi, notamment dans *La vie et demie*, où on note une décomposition dans l'organisation esthétique, peut se lire à la lumière des principes du nouveau roman en France depuis le début des années 50. Car l'écriture de Sony Labou Tansi, comme de celle de la plupart des écrivains de cette période, est une réelle expérimentation des formes littéraires, c'est-à-dire ce que Ricardou nomme la volonté de remplacer *l'écriture d'une aventure par l'aventure d'une écriture.* (115)

Les critiques qui se penchent sur l'écriture de Labou Tansi pour en montrer l'originalité et la valeur littéraire abondent. Seulement depuis la publication du livre de Devésa, *Sony Labou Tansi: écrivain de la honte et des rives magiques du Kongo*, une ombre semble s'être abattue sur l'auteur congolais.

Pour Devésa, quiconque veut sérieusement étudier l'œuvre de Labou Tansi devrait se référer aux manuscrits dans la mesure où les textes publiés "[ont] subi des corrections et des remaniements qui, pour correspondre aux normes de l'Académie et à celles de l'édition, n'en conduisent pas moins les chercheurs à débattre inutilement de ce qui n'est plus vraiment la langue de Sony" (113). D'après ses analyses, "Sony Labou Tansi s'est trouvé dans l'obligation de se couler dans le moule des canons littéraires français du moment pour échapper au silence et intégrer le cercle fermé des auteurs célébrés" (112). Lors

Awa C. Sarr

d'un entretien avec Boniface Bongo-Mboussa, Devésa affirme n'être pas le seul à faire cette remarque et cite le critique Mukala Kadima-Nzuji, qui a fait le même constat que lui. À la question de Mongo-Mboussa, qui lui demande s'il ne s'agissait pas de "travail de toilette", il répond que non: il s'agissait d'un "sérieux travail de réécriture" (*Désir d'Afrique* 288-89). Après avoir exprimé son indignation de ces réécritures, qui ont altéré l'écriture de Labou Tansi, il lui trouve des explications. "Si, en 1979" se demande-t-il, "le jeune Sony Labou Tansi inconnu de tous avait refusé ce travail de réécriture, aurait-il néanmoins publié? Quand on sait la difficulté pour un Africain d'être édité, on peut en douter" (289). Par ailleurs, Devésa affirme n'avoir jamais eu l'intention de discréditer l'œuvre de Labou Tansi, qu'il considère comme un ami. Il a seulement

> voulu informer le public. Peut-être pour permettre, demain, aux jeunes auteurs, qu'ils soient ou non africains, de ne plus céder automatiquement aux exigences et aux effets de mode d'une institution éditoriale qui, parfois, même lorsqu'elle prétend défendre l'authenticité d'une voix, cultive un exotisme de bon aloi. (*Désir d'Afrique* 289-90)

Devésa compare par la suite l'aventure de Labou Tansi à celle d'Ouologuem et avertit que "les principaux acteurs de la scène culturelle africaine auraient tort de se voiler la face, de feindre une vertueuse indignation ou de se gausser des mésaventures survenues à ces deux écrivains", puisque tant que les écrivains africains dépendront de l'édition parisienne, ils seront aussi à sa merci (*Désir d'Afrique* 217). On voit ainsi se poser la question de l'autonomie de certains écrivains africains qui, à cause de l'absence d'infrastructures adéquates dans leur pays d'origine et d'un lectorat substantiel, sont confrontés aux lois des institutions littéraires françaises qu'ils doivent souvent accepter au risque de paraître inauthentique, frauduleux même.

En conclusion, nous dirons que les pratiques frauduleuses dans la littérature africaine subsaharienne peuvent s'expliquer en partie par la condition de dépendance littéraire dans laquelle l'Afrique se trouve depuis la période coloniale jusqu'à nos jours. Comme l'ont montré Pierre Bourdieu et Jacques Dubois, l'univers littéraire se plaît à se donner une image sublime qui ne coïncide pas toujours avec la réalité des faits. Ainsi que l'affirme Jean-Pierre Bertrand dans sa préface à la seconde édition de *L'Institution de la littérature* de Dubois, "la littérature [est] à l'instar d'autres secteurs d'activités humaines, un lieu de pouvoir d'autant plus puissant qu'il ne s'avoue jamais comme tel" (13). Et comme le dit Devésa, au lieu de jouer "les cyniques" et de "s'esclaffer" selon l'argument que les fraudes sont monnaie courante dans la littérature africaine et

> que d'autres écrivains que Sony, en Afrique, aux Antilles ou en France, soient dans l'obligation de se plier à ces habitudes de travail pour voir leurs ouvrages publier ne change rien au problème [...]. Aussi est-il grand temps que se fassent entendre tous ceux qui, en Europe et en Afrique, regardent les livres autrement que comme des produits manufacturés (238-39).

Ouvrages cités

Béyala, Calixthe. *Le Petit Prince de Belleville*. Paris: Albin Michel, 1992.

_____. *Les Honneurs perdus*. Paris: Albin Michel, 1996.

Bisanswa, Justin Kalulu. "Littérature et représentation chez Sony Labou Tansi". *Littératures francophones: langues et styles*. Éd. Papa Samba Diop. Paris: L'Harmattan, 2001.

Blachère, Jean-Claude. *Négritures: les écrivains d'Afrique noire et la langue française*. Paris: L'Harmattan, 1993.

Bourdieu, Pierre. *Les Règles de l'art: genèse et structure du champ*. Paris: Seuil, 1992.

Casanova, Pascale. *La République mondiale des lettres.* Paris: Seuil, 1999.

Devésa, Jean-Michel. *Sony Labou Tansi: écrivain de la honte et des rives magiques du Kongo*. Paris: L'Harmattan, 1996.

Diallo, Bakary. *Force Bonté*. Paris: Rieder, 1926.

Dubois, Jacques. *L'Institution de la littérature.* 2ᵉ éd. Bruxelles: Éditions Labor, 2005.

Hitchcott, Nicki. "Calixthe Beyala: Prizes, Plagiarism, and 'Authenticity' ". *Research in African Literatures* 37 (2006): 100-109.

Kakpo, Mahougnon. "La vie et demie. L'Archaïque et le baroque dans le roman négro-africain d'expression française". *Littératures francophones: langues et styles*. Éd. Papa Samba Diop. Paris: L'Harmattan, 2001.

Kapanga, Kasongo Mulenda. "Criticism of the African Novel: a Conflict of Discourse". Diss. Vanderbilt U, 1992.

Kestloot, Lilyan. *Les écrivains noirs de langue française: naissance d'une littérature*. Bruxelles: Institut Solvay, 1963.

Kom, Ambroise. *Mongo Béti parle*. Bayreuth: Bayreuth University Press, 2002.

Midiohouan, Guy Ossito. *Écrire en pays colonisé*. Paris: L'Harmattan, 2002.

Mongo-Moussa, Boniface. *Désir d'Afrique*. Paris: Gallimard, 2002.

Ouologuem, Yambo. *Le Devoir de violence*. Paris: Seuil, 1968.

Randall, Marilyn. "Appropriate(d) Discourse: Plagiarism and Decolonization". *New Literary History* 22 (1991): 525-41.

Ricard, Alain. *Littérature d'Afrique noire: des langues aux livres*. Paris: Karthala, 1995.

Wise, Christopher. "In Search of Yambo Ouologuem". *Research in African Literatures* 29 (1998): 159-82.

Roxanna Curto

Illinois State University

Senghor and Heidegger: Negritude's Appropriation of German Phenomenology

This essay examines the influence of the German philosopher Martin Heidegger on the Senegalese writer and politician Léopold Sédar Senghor. Although Senghor studied Heidegger extensively throughout his life, the fundamental importance of this German philosopher for his work has not been recognized. This essay focuses on how Senghor appropriated Heidegger's ideas about "being-in-the-world" and the detrimental mindset created by technology ("Enframing") in developing his notion of Negritude and the dominance of an emotive perception of reality in black African culture. The final section explores some of the parallels between the politics of the two authors: National Socialism for Heidegger and the African Socialism invented by Senghor.

In the essays of *Liberté 1-5*, Senghor famously denounces discursive reason, which he associates with the West, and defends emotion, which he equates with a black African mode of being, stating: "L'émotion est nègre comme la raison est hellène" (*Liberté 1* 24). This statement is often cited as evidence of Senghor's essentialism and interpreted to mean that Senghor more generally rejects Western philosophy. Nevertheless, Senghor's critique of discursive reason is very much founded in his appropriation of French and German phenomenology, and far from rejecting Western philosophy, Senghor assiduously studied a number European thinkers (such as Nietzsche, Bergson, Sartre, and Heidegger) and embraced many of their ideas. In particular, critics have overlooked the extent to which Senghor's

28   FLS, Vol. XXXVII, 2010

extensive readings of the later Heidegger's writings on art and technology, especially "The Question Concerning Technology," shaped the key concepts of his work: Negritude, technology, and African socialism.

Senghor read the German phenomenologists, especially Martin Heidegger, extensively throughout his life and appropriated many of their ideas in his writings on Negritude. In "Senghor and the Germans," János Riesz writes, "Senghor's relationship to Germany and the Germans marks every phase of his life" (25). In "Négritude et Germanité I" and "II," Senghor states that he was drawn to the German phenomenologists because they described a way of relating to reality that resembled that of African culture, and he identifies himself as a "Negro-African" "qui a toujours été attentif aux Allemands, qui a toujours réagi au contact de leur civilisation" (*Liberté 3* 11, quoted in Riesz). While interned in a German prisoner of war camp from 1940 to 1942, Senghor studied German and spent much of his time reading Heidegger (Bâ 17). Regarding his experience there, he writes: "Et je trouvais chez les Allemands comme des échos aux appels que je lançais dans la nuit: comme les expressions expressives des idées et sentiments ineffables qui s'agitaient dans ma tête, dans mon cœur" (*Liberté 3* 13). After he was freed from the camp in 1942, Senghor continued to immerse himself in the reading of German philosophers, including Heidegger:

> Si, après ma réforme et ma démobilisation en 1942, je me suis plongé, de nouveau, dans les philosophes allemands en commençant par Marx, Engels et Hegel, si, après Sartre, j'ai découvert Heidegger, c'est, sans nul doute, que je sens, même chez les penseurs socialistes, ce *Wirklichkeitsinn* qui est le sceau du génie allemand. (*Liberté 3* 16)

In the only analysis of Senghor's appropriation of Heidegger, Sandra Adell asserts that Senghor

> blindly assumes that Heidegger — through his preoccupation with the relationship between (hu)man, Being, the *logos* and *poësis* — is engaged in a "modern universal humanism" with its emphasis upon the "role and action of Man in and upon the world." (36).

Adell argues that when Senghor claims Negritude has "already responded affirmatively" to this form of humanism, he is grossly misreading Heidegger, who "is concerned with what humanism, as it is articulated in twentieth-century discourses, obscures from man: his *essence* and its relation to the *truth* of Being" (37). Adell concludes, "[i]n accord with Heidegger, then, to think Negritude as a humanism is to further impede the questioning of the relation of Being to the essence of (the black) man" (38). According to her, Heidegger and Senghor's notions of humanism are incompatible, since for Heidegger, humanism is a negative force that blocks the nature of Being from man, while for Senghor, it is a positive entity capable of forming the basis of his utopian "civilisation de l'Universel."

Although Adell is right to point to Heidegger's influence on the notion of humanism that Senghor seeks to develop, her critique of Senghor does not explore the full extent of his use of Heidegger. In fact, a closer reading shows that Senghor advocated the one form of humanism accepted by Heidegger. Heidegger makes a clear distinction in his writings between the traditional humanisms he condemns, which assume a technical interpretation of the world and apply it to man, and the new humanism he would like to forge, which is separated from the instrumental view of reality, and thus more in touch with "Being." In his 1947 "Letter on Humanism," Heidegger writes, "every humanism which conceives man other than belonging to 'being' makes him non-human: only that humanism is true, which sees man as a function of 'being'" ("Letter on Humanism" 217). In order to forge this new kind of humanism, according to Heidegger "we must free ourselves from the technical interpretation of thinking" ("Letter on Humanism" 218). By associating his project with Heidegger's vision of a new humanism, Senghor is intent on showing that black African culture, due to its non-technical mode of perceiving reality, is well-positioned to realize it.

Heidegger's work in this area, which provides ideas that Senghor appropriates in his articulation of Negritude, is based on Aristotle's *Nichomachean Ethics* and his notion of four modes of causality. In Heidegger's analysis of the *Nichomachean Ethics*, he reviews the four modes of causality: *causa materialis*, *causa formalis*, *causa finalis*, *causa efficiens*. Heidegger states that of these four modes, the first three, which correspond to *poiesis*, or "creation," have been forgotten in the modern era. The only mode of causality that Aristotle describes that has not been forgotten, according to Heidegger, is the *causa effi-*

ciens, or "efficient cause," which resembles our modern notion of causality. According to Heidegger, the "forgottenness" of the first three modes corresponding to *poiesis*, and the dominance of the *causa efficiens* in the modern era, result in a worldview he calls "Enframing."

Heidegger describes "Enframing" as a technical perspective according to which objects in the world are considered purely in terms of their potential use value. The worldview of Enframing is characterized by the reduction of reality to an "inventory" that is available for "using up," the perception of the world as "standing reserve" ("Letter on Humanism" 35). Heidegger believes that the greatest danger of modern technology does not lie in the potentially destructive power of machines, but in the prevalence of "Enframing."

In Senghor's reading of Aristotle's text, he equates the three modes of causality that correspond to *poiesis* with intuitive reason, and the *causa efficiens* with discursive reason. Senghor, like Heidegger, claims that although the ancient Greeks founded Western civilization, their mode of Being and perception of reality differed greatly from the modern era in Europe: "Comme vous le savez, ce sont les anciens Grecs qui ont fondé ce que j'appelle la 'civilisation albo-européenne' " (*Liberté 5* 128). Senghor says that there is a common misunderstanding that the Greeks founded Western civilization solely on the notion of discursive reason: "On a trop souvent prétendu qu'ils l'avaient fondée sur la seule raison discursive: sur la *dianoïa*" (*Liberté 5* 128). This is not the case, according to Senghor, because *dianoïa*, or discursive reason, is only one factor among others leading to truth that Aristotle mentions in the *Nicomachean Ethics*:

> Ce n'est pas tout à fait exact. En effet, Aristote, le plus grand des philosophes grecs, nous apprend, dans son Éthique à Nicomaque, qu'il y a, dans l'âme, trois facteurs prédominants qui déterminent l'action et la vérité: "sensation, esprit et désir." J'ai traduit le mot noûs par "esprit." En vérité, c'est la symbiose de la raison discursive et de la raison intuitive, de la pensée et du sentiment. (*Liberté 5* 128)

Senghor substitutes discursive reason for Heidegger's interpretation of the *causa efficiens* in Aristotle:

> loin de privilégier la raison discursive, qui, nous venons de le voir, n'est qu'un des quatre instruments de la connaissance et de l'action, les anciens

Curto   *31*

> Grecs, en fondant la civilisation albo-européenne, ont voulu en faire la civilisation de la totalité du monde. (*Liberté 5* 128)

Much as Heidegger says that "Being" and *poiesis* are suppressed by Enframing in the modern era, Senghor writes that the factors that correspond to intuitive reason, especially feeling and spirit, have been forgotten by the West and discursive reason has come to dominate.

Senghor appropriates Heidegger's idea about the differences between the modes of "being-in-the-world" of "primitive" cultures, and those that have experienced the advent of modern technologies, and uses it as a basis for his description of the characteristics of black African culture. In both "The Question Concerning Technology" and *Being and Time*, Heidegger proposes two primary modes of *Dasein*: the technological outlook that characterizes societies with modern technologies, in which every object is viewed in terms of its potential instrumentality or use value (what Heidegger calls "Enframing"), and the viewpoint existing in pre-technological societies, which is best described as an "awareness" of our place in the world that is in touch with Being. A culture that has not assumed the worldview of Enframing, because it does not possess the modern technologies that destroy nature, is "primitive" in Heideggerian terms. Heidegger draws a distinction between technical instruments like hand tools and the windmill, which incorporate themselves into nature while leaving it intact, and modern technologies, which permanently consume natural resources. While the use of technical instruments does not obscure Being, the emergence of modern technologies leads to the dominance of Enframing as a worldview in the West. A culture that does not possess modern innovations, and has thus not assumed the *Weltanschauung* (worldview) of Enframing, possesses a "primitive *Dasein*" in Heideggerian terms, and is much more in touch with Being than Western man in the technological era.

Senghor attempts to show that a culture's mode of "being-in-the-world" is primarily determined by the extent to which Enframing has become dominant, as manifested in a culture's attitude towards technology and art. For Heidegger, cultural *Dasein* is reflected in the separation — or lack thereof — of technologies and the arts. Heidegger observes in "The Origin of the Work of Art" that in the worldview or *Weltanschauung* characteristic of ancient Greeks or medieval Europeans, art was not considered to be separate from technical inventions; the classical Greek temple and medieval cathedral, for instance, were, like art, formative to notions of self and reality, due to their place in the everyday life of a culture. In the era of the dominance of technological thinking, however, the nature and potential function of art changes. Heidegger finds that art's marginal place in modern society demonstrates the extent to which the technical perspective has come to dominate, and causes him to wonder whether it is technology, and not art, which constitutes the fundamental element in the West's outlook on everything. For him, the separation of art from the technical — as evidenced by the use of *poiesis* to refer only to art, and *techne* to industrial objects — is symptomatic of the dominance of "Enframing" as a mode of perceiving reality in the modern age.

In cultures with "primitive" *Dasein*, on the other hand, art is integrated into all aspects of living and plays a fundamental role in how society conceives of itself. According to Heidegger, neither "primitive" cultures nor the ancient Greeks — as pre-technological societies — make a distinction between the modes of production of *techne* and *poeisis*. In "Building, Dwelling, Thinking," Heidegger writes: "To the Greeks *techne* means neither art nor handicraft but, rather, to make something appear, within what is present, as this or that, in this way or that way" (*Technology* 36). For the Greeks, the term *poiesis* was used to denote both creation by man, and an emergence from nature: "Not only the making of a craftsman, an artist, or a poet, but also the rising up of 'nature' (*physis*) is described as *poiesis*" (*Technology* 35). In "The Question Concerning Technology" he writes, "The Greeks conceive of *techne*, producing, in terms of letting appear" (*Technology* 35). Heidegger appears to feel a sort of nostalgia for the time when *techne* referred at once to technology and art: "Once there was a time when the bringing-forth of the true into the beautiful was called *techne*. And the *poiesis* of the fine arts was also called *techne*"; "And art was simply called *techne*. It was a single, manifold revealing" (*Technology* 34).

In the essays of *Liberté 1* and *3*, Senghor associates Negritude with the mode of revealing characteristics of cultures untouched by modern technology, such as the ancient Greeks or cultures that are "primitive" in Heideggerian terms, by emphasizing the unity of art and the technical in black African life. He does so at first by highlighting the similarities between the Greek and "Negro-African" conceptions of art. Senghor states that the ancient Greeks used "poésie" to refer to all forms of creation and did not distinguish between art and technical creations. In "Pour un dialogue des disciplines et des cultures," Senghor, like Heidegger in "The Question Concerning Technology," highlights the Greek use of the terms *techne* and *poiesis* to refer to both artistic and scientific endeavors in order to demonstrate the unity of art and the technical in this culture: "Il est vrai qu'en grec le mot *technè* a signifié successivement 'habileté manuelle,' 'procédé,' 'art,' mais aussi 'connaissance théorique,' 'science'" (*Liberté 5* 125). Senghor then signals the etymological roots of the terms "ingénieur" to illustrate the ideal unity of the arts and sciences at the time of the ancient Greeks: "Au sens étymologique, mais surtout au sens moderne du mot, l'ingénieur est un homme habité par l'esprit: un poète, c'est-à-dire un créateur" (*Liberté 5* 124). When asked during a 1980 interview, "Au bout de ces années d'action et de poésie, quel est le mot que vous aimez le plus?," Senghor responds, "C'est le mot *poéisis*. C'est Aristote qui nous le dit dans *l'Éthique à Nicomaque*: la *poéisis*, c'est la fabrication, c'est-à-dire, par delà le mot 'poésie,' le mot 'création'" (*Poésie de l'action* 235). Senghor would like to see a return in the West to the Greek notion of *poiesis*; he believes that the influence of "Negro-African" culture on Europe can provide the means of doing so.

In his interviews and essays, Senghor frequently emphasizes the unity of the technical and the poetic in black African culture. In another interview, he declares, "la poétique est en même temps un art, une technique et une science," and calls the poet a "Maître-de-science" (*Poésie de l'action* 67). In "Le Musée dynamique," Senghor explains that in black African culture, no separation exists between the work of art and the industrial object — "l'œuvre d'art n'est pas un produit industriel" — and that "technique" is used to refer to practices that produce both artistic and more practical creations (*Liberté 3* 64). In "Fonction et Signification du Premier Festival Mondial des Arts Nègres," Senghor writes: "En parlant de la Négritude, je parle d'une civilisation où l'art est, à la fois, technique et vision, artisanat et prophétie" (*Liberté 3* 64).

In "Négritude et Modernité ou la Négritude est un humanisme du XXe siècle," Senghor writes about the lack of distinction between the technical and the artistic in black African culture: "dans cette civilisation négro-africaine, dont l'un des traits les plus caractéristiques est *l'unité dans la cohérence*, l'art est, essentiellement, une technique" (*Liberté 3* 224). According to Senghor, cultures south of the Sahara perceive no distinction between the technical and artistic domains, but view them as part of the same reality: "C'est qu'au sud du Sahara, les deux mondes, visible et invisible, matériel et spirituel, profane et religieux, technique et artistique, ne sont que l'avers et l'envers d'une même étoffe: d'une même réalité" (*Liberté 3* 227). He then declares that African art possesses two primary characteristics. The first is a "total art" because it incorporates all other artistic forms within it. The second is a "technique": "Le second caractère de l'art nègre est d'être une *technique*. Contrairement à ce que croient les Européens, chaque art — danse et musique, chant et poème, sculpture et poterie, peinture et tissage — est une technique précise" (*Liberté 3* 228). Here Senghor plays on the meaning of "technique" in French, which can mean either a skill ("technique" in English), or "technology." On the one hand, he appears to be referring to skills; on the other hand, the context of the passage, which is inserted into a discussion of the etymology of *techne* (the root of the word "technology") and a rereading of Heidegger's "The Question Concerning Technology," indicates that the French "technique" also denotes technology. By showing the lack of distinction between *techne* and *poiesis* in black African culture, and illustrating the extent to which art occupies a central place in everyday life, Senghor seeks to show that "Negro-African" culture possesses a mode of "being-in-the-world" that is akin to the cultural *Weltanschauung* Heidegger attributes to societies existing prior to, or without access to, modern technologies: primitive *Dasein*.

For Senghor, as for Heidegger, art is the ultimate expression of the ontology or mode of "being-in-the-world" of a culture. In "The Age of the World Picture," Heidegger states that the mimetic standard for judging art that exists in the West is a reflection of the technical worldview, which seeks to master reality by reproducing it exactly. He calls this phenomenon the "world picture," which, he explains, "when understood essentially, does not mean a picture of the world but the world conceived and grasped as picture" (*Technology* 129). According to Heidegger, "the fact that the world becomes picture at all is what distinguishes the essence of the modern age" (*Technology* 130), and the "fundamental event of the modern age is the conquest of the world as picture" (*Technology* 134). Heidegger considers the separation of art and function in European culture, and the predominance of the mimetic standard, in order to argue that this approach to art is the ultimate manifestation of Enframing as the dominant mode of perceiving reality in the West.

Senghor contrasts the ontology expressed in "art nègre" to the technological outlook reflected in the mimetic standard of art in the West. Senghor writes in "Négritude et Modernité ou la Négritude est un humanisme du XXe siècle": "L'art, comme la littérature, est toujours l'expression d'une certaine conception du monde et de la vie: d'une certaine philosophie et, d'abord, d'une certaine ontologie" (*Liberté 3* 75). According to Senghor, writing in the same essay, black African peoples have a particular way of living that is expressed in their art: "Qui niera que les peuples négro-africains n'aient, eux aussi, une certaine manière de concevoir la vie et de la vivre?" (*Liberté 3* 69). Senghor maintains that these differences in ontologies manifest themselves in diverse attitudes towards art. In Africa, according to Senghor, art is not relegated to the margins of society, as Heidegger claims it is in the modern West, but remains an integral part of life: "Car, en Afrique noire, l'art n'est pas une activité séparée: en soi ou pour soi. Il est une activité sociale, une technique de vie et, pour tout dire, un artisanat" (*Liberté 3* 76). Unlike Western art, African art, according to Senghor, does not seek to master nature by reproducing it, by "photographing" it: "l'art ne consiste pas à photographier la nature, mais à l'apprivoiser" (*Liberté 3* 77). For Senghor, the lesson that "art nègre" has to teach is that art and photography are not the same: "la leçon nègre est que l'art n'est pas photographie" (*Liberté 3* 77).

To illustrate the difference between the ancient Greek and black African conceptions of art, on the one hand, and those in the modern West on the other, Senghor uses the example of the Venus of Milo. At the time of its creation, according to Senghor, the statue was a goddess: "Bien sûr, les Venus — et c'est ce qu'indique le nom — représentaient une déesse autrefois, au temps de la ferveur hellène" (*Liberté 3* 95). She possessed a ritual function within society: "Les Vénus grecques étaient sculptées [...] pour aider à la fécondité des femmes, pour aider à l'action des ancêtres et de Dieu: elles étaient porteuses de *charme*, magiques" (*Liberté 3* 95-96). Since the time of the ancient Greeks, however, the perception of this work has changed: "Mais, depuis, on avait fait descendre la déesse du ciel sur la terre, de l'esprit dans la matière" (*Liberté 3* 95). Now, according to Senghor, this spiritual dimension has been forgotten, and the work is viewed in terms of its ability to represent a reality, that of the ancient Greek woman who posed for it: "On veut donc représenter une femme grecque et pas autre chose" (*Liberté 3* 95). Consequently, Senghor writes, "La Vénus de Milo est, pour résumer, une sculpture-photographie" (*Liberté 3*, 95). This is characteristic of what he calls "l'art de la raison discursive": "il imite la nature, il la photographie" (*Liberté 3* 96). Senghor echoes Heidegger's terminology in his description of the Venus de Milo as "sculpture-photographie"; for Heidegger, the development of modern technologies, like photography, is symptomatic of the mode of revealing in the modern era, in which the world is viewed as an image to be mastered through its reproduction in art.

Senghor thus appropriates Heidegger in a way that allows him to affirm the positive value of African cultural production and, at the same time, underscore the importance of acquiring what he believes African culture lacks: European technology. In order to justify his critique of the West's technical perspective all the while seeking to acquire its inventions, Senghor points to Heidegger's distinction between the instrumental use of technologies (considered by Heidegger to be relatively innocuous) and their "essence" as the "mode of revealing" of Enframing (the real danger, according to Heidegger). In "The Question Concerning Technology," Heidegger writes, "What is dangerous is not technology. There is no demonry of technology, but rather there is the mystery of its essence. The essence of technology, as a destining of revealing, is the danger" (*Technology* 28). Senghor attempts to draw a similar distinction between the use of modern innovations and the dominance of Enframing by showing that he is not against the transfer of machines to the colonies *a priori*. The primary role that modern technologies should play in culture, according to Senghor, is the satisfaction of these needs, and not the determination of the nature of things:

> Je crois, plus sérieusement, que les techniciens ont pour rôle, non pas de nous faire saisir l'essence des choses, mais de nous aider d'abord à satisfaire nos "besoins animaux," condition sine qua non de tout développement spirituel. (*Liberté 3* 42)

Curto 37

In advocating a transfer of technologies from the West to the colonies, Senghor seeks to allow African culture to take advantage of the utility of modern inventions, without assuming the framework of Enframing.

This contradiction, far from suggesting a misinterpretation of Heidegger, actually displays a profound internalization of his discourse. Senghor reads Heidegger so closely that some of the problems and contradictions that arise in "The Question Concerning Technology" manifest themselves in his own appropriation of the work. Heidegger never clearly indicates, for instance, whether Enframing brought modern technologies into existence, or the advent of these technologies produced the dominance of Enframing as a way of viewing reality. Similarly, Senghor does not explain whether the West's instrumental view of reality provided it with the means of developing new innovations, or whether it was the development of the inventions themselves that produced the total dominance of the technical perspective. In his discussion of black African culture, Senghor also fails to specify whether its spiritual, intuitive mode of perceiving reality resulted in a lack of technological development, or whether it was the inaccessibility of modern innovations that engendered this emotional state of being.

The absence of an adequate explanation in Senghor's writings of why the West developed technologies while Africa did not suggests that Senghor believes that this discrepancy is due to the inherent inferiority of black peoples. Although Senghor appropriates the basic principles of French and German phenomenology in order to describe differences in cultural modes of "being-in-the-world," he fails to provide an adequate explanation of their origins. This failure to problematize the origins of the discrepancy between the technical and primitive *Daseins* suggests that he has internalized a notion of inequality between the races that is primarily based on differences in their propensities towards technological development. Senghor's thinking on technology thus reflects the essentialism in his writings, since it implies that the origins of the positions of Europeans and Africans in the global capitalist hierarchy lie in a biological inequality between the capacities of white and black peoples to develop modern technologies.

Senghor insists that the acquisition of innovations by black African peoples is the fundamental means of instigating economic and social development in the former colonies. Following Heidegger, he believes that it is possible to obtain technologies without appropriating the perspective of Enframing, through the creation of a new humanism based on Being. For him, technological innovations will provide the means of establishing both the African socialist nation and the "civilisation de l'Universel" of the future, which he conceives of as modernized and industrialized societies in which the book — as an invention at the crossroads between the intuitive and the technical — plays a fundamental role.

For both Senghor and Heidegger, literature — which they associate with *poiesis* — provides the means of combating the dangers of Enframing. The two thinkers believe that literature constitutes the primary means by which a people expresses its particular *Dasein* or cultural "being-in-the-world." Senghor equates this cultural *Dasein* with Negritude, while Heidegger emphasizes the fundamental role of the "*Volk*" (which he equated with the collective German people) in creating a viewpoint capable of countering the technological mindset of Enframing.

According to Heidegger, the *Volk* could provide the means of overcoming the dominance of Enframing by conceptualizing Being as something different from the "present-at-hand" (an instrumental view of reality). In his 1953 "Introduction to Metaphysics," Heidegger makes it clear that he believes that the German people are the only group capable of realizing this goal. In Heidegger's 1933 speech, "The Self-Assertion of the German University," he praised the historical mission of the *Volk* and invoked "the power to preserve, in the deepest way, the strengths which are rooted in soil and blood" ("Self-Assertion" 468).

In his essays on Hölderlin, written in the 1930s, Heidegger attempts to restore the connection between the ancient Greeks and the Germans (much like Senghor tries to link ancient Greek, modern German, and black African cultures) in order to revitalize the idea of an original "German essence." Heidegger believed that Hölderlin "had offered to the Germans a program (spiritual reappropriation of the homeland) through which they would be able to discover their essence" (Farías 271). Heidegger considers the Germans a nation of poetry and thought, just as Senghor describes black African culture as dominated by *poiesis*. Heidegger's praise of the "essence" of the German people echoes Senghor's description of an "âme nègre" (black soul) as the essence of Negritude in the essays of *Liberté 1-5*.

Heidegger believed that the Nazi party had found a means of breaking free of the oppressive mindset of Enframing, by utilizing technology in an instrumental fashion, while emphasizing the importance of the *Volk*. In his "Introduction to Metaphysics," Heidegger writes that National Socialism strove for "a match between a planetary-determined technology and modern man" and claims that this political movement provides the only possible means of establishing "a satisfying relationship with technology" (*Metaphysics* 469). In his 1966 interview with *Der Spiegel* (published posthumously), Heidegger insists that his engagement with Nazism be considered in light of his struggle to find a means of confronting the newly emerging reign of modern technology:

> A decisive question for me today is: how can a political system accommodate itself to the technological age, and which political system would this be? I have no answer to this question. I am not convinced that it is democracy. (*Der Spiegel* 204)

In this same interview, Heidegger "claimed that technology had become independent of human control and that democracy was unable to regain control of it" (*Der Spiegel* 205). In the *Der Spiegel* interview, Heidegger cites America and Russia as countries where the widespread use of modern technology has led to a detrimental mindset.

Senghor's Negritude, which provides him with the means of countering discursive reason, is analogous to the Heideggerian principle of the *Volk*. Just as Heidegger believed that National Socialism would counter Enframing by glorifying the *Volk*, Senghor's African Socialism embraced the idea that Negritude would unite with the technological mode of Being of the West, to create the ideal, utopian "Civilization of the Universal." In the essays of *Liberté 1-5*, Senghor claims that German, Greek, and black African culture possess the same intuitive "being-in-the-world" and that the presence of these cultures in his "Civilisation de l'universel" will serve to counter the discursive reason brought by technological civilizations. Both Heidegger and Senghor write favorably about the instrumental functions of modern technology, all the while condemning the mindset (Enframing for Heidegger, discursive reason for Senghor) that it provokes; they affirm that the intuitive "being-in-the-world" of their cultures will counter the negative effects of the dominance of technology.

In conclusion, then, Senghor's African socialism was developed through the appropriation of ideas from a thinker who himself participated in National Socialism; this suggests some troubling parallels between the politics of these two thinkers. Both Heidegger and Senghor present the "being-in-the-world" of their respective cultures as the means of escaping the tyranny of the technological age as demonstrated in the notion of Enframing. Both seek a humanism more in tune to "Being" — but their response is to create "humanisms" grounded in the culture of a particular people and race. In his writings, Heidegger explicitly denounces the racial aspects of National Socialism, yet replaces the biological discourse of the movement with his own racially charged notion of "German *Dasein*." This strategic move by Heidegger is reflected in Senghor's own rhetoric: although Senghor repeatedly denies the biological component of Negritude, adamantly defending himself against accusations of essentialism, he presents the existence of an "âme nègre" as the basis of Negritude. In his search for a humanism to serve as a basis for his utopian "Universal civilization," Senghor thus commits some of the same mistakes as Heidegger; his choice of which aspects of Heidegger's thinking to appropriate — and which to ignore — reflects his own attempts to justify his politics of African Socialism, which sought to promote development in Senegal through technology transfer from Europe, all the while emphasizing the importance of safeguarding Negritude culture.

Works Cited

Adell, Sandra. *Double-Consciousness/Double Bind: Theoretical Issues in Twentieth-Century Black Literature*. Urbana: University of Illinois Press, 1994.

Bâ, Silvia Washington. *The Concept of Negritude in the Poetry of Léopold Sédar Senghor*. Princeton: Princeton University Press, 1973.

Farías, Victor. *Heidegger and Nazism*. Philadelphia: Temple University Press, 1989.

Heidegger, Martin. Interview. *Der Spiegel* 31 May 1976. 204.

_____. *Introduction to Metaphysics*. Trans. Richard Polt and Gregory Fried. New Haven and London: Yale University Press, 2000.

_____. "Letter on Humanism." *Basic Writings*. Trans. David Farrell Krell. New York: Harper Collins, 1977. 195-205.

_____. *The Question Concerning Technology and Other Essays*. Trans. and ed. William Lovitt. New York: Garland Publishers, 1977.

_____. "The Self-Assertion of the German University: Address, Delivered on the Solemn Assumption of the Rectorate of the University. Freiburg, the Rectorate 1933/34: Facts and Thoughts." Trans. Karsten Harries and Hermann Heidegger. *The Review of Metaphysics* 38.3 (1985): 467-502.

Riesz, János. "Senghor and the Germans." *Research in African Literatures* 33.4 (2002): 25-37.

Senghor, Léopold Sédar. *La Poésie de l'action: conversations avec Mohamed Aziza*. Paris: Stock, 1980.

_____. *Liberté 1: Négritude et humanisme*. Paris: Éditions du Seuil, 1964.

_____. *Liberté 3: Négritude et civilisation de l'universel*. Paris: Éditions du Seuil, 1977.

_____. *Liberté 5: le dialogue des cultures*. Paris: Éditions du Seuil, 1993.

FLS, Volume XXXVII, 2010

Patrick D. Murphree

Independent Scholar

Sentimental *Invraisemblance* and Post-revolutionary French Identity: Three Parodies of *Misanthropie et repentir*

> The parodies of Julie Molé's *Misanthropie et repentir* (1798), an adaptation of Kotzebue's *Misanthropy and Repentance* (1788), critique not only the sentimental excesses and departures from realism found in the work itself, but also the polarized audience reaction that it generated, ultimately advocating a moderate and rational response. In the context of the late Directory, these parodies participate in a cultural effort to construct a stable post-revolutionary French identity by othering the emotional extravagance of *sensibilité* as a lingering remnant of the enthusiasm that had led to the radical phase of the French Revolution.

By the late eighteenth century, the doctrinal tenets of *sensibilité* had become common cultural property in France, infiltrating not only the arts but also the political and social theories of the *philosophes*.[1] Their revolutionary descendants accordingly adopted *sensibilité* as a guiding principle, translating a literary ideal into political praxis and creating a culture of militant *sensibilité* that, particularly during the radical Revolution, equated sentimental practices with republican citizenship. When the Directory rejected the values of revolutionary radicalism, comic dramatists followed suit, questioning the political, social, and dramaturgical consequences of *sensibilité*.

---

[1] On eighteenth-century *sensibilité*, see Vincent-Buffault 1-96; Denby 1-138. On the politicization of *sensibilité* in the late eighteenth century, see Maza.

Sensibilité begins in an emotional experience of the world. When confronted with a touching scene, a virtuous person feels pity and sympathy and displays these emotions through signs of *sensibilité*, particularly tears. Because sentimental ideology holds that an automatic relationship exists between internal feelings and external signs, displaying *sensibilité* testifies to the displayer's virtue. According to their proponents, cultural forms such as the sentimental *drame* increase the virtue of their audiences by allowing them to express their *sensibilité*; by making the private experience of *sensibilité* public, theatrical performance transforms society by encouraging a public morality grounded in *sensibilité*. This social transformation, in turn, requires that all citizens participate in a mutual and fully transparent sharing of their emotions; the transparency is a necessary consequence of the presumed direct relationship between emotional displays and the states they signify. Thus, the *drame* presumes and anticipates a unified audience response of sentimental tears, attributing the failure of a particular performance to achieve this response to the corruption of audience members who refuse to allow themselves to feel.

In the theatre, eighteenth-century *sensibilité* climaxed in the works of August von Kotzebue, who became the most widely produced dramatist in Europe following the unprecedented international success of his 1788 pathetic drama, *Menschenhass und Reue*. In 1798, after several attempts by others to create a stageworthy translation of the play, Julie Molé, an actress working from a more literal translation by Bursay (Molé iii), used her theatrical experience to create *Misanthropie et repentir*. Her adaptation became the most performed play in Paris in 1799, its success spawning no fewer than five theatrical parodies (Kennedy et al. 386).[2] In *Cadet Roussel misanthrope et Manon repentante*, Joseph Aude, Alexandre Hapdé, and Augustin Flan attack Molé's sentimental excess and pretension to realism. *Comment faire?*,

---

[2] Kennedy et al. credit Antoine-François Rigaud as the author of the work that achieved ninety-three performances in 1799. While Rigaud did write a verse translation that was accepted for performance in 1795 by the remnants of the Théâtre de la Nation — the conservative branch of the *ci-devant* Comédie Française then performing at the Théâtre Feydeau — this version was never produced (Rigaud iii-iv). The version played to such success was Molé's prose version (Denis 431; Étienne and Martainville 161; Dorvo 3); on its production and reception, see Denis 341-478.

ou Les Épreuves de Misanthropie et repentir by Étienne Jouy and Charles Longchamps and Hyacinthe Dorvo's *La Veille des noces, ou L'Après-souper de Misanthropie et repentir* dramatize the polarized audience response to the *drame*, which was greeted with either sentimental tears or derisive laughter. The parodies articulate a post-revolutionary and distinctively French mode of social behavior that accepts both sentimental and ironic responses to Molé's play while simultaneously othering the sentimental response as foreign. Implicitly rejecting *sensibilité* as the origin of revolutionary radicalism, they call for its replacement by the moderate values of the classical comic tradition.

In *Misanthropie et repentir*, emotionally extravagant characters behave as sentimental paragons in a plot that limns the conflict between two sentimental principles: affective familial bonds and emotional fulfillment as a guide to moral action. After abandoning her husband and children to follow a seducer, repentant Eulalie has taken refuge as a housekeeper on the estate of Count and Countess Walberg. Misanthropic Meinau, wounded by his wife's infidelity, has abandoned society and now lives in a cottage on the estate. Unaware of each other's proximity and operating under assumed names, both have earned reputations for virtue and generosity. After the plot drives each to confess their identities to confidants, these characters force the couple to meet; despite still being in love, Meinau and Eulalie decide to spare each other's feelings by never meeting again. In the climactic scene, the Walbergs present Meinau and Eulalie with their children, who have been living with a guardian; overcome by a rush of parental sentiment, the couple agree to reconcile and re-form the family unit. Although praised for its touching sentimentality, *Misanthropie et repentir* was also acclaimed for its realism, as befits its generic designation as a *drame*. For theorists of the *drame*, lifelike theatrical representation promotes the genre's moral end because such a representation leads an audience to imitate the virtuous actions displayed on the stage.

As practitioners of the *genre poissard*, a popular comic form notable for its generally realistic representation of the lifestyle and colorful argot of the working class Parisians living in and around Les Halles, the authors of *Cadet Roussel misanthrope et Manon repentante* take great offense at the claim that Molé's weepy, sententious, moralistic, and idealized *drame* accurately depicts reality.[3] In *poissard* plays, stock characters shared among the dramatists working in the medium populate farcical plots frequently tinged with a satire made more effective by the realistic diction and behavior of the characters. Aude, Hapdé, and Flan replace Molé's aristocrats with popular *poissard* figures who behave in the lifelike manner associated with the genre. For instance, Molé's Countess becomes Mme. Angot, the most recent incarnation of the *poissarde parvenue* type (see Moore 236-83). A satire of the nouveau riche profiteers who were a fixture of Directory society, Mme. Angot apes the manners of the elite without true understanding; her comic mangling of correct speech and fashionable etiquette reinforces hierarchical class distinctions while also representing unsavory aspects of social reality normally elided in other theatrical genres. The authors further call attention to the *invraisemblance* of their target by emphasizing the consequences of the physical environment. Both plays are set along the shores of a small pond, but the parody contains a recurring gag in which characters swat at the mosquitoes that swarm in the marshy environment. At one point, Cadet Roussel, the *poissard* Meinau, rhapsodizes on the joys of fatherhood and just as he reaches an emotional climax shouts "ah!" and slaps his face (48). If this were an unironic *drame*, an audience might assume that the gesture reflects the extreme emotional turmoil appropriate to a sentimental hero, but in this case, it is prepared to laugh when Cadet reveals its true meaning: "Encore une mouche; on ne les détruira jamais" (48). By having Cadet puncture his display of paternal *sensibilité*, the authors call into question his professed tenderness, while the reminder of the physical environment highlights the absence of such concerns in Molé's supposedly realistic *drame*.

Aude, Hapdé, and Flan employ a parodic method of *reductio ad absurdum* when transposing the target text into a *poissard* key. When recasting the scene in which the penitent confesses her identity to her protector, they condense three pages of dialogue into dramatic action that had required ten pages in the original, thereby throwing Molé's unrealistic verbal expansiveness into sharp relief. Molé directs the

---

[3] Although designed for consumption by wealthier audiences, the success of the *genre poissard* depended to a large degree upon the accuracy of its representation, since any Parisian could readily compare the stage version of a *poissard* with the real thing. For an analysis of the form that emphasizes its realism, see Moore.

Murphree 47

actress playing Countess Walberg to respond to Eulalie's confession "*avec un mouvement involontaire d'horreur*"; yet after taking but a few steps, she returns to comfort the sobbing woman, rejecting "cette rigueur extrême qui fait repousser les malheureux" (75). In contrast, Mme. Angot responds to the confession of Manon, the *poissard* Eulalie, by cursing the fallen woman and raising her fists to strike. The physicality and vulgarity of the response comically undermine Mme. Angot's elitist veneer, while the motivations for the response — a *parvenu* concern for appearances and an established social pattern whereby older women are the upholders of propriety (see Garrioch 39 and Desan 451-54 and 461-62) — subtly suggest that *sensibilité* is not necessarily an instinctive reaction. Nevertheless, when Manon begs, "Ne tapez pas; écoutez," Mme. Angot immediately relents (34). Her sudden conversion from violent defender of traditional morality to comforting maternal presence parodies the cliché in which an initial reaction of horror immediately dissolves into sentimental tenderness.

As the scene continues, Eulalie's lengthy orations on her guilt become Manon's grief-stricken utterance: "Conscience, douleur, remords" (34). Mme. Angot replies, "Velà assez de paroles comme ça: je ne t'en veux plus [...]" (35), a deflated rendering of the Countess's, "Laissons là ces souvenirs pénibles. Je devine la fin de votre triste aventure" (79). Mme. Angot's speech highlights Molé's artificial diction while subtly changing the intention behind the speech from protecting Eulalie from the pain of her conscience to protecting the listener from having to hear it. At the conclusion of the scene, the Countess leads Eulalie to dinner so as not to arouse the suspicions of the other characters, a virtuous act made ridiculous by the gluttonous Mme. Angot, who abruptly announces to the sobbing Manon: "Ecoute: j'allons manger un morceau; après dîner, nous verrons à te tirer d'affaire" (35). Although callous, Mme. Angot's behavior reinforces Aude, Hapdé, and Flan's contention that a lifelike theatrical representation must include the unpleasant aspects of reality while the representation of this believable, if unappealing, interpersonal interaction calls into question the status of *sensibilité* as the natural mode of human behavior.

Typical of its genre, *Misanthropie et repentir* concludes with the formation of a community united by *sensibilité* and sustained by emotional transparency; ideologically, *sensibilité* presumes that all individuals will want to live in such a sentimental utopia. For the revolutionaries, engaged in their own utopian project, *sensibilité* was not merely a model; the Republic of Virtue was itself a sentimental ideological construct.[4] Following the logic of *sensibilité*, revolutionaries advocated an emotional relationship with the world. In pursuit of positive emotional sensations, individual citizens would perform virtuous actions. Those witnessing these actions would be inspired to perform similar actions out of a desire for similar emotional experiences, leading to increasingly virtuous behavior on the part of all citizens. The accumulated pressure of these behaviors would transform France not merely into a Republic, but into a utopia that would resemble nothing so much as the hermetic community of the sentimental denouement whose survival depends upon the complete emotional transparency of its members. For the revolutionaries, "shared emotion created moral and political collectivity" (Maslan 238); a refusal to share one's emotions was thus not merely antisentimental, it was counterrevolutionary. The sentimental community requires a mechanism to neutralize the threat posed by individuals who refuse to embrace *sensibilité*; in a *drame*, expulsion of such individuals is the usual method, but a dramatic community can expel an individual who refuses to accept the sentimental order far more easily than can a political one. Thus, the transposition of literary ideals into political reality led inexorably to the Terror, the violent amputation of those parts of the social body that would not participate in the sentimental utopia. Any debate about *sensibilité* in the late 1790s was thus also a debate about the causes of the Terror, the mechanisms necessary to avoid its return, and the need to disentangle emotional experiences from political radicalism.

Writing in 1802, theatre historians Charles-Guillaume Étienne and Alphonse Martainville describe the reactions that greeted *Misanthropie et repentir*: men wept, women fainted, marital spats erupted, and sentimentalists, "convaincus que la vue seule du malheur doit exciter la commisération, et que l'insensibilité est un vice du cœur, refusèrent d'épouser des femmes qui avaient ri ou affecté de rire pendant la représentation de la pièce" (168). These extravagant responses and the "foule de plaisanteries" to which they gave rise polarized

---

[4] My argument here draws heavily upon Vincent-Buffault 77-96, Denby 139-65, and Maslan, especially 74-124 and 183-215.

Murphree 49

audiences into two camps (Étienne and Martainville 168). On one side stood those who treated the play ironically and used wit as a weapon to mock those who allowed the *drame* to send them into emotional transports. On the other stood those who, touched by the play and unable to comprehend the experience of those who were not, lashed out with violent rhetoric that denied the humanity of their opponents and recalled nothing so much as the rigor of Robespierre.

Inspired by the stories of broken engagements proceeding from divergent responses to *Misanthropie et repentir*, both *Comment faire?* and *La Veille des noces* begin with two mismatched young couples, each composed of a sentimental partner and a more worldly one.[5] In *Comment faire?*, Agathe and Adèle relate contrasting summaries of *Misanthropie et repentir* in musically contrasting vaudevilles. Agathe's description reflects the sentimental party line:

> Une femme faible et bonne,
> Dupe d'un moment d'erreur,
> Pour un mari qui pardonne,
> Abjure un vil séducteur... (303)

While Agathe portrays Eulalie as a good but misguided woman, Adèle undermines Agathe's defense of Eulalie's motivations by character-izing her as vain and flighty:

> L'intéressante personne
> Fuit un mari qu'elle aimait,
> Et tendrement abandonne
> Deux enfans pour un bonnet. (304)

This response has much in common with the charges of immorality

---

[5] *Comment faire?* premiered on March 16, 1799, and played 57 times by year's end, making it the fifth most performed play of that year (Kennedy et al. 386). Open-ing a month later (April 14, 1799), *La Veille des noces* was less successful, achieving only six performances (Kennedy et al. 149). The earlier play had robbed *La Veille des noces* of some of its novelty, while the more sedate tone of Dorvo's verse comedy was likely less appealing than the musical numbers and farcical exaggeration in *Comment faire?*. There were also apparently charges of plagiarism circulating as Dorvo takes pains to clarify his independent conception by citing a letter from Molé dated March 1, 1799, in which she responds to an earlier letter of his in which he had described his idea for the play (3).

that haunted every version of Kotzebue's play. For more conservative audience members, the social rehabilitation of the fallen woman encouraged a dangerous moral laxity; by the nineteenth century, this argument had carried the day and in dramatic literature, death became the only means by which a fallen woman could attest to her repentance (Metayer 239). Sophie, Adèle's counterpart in *La Veille des noces*, ironically praises Eulalie before demanding blood, revealing that audience attitudes toward moral failure had already begun to harden:

> SOPHIE.
>
> Je suis loin d'accuser la modeste Eulalie,
> Mais je n'estime pas une femme avilie;
> Et loin qu'à son époux elle eut du recourir,
> À sa place, il faillait.....
>
> VERSAC.
> Se consoler.
>
> SOPHIE.
> Mourir. (21)

Ironically, Molé had attempted to forestall charges of immorality by altering the characterization of her heroine from that found in Bursay's translation. "Sûrement," writes Molé in her author's preface, "la sévérité de nos mœurs n'aurait pas souffert sur la scène un être trop coupable, pour intéresser, malgré ses remords" (v-vi). Molé seeks to raise Eulalie's moral standing by having the character consistently emphasize her own culpability rather than that of her seducer and by representing her as a naïve victim of seduction rather than as a woman easily manipulated by vanity and sexual desire. By using the first-person plural to address her audience, Molé constructs an identity group that includes herself and her readers and, by referencing shared mores and the practices of the French stage, marks this identity group as specifically French. Ignoring Molé's protestations, the parodies, particularly *Comment faire?*, treat the work as if it were entirely foreign, erecting their opposition to the work on the grounds of an innate French identity. In 1799, no claim about French identity could ignore the chaos of the preceding decade. As a result, the patriarchal panic encoded in the increasingly intolerant response to the fallen woman

Murphree
51

reflects the desire to move towards a social order marked by strict conformity to a relatively narrow moral code as one route by which to avoid repeating the revolutionary experience.

In *Comment faire?* and *La Veille des noces*, the young people return from a performance of *Misanthropie et repentir*, each thoroughly disgusted by the differing response of his or her prospective spouse. By exchanging partners, the couples resolve their nuptial crises without abandoning their polarized positions, both of which the parodies subject to ridicule. In these plays, the worldly ironists are too dissociated from their own feelings; their flippancy represents a social danger because it can easily lead to callousness. While in the aftermath of the Terror firmness in defending social order became a virtue (Baczko 129-30), under the lingering influence of *sensibilité*, callousness continued to be rejected as immoral. The sentimentalists, by contrast, are too immersed in their own emotional experiences to behave as fully integrated members of society. While advocates for the *drame* claimed that shared sentimental experiences led to communion and a renewed sense of the social bond, these experiences originate in individual emotional reactions. Furthermore, to protect the normative status of their tears, the sentimental characters attack those who do not share their response, inadvertently calling into question the inevitability of that response. Thus, the problem addressed by these parodies is not so much an individual audience member's response, whether sentimental or ironic, but rather the tendency of those responses to lead to intolerance and social division. As the sociopolitical project of the Directory was to create some kind of closure to the revolutionary experience, anything that interfered with that process (in particular, extremism of any variety) was suspect. In these parodies, the intense arguments between the lovers and their refusal to compromise allegorically represent the factionalism of the Revolution, which had been driven by the youthful enthusiasm of its leaders. Although there is no direct evidence that the parodies' authors intended this reading, revolutionary audiences were noted for their tendency to seek out allegory in stage productions, and the use of the home to represent the nation was a favorite technique.[6]

---

[6] On allegorical readings by revolutionary audiences, see Johnson 99-161. On the allegorical use of the domestic environment to represent the politics of *sensibilité*, see Maslan 183-215.

Through subplots involving older couples, the parodies address the risk of intolerance and the limited applicability of the segregationist solution adopted by the young people. In *Comment faire?*, the Bonnevals get into a foolish argument after he misinterprets her extravagant emotional reaction to a performance of *Misanthropie et repentir* as an implicit confession of adulterous guilt; they reconcile by agreeing to treat emotional responses as secondary to the business of existing as a couple, implicitly rejecting the idea, beloved of radicals, that enthusiasm promotes social cohesion. In the final line of spoken dialogue, Bonneval replies to the suggestion that every bridegroom in Paris should take his intended to see the play the night before the wedding by agreeing but with a caveat: "mais non pas le lendemain," thereby making explicit the idea that marital (and by extension, social) stability is best achieved by a decorous avoidance of emotionally charged experiences (311).

In *La Veille des noces*, Félix and Bélise are longtime friends who intend to marry the next day as part of the wedding festivities for their daughters from previous marriages. Like their daughters, Félix and Bélise have divergent reactions to the play. She finds the play touching in the typically sentimental way, while he reacts with mild frustration to its uncommon length and refuses to indulge himself in what he considers "inutiles alarmes" (12). When recounting their unhappy first marriages, they blame mismatched personalities and their late spouses' immoderate behavior; Bélise's miserly husband had never liked her love of fashion, while Félix's coquettish wife had been endlessly frustrated by his tendency towards moral rectitude. Realizing that marrying one another would simply recreate the unpleasantness of their first marriages, the pair decide to forgo matrimony in order to maintain their friendship. Dorvo thus acknowledges the *invraisemblance* of the denouement of his target, in which *sensibilité* overrides all other emotional and practical considerations. Employing a traditional argument revivified by advocates for the *drame*, a family friend announces that the pair's decision demonstrates that "le spectacle est l'école des mœurs" (40); nevertheless, their decision hinges on an interpretation of *Misanthropie et repentir* that effectively rejects *sensibilité*. Rather than allowing their emotions to guide them as Molé intends, Félix and Bélise elect to remain in conscious control of their actions. By choosing friendship rather than love, and basing this friendship on mutual respect and a healthy distance, they reject the sentimental imperatives of transparency and unity. An allegorical reading suggests that French society must similarly move away from sentimental dogmatism in order to transcend the divisiveness of the revolutionary experience. By concentrating upon social consequences rather than dramaturgical inadequacies, Dorvo intensifies the allegorical force of his call for an adoption of the moderation displayed by Félix and Bélise to solve the sociopolitical impasse facing Directory society.

Although accepting the validity of both the sentimental and ironic responses to *Misanthropie et repentir*, by parodying a sentimental play, the parodies also suggest that the sentimental response is particularly problematic, since the demand that every audience member prove his or her virtue by displaying *sensibilité* in response to the *drame* can easily lead to hypocrisy. The *poissards* in *Cadet Roussel misanthrope* demonstrate that emotion does not always lead to sentimental behavior, while the conversion of Mme. Angot into a sentimental protector suggests that *sensibilité* is an artificial construct that conceals a more intolerant human nature. In *Comment faire?*, clever servant Justin explains the popularity of Molé's work as a product of the desire for respectability: "ceux qui en disent beaucoup de bien espèrent qu'on en pensera moins mal d'eux" (272). If *Misanthropie et repentir* encourages such hypocrisy, perhaps it is, in the words of the fop Delville, "vraiment une pièce anti-sociale" (284). According to Delville, marital fidelity is so rare that if every French husband followed Meinau's example, "Nos forêts ne suffiraient pas/ Pour loger nos ermites" (285). While hardly approving of Delville's modish flippancy, Jouy and Longchamps use his ironic stance to undermine the position of moral authority taken by the misanthrope who rejects corrupt society. In other words, Delville may be a fop, but at least he remains committed to preserving the social bond.

By parodying a play strongly identified with a German creator, all three parodies participate in a cultural movement characteristic of the late 1790s that sought to distance the French people from revolutionary excess by othering emotional extravagance. Étienne and Martainville argue of the *drame*: "C'est surtout chez le peuple Germain qu'on vient sacrifier sur ses autels" (160-61), suggesting that the Germanic character is peculiarly susceptible to sentimental tendencies foreign to the people of France. Underlying the historians' dramaturgical criticism is a two-fold fear. First, by promoting the ideology of *sensibilité* that had also produced revolutionary radicalism, emotional extravagance may lead to a return of the Terror. Second, a cultural system that encourages the experience and expression of emotion without the tempering involvement of the rational faculties betrays the distinctive qualities of the French classical tradition. Thus, for critics like Étienne and Martainville, opposed to the *drame* as a corrupting influence, to praise Kotzebue is practically treasonous.

The parodies similarly critique an unreflective reliance upon emotional response, but without the hyperbolic rancor of the historians. Although as working artists, the authors of these parodies accept the commercial value of an audience's emotional experience, they also insist that allowing feelings to override the rational faculties dangerously imperils an audience's ability to make determinations of artistic quality. In the verse prologue that opens the published version of *Cadet Roussel misanthrope*, three characters debate the appropriate response to Molé's *drame*. Valmin defends the right of the *parterre* to laugh at anything it likes, while Fontable defends the tears of those touched by the *drame*, but the victory goes to Dacier, who argues for critical moderation in the treatment of the play:

> J'ai pour l'heureux progrès des arts et des talents,
> Séparé de l'or pur quelques faux ornemens,
> D'autant plus dangereux qu'ils brillent dans l'ouvrage
> Dont les seules beautés ont droit à notre hommage. (5)

By warning against an uncritical embrace of foreign taste, Aude, Hapdé, and Flan suggest that at this critical moment, France must seek its own unique cultural identity.

The practice of parody, based on the incorporation of the parodied subject, reflects a desire to engage with rather than repulse the critical target. Like French comedy since Molière, these parodies promote a pragmatic ideology that embraces a wide variety of behaviors and perspectives, provided that these do not become so extreme as to be detrimental to the social bond. While Molière's comedies criticize certain behaviors, very little in the work of Molière and his successors suggests the possibility of an absolute cure for the *caractères* portrayed; in most cases the flawed individual is reincorporated into

Murphree 55

the social order but deprived of the authority to adversely affect the other characters or else is simply cordoned off and left to his or her own delusional devices. By contrast, sentimental drama favors either the miraculous transformation of a flawed individual into a virtuous and sentimental being or the expulsion from the dramatic community of a character who rejects such a transformation. Comic dramatists avoid these devices in favor of conclusions that tolerate flawed individuals and absorb them within the social fabric because, according to Robert Heilman, "Inflexible rules for the good are anticomic, as is any utopian dreaming which treats defections from the ideal as intolerable errors rather than expectable shortcomings" (244). By endorsing the social compatibility of diametrically opposed positions on the question of sentimental drama, these parodies ultimately endorse the comic value of acceptance rather than the intolerance of *sensibilité* and revolutionary radicalism.

When Aude, Hapdé, and Flan argue that one can praise the achievements of *Misanthropie et repentir* while vigorously criticizing its *invraisemblance*, they acknowledge the value of representing virtue but demand that this representation acknowledge the flawed nature of the world in which that virtue must exist, thereby rejecting the utopian impulses of *sensibilité*. When Dorvo gives to the older generation the wisdom of experience to avoid the pitfalls of emotion in favor of cordial stability, he argues for a consensus that embraces comic values that stress inclusion and reject the youthful idealism and intolerance of the Revolution. When Jouy and Longchamps write jokes that render the worldly and the sentimental responses equally ridiculous, they dissolve difference in the *communitas* of laughter, allowing the audience to assent collectively to a social vision marked by moderation, adaptability, and social continuity — a vision made more attractive after the horrors of the revolutionary experience. By avoiding extremes while lampooning a foreign import, the parodies promote moderation as a quintessentially French value, implicitly marking revolutionary excess as an aberration and preparing the groundwork for the Imperial consensus that would reject political, social, and cultural extremism. The success of *Misanthropie et repentir* and its parodies reveal the desire to reconstruct French society in the aftermath of the Revolution on the basis of a flexible ideological structure that could incorporate, and thereby neutralize, both *sensibilité* and its discontents.

Works Cited

[Aude, Joseph, Alexandre Hapdé, and Augustin Flan.] *Cadet Roussel misanthrope et Manon repentante*. Paris, An VII [1799].

Baczko, Bronislaw. *Ending the Terror: The French Revolution after Robespierre*. Trans. Michel Petheram. Cambridge: Cambridge University Press, 1994.

Denby, David J. *Sentimental Narrative and Social Order in France, 1760-1820*. Cambridge: Cambridge University Press, 1994.

Denis, Andrée. *La Fortune littéraire et théâtrale de Kotzebue en France pendant la Révolution, le Consulat et l'Empire*. Diss. Université de France IV, 1973. Lille: Reproduction des thèses, Université Lille III. Paris: Diffusion-Champion, 1976.

Desan, Suzanne. "The Role of Women in Religious Riots During the French Revolution." *Eighteenth-Century Studies* 22 (1989): 451-68.

Dorvo, [Hyacinthe]. *La Veille des noces, ou L'Après-souper de Misanthropie et repentir*. Paris: [1799?].

Étienne, C[harles]-G[uillaume] and A[lphonse] Martainville. *L'Histoire du théâtre français, depuis le commencement de la révolution jusqu'à la réunion générale*. Vol. 4. Paris, 1802.

Garrioch, David. *The Making of Revolutionary Paris*. Berkeley: University of California Press, 2002.

Heilman, Robert Bechtold. *The Ways of the World: Comedy and Society*. Seattle: University of Washington Press, 1978.

Johnson, James A. *Listening in Paris: A Cultural History*. Berkeley: University of California Press, 1995.

Jouy, [Victor-J. Étienne de], and [Charles de] Longchamps. *Comment faire? ou Les Épreuves de Misanthropie et repentir. Œuvres compètes d'Étienne Jouy*. Ed. Étienne Jouy. Vol. 4. Paris: 1825. 267-313.

Kennedy, Emmet, et al. *Theatre, Opera and Audiences in Revolutionary Paris: Analysis and Repertory*. Westport: Greenwood, 1996.

Maslan, Susan. *Revolutionary Acts: Theater, Democracy, and the French Revolution*. Baltimore: Johns Hopkins University Press, 2005.

Maza, Sarah. *Private Lives and Public Affairs: The Causes Célèbres of Pre-revolutionary France*. Berkeley: University of California Press, 1993.

Metayer, Leon. "What the Heroine Taught, 1830-1870." *Melodrama: The Cultural Emergence of a Genre*. Ed. Michael Hays and Anastasia Nikolopoulou. New York: St. Martin's Press, 1996. 235-44.

Molé, Julie. *Misanthropie et repentir*. Paris, An VII [1799].

Murphree

Moore, A. P. *The* Genre Poissard *and the French Stage of the Eighteenth Century*. New York: Columbia University Institute of French Studies, 1935.

Rigaud, A[ntoine]-F[rançois]. *L'Inconnu, ou, Misanthropie et repentir*. Paris, 1799.

Vincent-Buffault, Anne. *The History of Tears: Sensibility and Sentimentality in France*. Trans. Teresa Bridgeman. New York: St. Martin's, 1991.

Fayçal Falaky

Tulane University

L'originalité du plagiat

La question du plagiat est tellement liée à celle de l'originalité que les deux notions semblent partager un destin commun. Si la création ex nihilo n'est pas possible, est-ce que toute littérature n'est donc que l'expression renouvelée d'idées rebattues? Comment donc se faire un nom, comment se distinguer de ceux qui nous ont précédés? Quand la critique dix-neuviémiste se penche sur les larcins littéraires commis par les écrivains de siècles passés, elle semble aussi dresser un miroir dans lequel se reflète une obsession qui hante l'auteur contemporain: comment être original quand on a déjà tout écrit et réécrit? En écrivant *Les Questions de littérature légale* en 1812, Charles Nodier, loin d'apporter les réponses promises par le titre de son essai critique, nous livre un ouvrage dont le but est de se montrer ironiquement original par le biais d'une étude sur le plagiat.

Dans les *Éléments de littérature*, ouvrage écrit en 1787, Marmontel réserve un article au plagiat pour en faire plutôt l'apologie, et nous offre, ce faisant, un portrait auctorial annonçant déjà la fonction-auteur telle que conçue au dix-neuvième siècle. Si ce n'est que les "pédants, les envieux et les sots" (3: 556) qui se plaisent à accuser de plagiat les écrivains célèbres, la notoriété même de ces derniers semblent leur pardonner tout crime littéraire. Marmontel note ainsi que le plagiat est excusable lorsqu'utilisé par un génie pour rendre public un trésor enterré dans les mots d'un écrivain médiocre qui n'a pu être sauvé de l'oubli: "si celui qui a eu quelque pensée heureuse et nouvelle, n'a pas su la rendre, ou l'a laissée ensevelie dans un ouvrage obscur et méprisé, c'est un bien perdu, enfoui; c'est la perle dans le fumier, et qui attend un lapidaire" (3: 557). La question du plagiat est ainsi reléguée au plan secondaire au profit de la renommée de l'écrivain. Qui se soucie du plagiat quand le plagié n'est plus? De cette question légale s'esquisse une figure auctoriale inextricablement liée au public. Pour être auteur, il faut être connu. Pour avoir une renommée, il faut mettre au jour ses idées (ou à défaut, celles des autres): "Quiconque met dans son vrai jour, soit par l'expression, soit par l'à-propos, une pensée qui n'est pas à lui, mais qui sans lui serait perdue, se la rend propre en lui donnant un nouvel être; car l'oubli ressemble au néant" (3: 557). Et c'est la peur de ce néant qui excuse un type de vol qui ne peut donc se faire qu'aux dépens d'écrivains oubliés. "On dit que l'on pardonne le vol en littérature, à la condition, pour le voleur, de tuer le volé", écrit Louis-Gustave Vapereau dans l'*Année littéraire et dramatique* et donne comme modèle Molière, qui "s'est donné cette circonstance atténuante. Tous ceux à qui il a pris quelque chose sont morts et bien morts" (6: 309). Tuer pour devenir immortel, voilà le dilemme de l'auteur qui prend conscience de sa fonction et de sa place dans l'Histoire. Dans un siècle où la critique sainte-beuvienne et lansonienne attachait le jugement littéraire à la figure de celui qui écrit, l'auteur deviendra lui-même une construction discursive. Comment peut-on donc délimiter cette construction (ou destruction) de soi si d'autres se mêlent dans l'acte intime? Et si l'auteur peut se défendre de son vivant, que pourra-t-il faire après sa mort pour s'opposer aux calomnies ou, pire encore, au silence de l'indifférence? N'est-ce pas cela le combat de Rousseau, cet ennemi de l'amour-propre, qui écrit trois autobiographies pour avoir le monopole de son propre jugement?[1] À cet égard, le fait que l'écrivain puisse ne plus appartenir à lui-même semble déjà indiquer le paradigme foucaldien de l'effacement et de l'insignifiance littéraire de l'auteur. Que cela soit passé pendant une époque où la fonction auctoriale est mise en valeur ne fait que mettre l'accent sur le paradoxe de la critique sainte-beuvienne. En encensant certains écrivains pour en négliger d'autres, en cherchant l'intention ou les intentions poétiques de l'auteur, Sainte-Beuve avait, sans le vouloir, permis à la fonction auctoriale d'être d'abord variable et incertaine pour qu'elle soit ensuite insignifiante. Face à la multiplicité des

---

[1] Ce désir est explicite dans le titre de son avant-dernière autobiographie, *Rousseau juge de Jean-Jacques.*

Falaky 61

jugements, l'éclatement critique de l'auteur fera taire sa voix pour hausser celle des lecteurs, critiques ou pas.

Nonobstant, si le dix-neuvième siècle semble s'intéresser à la question de la mort de l'auteur, ce n'est pas tout à fait selon les prémisses posées par les articles de Barthes et Foucault.[2] La mort hante l'auteur du dix-neuvième parce qu'elle ne dépend pas seulement de lui. D'une part, il est obligé de faire valoir son talent et son originalité au public, d'autre part, c'est au public de décider de son sort. Quand Vapereau dit que les victimes de Molière sont bien mortes, il présente un dilemme angoissant qui dépasse la question du plagiat. On est là devant un type de difficulté plus essentiel où l'auteur se demande si son sort sera de vaincre ou périr, de devenir immortel ou mourir.

En mettant en scène dans son *Cyrano* des membres de l'Académie française, le but d'Edmond Rostand est de les mettre en ridicule. Lui-même académicien, Rostand n'évoque que ceux des immortels que l'on ne se rappelle plus. Rostand ironise en faisant répondre au père d'un jeune homme voulant savoir si l'Académie est présente à une pièce de Baro: "Porchères, Colomby, Bourzeys, Bourdon, Arbaud... Tous ces noms dont pas un ne mourra, que c'est beau!" (20). Même l'Académie ne garantit pas l'immortalité à ses membres, et l'ironie du vers de Rostand n'est que plus palpable dans une pièce sur Cyrano de Bergerac, auteur pratiquement inconnu au dix-neuvième siècle. On pourrait se demander aussi si Rostand n'y met pas autant d'ironie en identifiant la pièce comme comédie héroïque; le héros, en fin de compte, n'est-il pas, au moins dans le sens grec du mot, celui qui survit à la mort? Rostand, en choisissant un tel sujet, a dû se poser les mêmes questions sur sa propre destinée. Dans la République des Lettres, sera-t-il tel Cyrano, celui que l'on tue et que l'on voue à l'oubli, ou tel Molière, l'immortel voleur d'éclat? Cette dialectique se retrouve dans la pièce même et toujours autour de la question du plagiat. Juste avant de succomber à ses blessures, au milieu d'un délire pré-mortel, Cyrano récite un vers d'une scène que Molière lui avait prise. Devant le chagrin et les protestations de ses amis, Cyrano répond que l'auteur de Scapin a bien fait et compare ce vol littéraire à

---

[2] Avec "La mort de l'auteur", article publié par Barthes en 1968, et "Qu'est-ce qu'un auteur", titre d'une conférence donnée par Foucault en 1969, l'importance de l'auteur dans la critique littéraire traditionnelle fut remise en question.

l'élan coupé d'un amour resté sur sa faim, "ma vie, ce fut d'être celui qui souffle, — et qu'on oublie!" (221).

Si le personnage de Rostand se montre débonnaire par rapport au pillage qui s'est fait de son texte, Cyrano — le vrai — aurait été moins clément si l'on se fie à l'épître dédicatoire de *L'Histoire comique* qu'avait écrite son ami et éditeur Henri Le Bret:

> quand je lui demandais pourquoi il lisait les ouvrages d'autrui, il me répondait que c'était pour connaître les larcins d'autrui; et que s'il eût été juge de ces sortes de crimes, il y aurait établi des peines plus rigoureuses que celles dont on punit les voleurs de grands chemins (55).

Si on considère le siècle où se profèrent ces paroles, le ton de cette diatribe à l'encontre du plagiat est inouï. Plusieurs auteurs du grand siècle se sont plaints de ce qu'on appelait à l'époque le larcin littéraire sans pourtant aller jusqu'à vouloir le rendre passible de poursuites et de peines judiciaires. Dans son sens légal, en tant que vol ou empiètement sur la propriété d'autrui, le plagiat naît au dix-neuvième siècle. C'est au moins la conclusion à laquelle arrive Marilyn Randall qui, pour pasticher la célèbre phrase de Thibaudet sur la critique, affirme que: "Le plagiat, tel que nous le connaissons et le pratiquons, est un produit du XIXème siècle" (91). Dans la définition que donne le *Grand dictionnaire universel du XIXème siècle,* il y est également attesté que ce siècle "a tout renouvelé". Il a proscrit, comme plagiat, ce qui dans les trois siècles précédents n'était regardé que comme une *imitation* licite, un "heureux larcin".[3] Il faut dire que les origines de la chasse aux faussaires littéraires pendant le XIXème — provoquée par des publications de livres tels que les *Supercheries littéraires dévoilées* de Barbier et Quérard ou *Les Curiosités littéraires* de Ludovic Lalanne — sont assez troubles. Afin de compiler leurs anecdotes, Barbier, Quérard et Lalanne puisent librement dans les *Questions de littérature légale* de Charles Nodier (Randall, *Pragmatic* 109). Ce texte publié en 1812 et dont le sous-titre nous laisse entendre qu'il y est question de "plagiat, de la supposition d'auteurs, [et] des supercheries qui ont rapport aux livres" est un commentaire sur des exemples de crimes littéraires allant de l'imitation au plagiat de titres. Plus que tout, cependant, le livre de Nodier est une exégèse facétieuse sur l'impos-

---

[3] Citation tirée de l'article de Randall (91).

Falaky   *63*

sibilité d'être original. À titre de preuve on peut remarquer son goût pour l'imposture et le plaisir qu'il prend à inclure parmi les centaines de références citées les noms d'écrivains imaginaires comme Maxime Odin, le chevalier d'Orsain et Clotilde de Surville.[4] Loin donc d'être le réquisitoire contre le plagiat dont se sont inspirés Quérard et Barbier, *Les Questions de littérature légale*, malgré le titre pompeux, n'est que l'exercice ludique et dérisoire d'un bibliothécaire féru de fantaisies bibliologiques et de mystifications littéraires. Si la manie de Nodier fut prise au sérieux par les vrais amateurs de la littérature légale, cela veut dire qu'il a réussi son coup. La mystification est encore plus énorme quand on la considère comme point de départ d'un siècle qui a scellé la soumission de l'imitation littéraire à la question légale.

Le texte de Nodier se veut original à plus d'un titre. Il va sans dire que le genre — critique littéraire mi-vraie, mi-fausse — est insolite, mais il est également d'une originalité plus que singulière, vu que le sujet traité est le plagiat. Entre originalité et plagiat se trouve toute l'angoisse de l'influence littéraire, une angoisse qui ne pouvait être qu'obsédante pour un écrivain de littérature fantastique dont le but principal était d'imaginer et de se créer de nouveaux mondes. Dans la préface de l'*Histoire du roi de Bohème et de ses sept châteaux*, Nodier, imaginant déjà les accusations de plagiat à l'encontre de son conte, déclare:

> Et vous voulez que moi, plagiaire des plagiaires de Sterne —
>> Qui fut plagiaire de Swift —
>> Qui fut plagiaire de Wilkins —
>> Qui fut plagiaire de Cyrano —

---

[4] Clotilde de Surville n'est autre qu'une prétendue écrivaine du Moyen-Âge dont les poèmes furent découverts et se publièrent au début du XIXème siècle. Après un premier enthousiasme suscité par la publication, on découvrit très vite qu'il s'agissait d'une fraude. Celui qui publia les manuscrits de la fictive poétesse, Charles Vandenbourg, se défendit contre les accusations. Charles Nodier, qui fut d'abord un des accusateurs, décida de soutenir l'aveu de Vandebourg avant de publier lui-même, avec le concours d'un autre blagueur, le baron de Roujoux, un deuxième manuscrit de ladite Surville. À ce propos, Jean-François Jeandillou, spécialiste dans les supercheries littéraires et brillant éditeur des *Questions de littérature légale* de Nodier, écrit que "pour prouver, dans son *Dictionnaire des onomatopées*, que le verbe *bramer* s'employait dans le "vieux langage", Nodier n'hésite pas à citer quelques vers "attribués à Clotilde de Surville (XVIII)".

> Qui fut plagiaire de Reboul —
> Qui fut plagiaire de Guillaume des Autels —
> Qui fut plagiaire de Rabelais —
> Qui fut plagiaire de Morus —
> Qui fut plagiaire d'Erasme —
>
> Qui fut plagiaire de Lucien — ou de Lucius de Patras — ou d'Apulée — car on ne sait lequel des trois a été volé par les deux autres, et je ne me suis jamais soucié de le savoir...
>
> Vous voudriez, je le répète, que j'inventasse la forme et fond d'un livre! le ciel me soit en aide! Condillac dit quelque part qu'il serait plus aisé de créer un monde que de créer une idée. (26-27)

La page du titre d'une version pastiche de son Histoire nous apprend que le livre est publié chez les "Libraires qui ne vendent pas de nouveautés" (55). On retrouve le même souci d'originalité dans l'Épitre dédicatoire à Charles Weiss qui précède les *Questions de littérature légale:*

> Je suis bien sûr d'avance que les pages que tu vas parcourir ne t'apprendront pas une seule circonstance utile, et il y en a deux bonnes raisons: la première, c'est qu'il est très difficile, à ce que disent les plus savants hommes de notre temps, de t'apprendre quelque chose; la seconde, c'est que cet écrit est d'une érudition fort médiocre, et qu'il ne mériterait certainement pas les honneurs de l'impression, s'ils n'étaient accordés qu'aux notions nouvelles et intéressantes, comme cela devrait être. (XLVI-XLVII)

La notion que l'impression ne doit être réservée qu'aux nouvelles idées, on la trouve également dans l'autre épître dédicatoire citée ci-dessus, celle d'Henri Le Bret à la mémoire de Cyrano de Bergerac. Après avoir comparé le larcin littéraire aux crimes des voleurs des grands chemins, Le Bret note que:

> si chacun eût travaillé à ne dire que ce qui n'eût point été dit, les bibliothèques eussent été moins grosses, moins embarrassantes, plus utiles, et la vie de l'homme (quoique très courte) eût presque suffi pour lire et savoir toutes les bonnes choses; au lieu que pour en trouver une qui soit passable, il en faut lire cent mille, ou qui ne valent rien, ou qu'on a lues ailleurs une infinité de fois, et qui font cependant consommer le temps inutilement et désagréablement. (56)

Falaky   65

On est en droit de se demander si Henri le Bret parle en son nom ou au nom du défunt Cyrano, puisque même s'il dit rapporter les propos de son ami, l'éditeur semble directement peiné. Juste avant sa mort, Cyrano s'est fait voler un manuscrit et ce n'est pas d'emprunt littéraire qu'il s'agit mais bel et bien d'un vol à prendre au pied de la lettre. Le Bret se retrouve donc sans l'opportunité de publier un ouvrage qu'il croit meilleur que celui qu'il préface:

> Son *Histoire de l'étincelle* et *de la république du Soleil*, où en même style qu'il a prouvé la Lune habitable, il prouvait le sentiment des pierres, l'instinct des plantes et le raisonnement des brutes, était encore au-dessus de tout cela et j'avais résolu de la joindre à celle-ci: mais un voleur qui pilla son coffre pendant sa maladie m'a privé de cette satisfaction et toi, de ce surcroît de divertissement. (57)

Volé à sa mort, Cyrano le fut également de son vivant. Quand il se croyait victime de plagiat ou voyait d'autres écrivains se couvrir d'une gloire injuste, Cyrano ne cachait pas son courroux; son style ne lui permettait pas une telle discrétion. De sa plume aguerrie, il écrit dans une lettre contre La Mothe Le Vayer:

> Puis que nostre amy butine nos pensées, c'est une marque qu'il nous estime, il ne les prendroit pas s'il ne les croyoit bonnes; et nous avons grand tort de nous estomaquer de ce que n'ayant point d'enfans, il adopte les nostres; pour moy, ce qui m'offence en mon particulier (car vous sçavez que j'ay un esprit vangeur de torts, et fort enclin à la justice distributive) c'est de voir qu'il attribue à son ingrate imagination les bons services que luy rend sa mémoire, et qu'il se dise le pere de mille hautes conceptions, dont il n'a esté au plus que la Sage-femme. (Bergerac, *Lettres* 114)

Et à Cyrano, bretteur en prose comme en escrime, d'ajouter:

> en dépit de tous ses grands manuscrits, que si quelque jour apres [s]a mort, on inventorie le Cabinet de ses Livres, c'est-à-dire de ceux qui sont sortis de son génie, tous ces ouvrages ensemble, ostant ce qui n'est pas de luy, composeront une Bibliothècque de papier blanc. (114-15)

Dans une autre lettre contre Chapelle, Cyrano reprend la métaphore du père orphelin de ses enfants pour l'accuser de plagiat: "Si maintenant vous me demandez la définition de cét homme, je vous respondray que c'est un Echo qui s'est fait penser de la courte haleine, et qui auroit esté muet, si je n'avois parlé. Pour moy, je suis un misérable père, qui pleure la perte de mes enfans" (119). Étant donné que le plagiat fut monnaie courante pendant le dix-septième siècle, le fait que Cyrano aborde le thème de manière critique est en soi original. Dans les *Supercheries*, Quérard note que "Le plagiarisme fut tellement à l'ordre du jour au dix-septième siècle qu'il eut jusqu'à une chaire".[5] Nodier, lui aussi, observe dans ce sens que "La comédie françoise, du temps de Cyrano, n'étoit qu'un imbroglio à l'italienne ou à l'espagnole" (Nodier, *Cyrano* 107). Chacun subtilisait les écrits et pensées d'autrui sans qu'il y eût de véritables reproches. Il fallait juste que l'emprunt ne soit trop abusif. "L'on peut dérober à la façon des abeilles, sans faire tort à personne; mais le vol de la fourmi qui enlève le grain entier ne doit jamais être imité" dit La Mothe Le Vayer (142). Il y avait aussi des conventions implicites qui se rapportaient à l'ancienneté et à l'origine nationale de la source empruntée. On pouvait voler aux anciens (ce qui était même encouragé) mais il ne fallait pas toucher aux modernes. Et s'il fallait piller les modernes, il était préférable de prendre, comme le rapporte Nodier, aux "voisins de par-delà les Alpes et de par-delà les Pyrénées" (*Cyrano* 108). À ce propos, Georges Scudéry, rapportant lui-même les paroles de Gianbattista Marino, écrit dans la préface d'*Alaric*: "Le Marin disoit, que prendre sur ceux de la Nation, c'estoit larcin: mais que prendre sur les Estrangers, c'estoit conquette, et je pense qu'il avait raison" (page 17 de la préface). Il n'empêche que Scudéry ne participe pas à ce butinage transnational et comme il sait "que l'invention est plus approuvée que l'imitation, [il ne s'est] servi que rarement de cette dernière" (page 18 de la préface). En effet, malgré la citation du Marin en faveur des emprunts aux étrangers, lors de la Querelle du *Cid*, Scudéry s'est prestement attaqué à Corneille sur ce même point. Dans ses *Observations sur le Cid*, Scudéry écrit:

> Le Cid est une Comédie Espagnole, dont presque tout l'ordre, Scène pour Scène, et toutes les pensées de la Françoise sont tirées: et cependant, ni Mondory,[6] ny les Affiches, ny l'Impression, n'ont apellé ce Poeme, ny traduction, ny paraphrase, ny seulement imitation: mais bien en ont-il parlé,

---

[5] Citation tirée de *Pragmatic Plagiarism* de Marilyn Randall (149).
[6] L'acteur qui a interprété Rodrigue lors de la première du *Cid*.

Falaky   *67*

comme d'une chose qui seroit purement, à celuy qui n'en est que le traducteur: et luy-mesme a dit (comme un autre a desja remarqué)

> *Qu'il ne doit qu'à luy seul, toute sa renommee.* (103)

Bien que l'intention du libelle soit surtout de dénoncer le manque de
vraisemblance dans la pièce et le mépris de Corneille à l'égard des
principales règles du théâtre, ce qui a dû enrager Scudéry le plus c'est
de voir Corneille se revêtir d'une gloire qu'il croyait imméritée. Scudéry n'était pas le seul à partager ce point de vue. Plusieurs auteurs
ont considéré le *Cid* comme un vol fait à un contemporain[7] et en voulaient à Corneille pour s'être octroyé une renommée qui n'était pas la
sienne.[8] Une lettre intitulée de "L'Autheur du vray Cid espagnol à son
traducteur françois", écrite par Mairet mais signée Don Balthazar de la
Verdad,[9] entend contester précisément la prétendue gloire de Corneille. Le faux auteur espagnol écrit:

> Je parle à toy Vanteur, dont l'audace achevée,
> S'est depuis quelques jours dans le Ciel eslevée.
> Au mépris de la Terre, et de ses Habitants,
> A Toy dont l'insolence en tes écrits semée
> Et bien digne du faste des plus fous Capitans,
> Soutient que ton merite a faict ta Renommée.
> [...]
> Donc fier de mon plumage, en Corneille d'Horace,
> Ne prétens plus voler plus haut que le Parnasse,
> Ingrat rens moy mon Cid jusques au dernier mot,
> Apres tu cognoistras, Corneille déplumée,
> Que l'Esprit le plus vain est souvent le plus sot,
> Et qu'enfin tu me dois toute la Renommée. (67-68)

Encore plus que le plagiat, ce qui avait exaspéré certains auteurs était
la vantardise du jeune Corneille. Dans un siècle qui se plaisait encore
à imiter les anciens, la fanfaronnade de Corneille — son désir "de
voler plus haut que le Parnasse" — choque. Dans la querelle du *Cid*,

---

[7] Quoiqu'il reste encore des doutes sur la date exacte qu'on assigne à la pièce de
Guillén de Castro — *Las Mocedades del Cid* — elle fut très probablement écrite en
1605.

[8] L'affirmation de Corneille "*Qu'il ne doit qu'à luy seul, toute sa renommee*" se
trouve dans l'"Excuse à Ariste".

[9] Nom inventé mais qui laisse entendre que la vérité sur l'affaire va éclater.

on voit également se dessiner les factions qui vont s'opposer plus tard lors de la querelle des anciens et des modernes. Ces derniers qui, comme Scudéry, croyaient que "l'invention est plus approuvée que l'imitation", cherchaient à se débarrasser des conventions littéraires héritées de l'Antiquité et voulaient privilégier l'originalité et l'innovation. Dans ce sens, il n'est pas surprenant que la querelle des anciens et des modernes ait éclaté à l'instigation de Charles Perrault, conteur et fantaisiste, créateur de mondes au même titre que Cyrano.

En 1657, bien avant *Le Siècle de Louis le Grand* de Perrault, la préface écrite par le Bret de l'*Histoire comique* fleure déjà une irrévérence palpable envers les Anciens. Si Cyrano surpasse les Héraclites, les Xénophanes et les Anaxagores, c'est bien parce qu'il a une imagination plus fertile. Il a mieux imaginé la Lune:

> Lucien [y avait] vu des hommes avec lesquels il avait conversé et fait la guerre contre les habitants du Soleil; ce qu'il conte toutefois avec moins de vraisemblance et de gentillesse d'imagination que Monsieur de Bergerac. En quoi, certainement, les modernes l'emportent sur les anciens, puisque les gansars qui y portèrent l'Espagnol dont le livre parut ici il y a douze ou quinze ans,[10] les bouteilles pleines de rosée, les fusées volantes et le chariot d'acier de Monsieur de Bergerac sont des machines bien plus agréablement imaginées que le vaisseau dont se servit Lucien pour y monter. (Le Bret 49-50)

La gloire devait donc revenir non pas à ceux qui suivent ce qui est déjà tracé par les anciens mais plutôt à ceux qui peuvent recréer, imaginer et produire de nouveaux mondes. Dans ce goût pour l'originalité, pour un "bien neuf", se dessine déjà la figure de l'auteur moderne et de ses droits telle qu'elle se développera plus tard entre la fin du dix-huitième et le début du dix-neuvième siècle.

Quand Anatole France fait l'apologie du plagiat en 1891, il se montre nostalgique d'un monde révolu où l'esprit du bien commun l'emportait sur l'individualisme moderne. Du point de vue littéraire,

---

[10] Le Bret parle d'un livre de l'Anglais Francis Godwin dont le titre français est "L'Homme dans la Lune, le Voyage chimérique fait au monde de la Lune nouvellement découvert, par Dominique Gonzalès, aventurier espagnol". Les gansars sont de grosses oies d'Amérique qui portèrent l'aventurier espagnol jusqu'à la lune (Bergerac, *Histoire comique* 11).

Falaky 69

ce changement a crée des auteurs obsédés par l'originalité et qui ne se lassent pas de prétendre à la gloire:

> La littérature contemporaine n'est ni sans richesse ni sans agrément. Mais sa splendeur naturelle est altérée par deux péchés capitaux, l'avarice et l'orgueil. Avouons-le. Nous nous mourons d'orgueil. Nous sommes intelligents, adroits, curieux, inquiets, hardis. Nous savons encore écrire et, si nous raisonnons moins bien que nos anciens, nous sentons peut-être plus vivement. Mais l'orgueil nous tue. Nous voulons étonner et c'est tout ce que nous voulons. Une seule louange nous touche, celle qui constate notre originalité, comme si l'originalité était quelque chose de désirable en soi et comme s'il n'y avait pas de mauvaises comme de bonnes originalités. Nous nous attribuons follement des vertus créatrices que les plus beaux génies n'eurent jamais; car ce qu'ils ont ajouté d'eux-mêmes au trésor commun, bien qu'infiniment précieux, est peu de chose au prix de ce qu'ils ont reçu des hommes. L'individualisme développé au point où nous le voyons est un mal dangereux. On songe, malgré soi, à ces temps où l'art n'était pas personnel, où l'artiste sans nom n'avait que le souci de bien faire, où chacun travaillait à l'immense cathédrale, sans autre désir que d'élever harmonieusement vers le ciel la pensée unanime du siècle. (164)

Si Corneille et Molière sont devenus les grandes figures littéraires du dix-septième siècle, c'est précisément parce qu'ils ont vécu lors d'un siècle où "l'art n'était pas personnel". Ils ont su subtiliser les idées des autres pour leur donner une meilleure forme. Si la question de l'originalité n'était que secondaire lors du Grand Siècle, elle deviendra au dix-neuvième, malgré les protestations d'Anatole France, une préoccupation grandissante allant de pair avec l'individualisme post-révolutionnaire. La redécouverte d'artistes oubliés, tel Cyrano de Bergerac, va donc refléter le goût de ce siècle pour une création littéraire sui generis, mais l'angoisse aussi de savoir que cette originalité, tel que le prouve l'exemple de Cyrano, n'accorde pas forcément l'immortalité. Toutes ces caractéristiques attireront Nodier à l'auteur du *Pédant joué* et le pousseront à écrire, en 1831, une monographie d'un auteur qui était complètement tombé dans l'oubli. Au début de son étude sur Cyrano, Nodier parle cependant de lui-même:

> Hélas! disois-je l'autre jour en pensant tristement à ce qui reste d'éventuel dans ma laborieuse vie, c'est donc là qu'aboutit ce qu'on appelle

70 *FLS, Vol. XXXVII, 2010*

une carrière d'homme de lettres? Un oubli éternel après la mort, si ce n'est auparavant! C'étoit bien la peine d'écrire!

Cependant j'ai été banni comme Dante, prisonnier comme Le Tasse, et plus sottement amoureux que Pétrarque. Me voilà bientôt aveugle comme Homère et le divin Milton. Je ne suis pas tout-à-fait aussi boiteux que Byron, mais je tirois le pistolet mieux que lui. Je sais au moins autant d'histoire naturelle que Goethe, je me connois en vieux livres aussi bien que Walter Scott, et je prends tous les jours une tasse de café de plus que Voltaire. Ce sont là des faits incontestables et dont la postérité ne saura jamais un mot, au cas qu'il nous advienne une postérité.

Il faut bien, repris-je après un quart d'heure de méditation, qu'il m'ait manqué quelque chose.

Il m'en a manqué deux, ajoutai-je quand la demi-heure sonna.

La première, c'est le talent qui mérite la renommée.

La seconde, c'est le bénéfice inexplicable du hasard qui la donne.

Et il arriva, par ce phénomène de psychologie, qui est inexplicable aussi, mais qu'on est convenu d'appeler la liaison des idées, que je commençois une notice.

Ce seroit une biographie assez curieuse que celle des hommes de talent, que dis-je? des hommes de génie, qui ont été victimes de la fatalité des réputations. On pourroit lui donner pour épigraphe: *Diis ignotis*. (Nodier, *Cyrano* 95-96)

L'injustice née d'une plume méritoire et laborieuse à laquelle on refuse le mérite et la gloire, Nodier la vivait mais ne pouvait l'analyser qu'en étudiant la fortune qui fut réservée à Cyrano. Oublié de la littérature et accusé par ses contemporains et ensuite par Voltaire d'être fou, Cyrano fut cependant plagié par un nombre d'écrivains qui ont brillé plus que lui. Si l'on en croit Nodier, à part Molière, parmi ceux-ci figurent Fontenelle, Swift et même Voltaire, qui "avoit pris *Micromégas* dans le *Voyage de la Lune*".[11] Le projet de Charles Nodier sera donc de réhabiliter Cyrano ainsi que les autres génies oubliés, tel Bonaventure des Périers, dans un canon littéraire où le plus souvent les règles ne sont dictées que par les mystères du hasard et suivies par "une foi moutonnière à la parole du maître" (Nodier, *Cyrano* 97).

Cela dit, la raison principale pour laquelle Nodier se penche sur Cyrano est que la littérature de ce dernier, fantaisiste et fabuleuse, ne

---

[11] Citation tirée de la préface de *Cyrano de Bergerac dans tous ses états* de Laurent Calvié (25).

Falaky 71

se conforme pas aux consignes littéraires de son époque. Dans ce sens, Cyrano était un homme de génie. Nodier ajoute que "c'étoit un talent irrégulier, inégal, capricieux, confus, répréhensible sur une multitude de points; mais c'étoit un talent de mouvement et d'invention" (98). Il faut dire que dans ce court texte censé être monographique mais où la biographie de Cyrano s'imbrique avec celle de son biographe, Nodier conçoit son projet de la même manière. Pour excuser sa curieuse biographie, Nodier affirme qu'"Il en est de l'audace littéraire comme des conspirations: sous peine d'ignominie, il faut qu'elle réussisse. Un fait certain, cependant, c'est que, dans la littérature, dans les sciences, dans les arts, les audacieux sont les précurseurs de la pensée, les conquérants de l'avenir" (96). Et c'est dans cette optique finalement qu'il faut lire *Les Questions de Littérature Légale*. Écrites d'un ton toujours facétieux et enjoué, elles ne sont censées ni être un traité sur l'imitation littéraire ni le précurseur de travaux juridiques sur le plagiat, mais bel et bien la conception d'un genre absolument original où l'érudition bibliographique et l'imitation littéraire sont traitées de manière ironique. Ce désir de nouveauté, inspiré de la folie de ceux qui ont refusé la conformité, naît aussi d'une aspiration, tout aussi facétieuse, à la gloire littéraire, à pouvoir survivre la mort. Le fait que ce livre ait initié une vague de travaux sérieux concernant le plagiat fait preuve non seulement de la mystification recherchée par l'auteur mais aussi, et ironiquement faut-il ajouter, de son originalité.

Ouvrages cités

Bergerac, Cyrano de. *Histoire comique des états et empires de la lune et du soleil*. Éd. P. L. Jacob. Paris: Adolphe Delahays, 1858.

_____. *Lettres*. Éd. Luciano Erba. Milan: V. Scheiwiller, 1965.

Bret, Henri Le. "Épître dédicatoire et préface de *L'Histoire comique* de Cyrano de Bergerac". Calvié 43-65.

Calvié, Laurent. *Cyrano de Bergerac dans tous ses états*. Toulouse: Anarchasis, 2004.

France, Anatole. "Apologie du plagiat". *La vie littéraire*. Paris: Calmann Lévy, 1892.

Gasté, Armand. *La Querelle du Cid*. Paris: H. Welter, 1898.

La Mothe Le Vayer, François de. *Œuvres*. Dresde: Michel Groell, 1758.

Mairet, Jean. "L'autheur du vray Cid espagnol à son traducteur françois". Gasté 67-69.

Marmontel, Jean-François. *Éléments de littérature*. 3 vols. Paris: Verdière, 1825.

Nodier, Charles. "Cyrano de Bergerac". Calvié 95-119.

_____. *Histoire du Roi de Bohème et de ses sept châteaux*. Paris: Delangle Frères, 1830.

_____. *Questions de littérature légale. Du plagiat, de la supposition d'auteurs, des supercheries qui ont rapport aux livres.* 1812, 1828. Éd. Jean-François Jeandillou. Genève: Droz, 2003. Histoire des idées et critique littéraire 404.

Randall, Marilyn. "Critiques et plagiaires". *Le Plagiat*. Éd. Christian Vandendorpe. Ottawa: Presses de l'Université d'Ottawa, 1992. 91-104.

_____. *Pragmatic Plagiarism*. Toronto: University of Toronto Press, 2001.

Rostand, Edmond de. *Cyrano de Bergerac*. Paris: Charpentier et Fasquelle, 1898.

Scudéry, Georges de. *Alaric ou Rome vaincue*. La Haye: Jacob van Ellinckhuysen, 1685.

_____. "Observations sur le Cid". Gasté 71-111.

Vapereau, Gustave. *L'année littéraire et dramatique*. 11 vols. Paris: Hachette, 1858-68.

Barbara T. Cooper

University of New Hampshire

Purloined Property: A Study of Madame Reybaud's *Les Épaves* and Its Theatrical Adaptation, *Le Marché de Saint-Pierre*

> This essay examines the practice of theatrical adaptation of narrative texts in early nineteenth-century France. A comparison of Madame Charles Reybaud's short story, *Les Épaves*, first published in 1838, and Antier and Decomberousse's five-act melodrama, *Le Marché de Saint-Pierre*, performed at the Théâtre de la Gaîté in 1839, shows that a text adapted for the theater is no mere reproduction of its narrative source. Various types of modifications and adjustments are required to make the narrative text intelligible to a theater audience, to make it fit within the generic norms and performance conventions of drama.

As numerous studies have clearly shown, appropriation, adaptation, and parody were regular features of the literary landscape in nineteenth-century France.[1] At that time, short stories and novels were routinely transformed into dramatic works and successful plays were often parodied or replicated. Whether such "borrowings" were openly acknowledged or not, they were almost always recognized by drama critics and by audience members whose appreciation of the resulting work depended to a considerable extent on its individual merits rather than its origins. Only rarely did the comments about these derived or

---

[1] For a brief overview of theatrical adaptation in nineteenth-century France and a select bibliography on the subject, see Cooper.

74   *FLS, Vol. XXXVII, 2010*

imitative texts include a condemnation of the appropriative practices that led to their creation.[2]

Consider, for example, the case of Frédéric Soulié, whose short story, *Le Lion amoureux*, was adapted for the stage — without his consent or collaboration — by Eugène Scribe under the title *Cicily ou le lion amoureux* (Théâtre du Gymnase, 8 December 1840). The drama critic for *L'Artiste*, like many of his peers, was perfectly aware of the source of Scribe's play. Indeed, he began his review of *Cicily* by reminding his readers that

> Il y a un an ou deux [1839], M. Frédéric Soulié a consacré *le Lion* dans une nouvelle du meilleur goût insérée dans le *Journal des débats*. M. Scribe a pris l'idée de M. Soulié; il l'a arrangée à sa façon, et chose inouïe, il en a fait quelque chose de charmant [...] (403).

The critic then went on to outline the plot of the play and to applaud the skill of its actors. "Cependant," the reviewer concluded, "pour notre compte, nous aimons mieux la nouvelle de M. Frédéric Soulié" (404). His preference for the original story was not, however, accompanied by a denunciation of the unauthorized use of Soulié's narrative.

I begin this examination of dramatic adaptation with the example of Soulié's *Lion amoureux*, not because I intend to study that work in detail, but because, in this instance, we have a record of the original author's feelings about the appropriation of his text. According to Jules Janin, the celebrated drama critic of *Les Débats*, Soulié was much distressed by Scribe's unsanctioned reworking of his story, but had too much "respect" for the dramatist-Academician to express his views on the matter straightforwardly. Soulié thus used the example of other authors who had fallen victim to the same kind of infringement of their artistic property rights to publicly denounce the practice. Janin records Soulié's position on such unauthorized borrowings in his *Histoire de la littérature dramatique*, from which I shall quote at some length here.

> Il se passe, dit [Soulié], en ce moment, un grand mystère littéraire. Madame Charles Reybaud rencontre une idée dramatique et pleine de situations vives et compliquées; elle en a fait une nouvelle; ceci est bien. À peine la

---

[2] For one denunciation of this practice, see Luchet.

Cooper 75

> nouvelle a-t-elle paru que deux hommes s'en emparent et en font un drame; voilà qui va le mieux du monde. En même temps M. Paul de Musset écrit dans la *Revue de Paris* un conte assez galamment troussé; ceci est encore très bien. Le conte est à peine achevé qu'il est mis sur le métier pour en faire un vaudeville; voilà qui va à merveille. En troisième lieu l'illustre M. Paul de Kock publie un roman de sept cents pages; ceci est toujours la même chose. Le roman est découpé en trois actes; il n'y a rien de plus commode (97).

Soulié momentarily sets aside "la question du vol littéraire" which, he notes, is under legislative review as he writes.[3] "Je ne veux pas, non plus," he says,

> faire honte à la littérature dramatique de ses emprunts perpétuels à la littérature romancière; car il n'y a guère que les gens qui ne sont pas volés qui se plaignent; je veux constater que la plupart des auteurs dont l'imagination est féconde en sujet de pièces, ne font aucune de ces pièces (97).

This observation brings Soulié to the crux of the matter as he sees it: the disparity in wealth, reputation, and status that separates playwrights from the novelists whose texts they pillage without permission. Soulié claims, with obvious bitterness in his voice, that

> [...] l'exploitation théâtrale est plus productive cent fois que celle de la librairie. La renommée s'y acquiert aussi plus facilement; car à chaque production, si misérable qu'elle soit, trente feuilletons proclament le nom de l'auteur, six cents affiches l'inscrivent, tous les jours, sur tous les coins de Paris; l'Académie s'ouvre pour lui, les décorations lui pleuvent, rien ne lui manque enfin; et cependant les hommes de style et d'imagination, les romanciers dédaignent cette carrière où l'argent, la renommée, les honneurs sont si faciles à acquérir; ils préfèrent jeter leurs idées dans un livre, les éparpiller dans des *nouvelles*, et cela pour en obtenir un faible salaire, pour demander vainement à un journal quelques lignes où se trouvent leurs noms, et pour être classés, dans la bonne opinion des protecteurs des arts, immédiatement au-dessous des auteurs de la *Marchande de Goujons* ou de *Mademoiselle Marguerite* (98).

---

[3] A law on literary property was enacted on 29 May 1839. See A.-C. Renouard, Cochut, and Vigny.

76 FLS, Vol. XXXVII, 2010

Soulié's remarks on this subject cover several more pages in Janin's volume, where I shall leave them to be discovered by those who wish to read further. Having established some sense of the ubiquity of appropriation and theatrical adaptation as cultural practices in nineteenth-century France, I want to turn my attention now to one of the authors Soulié cites in his comments above: Henriette-Étiennette-Fanny Arnaud (1802-1870), who published some of her works as H. Arnaud and others under her married name, Mme Charles Reybaud. Mme Reybaud is largely forgotten today, but during her lifetime she enjoyed a measure of fame and saw several of her narratives adapted as plays.[4] In what follows, I shall focus on one particular text by Reybaud that underwent numerous transformations: *Les Épaves*.

It was in February, 1838, that Mme Reybaud first published the short story *Les Épaves* in the pages of the *Revue de Paris*. She later incorporated the tale, along with other works, in a two-volume collection titled *Valdepeiras* (1839). Set in Martinique, in the eighteenth century, *Les Épaves* tells a story about race, gender, and power and, most interestingly for my purposes here, concerns itself with matters of possession and property. While it is unlikely Reybaud imagined that the questions about the custody and disposition of "property" she raises in her Martinican tale would also pertain, in the real world, to the enjoyment of her authorial privileges, it is certainly the case that she soon lost sole possession of her work. Indeed, *Les Épaves* was rather quickly adapted as a drama by Benjamin Antier and Alexis Decomberousse; it was performed under the title *Le Marché de Saint-Pierre* at the Théâtre de la Gaîté on 20 July 1839.[5] Three years later, Reybaud's story likewise served as the inspiration for a comic opera,

---

[4] An anonymous author in *The Dublin University Magazine* (1852) wrote that "Although she is far from faultless as a writer, we are disposed to allot to this lady a high position in the ranks of living French novelists. [...] Madame Reybaud's *forte* is the *Roman-de-mœurs*. She deals in pictures of society. Her touch is light and elegant; and, whilst adorning a tale, she rarely neglects an opportunity of pointing a moral, or striking at a prejudice" (235, emphases in original). See, too, the article by Montégut and n. 10 *infra*. Quérard (254-57) lists the many pirated editions of Reybaud's work printed in Belgium.

[5] The authors did acknowledge the play's origins when it was republished in the *Théâtre de Alexis Decomberousse*, where one reads: "Ce drame est imité d'une nouvelle de Mme Charles Reybaud (*L'Épave*)" (II: 370). However, that fact is not mentioned in the 1839 edition of *Le Marché de Saint-Pierre* from which I shall be quoting in this essay.

Cooper 77

Le Code noir, by Eugène Scribe (Théâtre de l'Opéra-Comique, 9 June 1842). According to the *Catalogue général des oeuvres dramatiques et lyriques* published by the Société des auteurs et compositeurs dramatiques, Reybaud received no part of the profits from either of these two plays (71, 217). Neither would she profit from Hans Christian Andersen's *Mulatten* (1840), an adaptation of her tale for the Danish stage, nor from a later reworking of her story by a little-known Belgian author, Mme Massart, who published a play titled *L'Épave* in 1854.[6] It will not be possible for me to examine all of these adaptations in the course of this one essay.[7] After a brief summary of Reybaud's tale, I shall therefore concentrate on the earliest adaptation of her narrative, Antier and Decomberousse's *Le Marché de Saint-Pierre*.

Reybaud's *Les Épaves* is a sentimental story set in an exotic locale — the French colony of Martinique — during the early part of the eighteenth century ("vers les fêtes de Noël, en l'année 1720" [122]).[8] The tale begins with an evocation of its physical backdrop ("À quelques lieues de Saint-Pierre, au pied de ces volcans éteints qu'on appelle les pitons du Carbet, il y avait autrefois une habitation, la plus belle et la plus considérable de la Martinique" [121]) and then intro-

---

[6] In 1845, A. de Roosmalen included an excerpt from *Les Épaves* in his *Études littéraires* (154-57). That appropriation of Reybaud's narrative left her "ownership" of the story intact and, in contrast to the various dramatic adaptations cited above, was likely beneficial to Reybaud's personal reputation as an artist. It is useful to note that *Les Épaves* was not the only text by Reybaud adapted for the stage. Both Labiche's three-act drama *L'Avocat Loubet* (1838) and Boulé and Chabot de Bouin's *Adriane Ritter* (1838) were inspired by Reybaud's short story, *L'Avocat Loubet*, published in the *Revue de Paris*. *Béatrix*, a drama by Lefebvre and Saint-Yves (1839), was derived from a story with that title by Reybaud. In his review of Narcisse Fournier's *Claude Stocq*, Vauclare wrote: "C'est encore une nouvelle de Mme Charles Reybaud, qui a fourni le sujet du drame de la Porte-Saint-Martin. Cette dame jouit depuis quelque temps du privilège de voir la plupart de ses productions arrangées pour les scènes de drame et de mélodrame" (45-46).

[7] Sollors has already discussed *Le Code noir* and the Andersen play in ch. 6 of his book.

[8] All page references are to the Belgian edition of *Valdepeiras*. One reads in *The Dublin University Magazine* (1850): "Madame C. Reybaud excels especially in her descriptions of the landscapes of the tropics. Many of her best scenes are enacted in those glowing countries. She makes us sigh amid our fogs and frosts for the clear moonlight heavens, the luxuriant foliage, and the luscious fruits and gorgeous flowers of Southern America, Mexico, and the West Indian Isles" (355).

duces three of its main characters: M. de La Rebelière, a wealthy and politically powerful planter who was born in Belgium to a family of modest means; his French Creole wife, Eléonore de La Rebelière, whose socially prominent family has lived in Martinique for several generations; and his ward, Mlle Cécile de Kerbran, who is recently arrived in Martinique from France, where she had been educated by Mme de Maintenon at the convent of Saint-Cyr. Upon reaching the age of majority (eighteen), Cécile will inherit the fortune and the Martinican plantation of a distant relative, M. de Rethel, but for the moment she is dependent on her guardian.

In the pages that follow, the reader learns about the domestic life of the La Rebelière family. There is information about their everyday routine as well as about M. de La Rebelière's racial prejudice, cruelty, and jealousy and about Madame's feelings of boredom and confinement at her home. One likewise learns something about the socioeconomic and political aspects of colonial life in Martinique,[9] including the hard work and mistreatment of slaves, the practice of marronnage, the meaning of the term "*épave*," and the role played by the body of laws (*Le Code noir*) and social customs that dictate whites' relations with blacks and mulattos. When M. de La Rebelière announces that he will be going to Fort-Royal but that he will not take his wife with him or allow her to go to their home in Saint-Pierre while he is away, Mme de La Rebelière insists that she and Cécile will travel to another, more isolated family residence located a day's journey away.

Their trip through the "wilderness" to Eaux-Chaudes turns out to be, as Monsieur predicted,[10] both arduous and dangerous, and a violent storm forces the two women to seek shelter in a cabin (*case*) inhabited by Donatien, a handsome, hospitable, deferential, well-spoken, and well-educated man who has lived in France. Cécile believes their host to be white, but Mme de La Rebelière recognizes that he is a mulatto and considers him her social inferior. When the two

---

[9] The island's governor-general is married to a close relative of M. de La Rebelière's, a fact that explains the planter's political influence.

[10] To discourage them from going, La Rebelière had exclaimed: "Mais il y a pour une journée de marche dans des chemins affreux, à travers un pays désert où vaguent des nègres marrons. Il n'y a point d'autre habitation aux Eaux-Chaudes qu'une case abandonnée, et qui était en fort mauvais état il y a deux ans, lorsque j'y suis allé pour la dernière fois" (125).

Cooper 79

women finally arrive at Eaux-Chaudes the next day, the narrator observes: "Il [Donatien] était ainsi le plus proche voisin de madame de La Rebelière, mais un abîme les séparait; et pour aller d'une possession à l'autre il fallait suivre un long détour" (144). During the remainder of their stay, this chasm, symbolic of the social distance between the white women and the mixed-race man, is reduced whenever Cécile and Eléonore encounter Donatien during their walks, but it is never entirely bridged.

One evening, while they are out walking alone, the two women come upon Palème, a former slave of M. de La Rebelière's who has run away to the hills ("s'en est allé marron" [145]). As darkness falls, Palème insists that the women spend the night in his *ajoupa* (thatched hut) but, in what is both a cruel parody of true hospitality and the antithesis of Donatien's deference, he fails to show them the slightest respect. Donatien arrives on the scene just in time to save Cécile and Eléonore from the "danger" Palème represents — the mere fact of spending the night alone in his company could have sullied their reputation — and to escort them safely home (145-48). This second "rescue" marks a major turning point, as both women now experience tender feelings for Donatien, though neither confesses this to the other or to him. On another occasion, Donatien will again save Cécile, who has gone out on her own, lost her way, and taken shelter beneath a mancenillier tree — a tree whose fruit and leaves are poisonous (157). This incident allows Cécile to understand the true nature of her feelings for Donatien and his for her.

Their chaste wilderness idyll has no time to develop, however, since M. de La Rebelière has recently arrived unannounced at Eaux-Chaudes and plans to return home with his wife and ward the next day. Though he can prove nothing, the ever jealous La Rebelière suspects his wife has been unfaithful — a fact she of course denies. Still, Monsieur continues to doubt her and to spy on her. Before their departure, he discovers a letter that Eléonore has written in secret to Donatien. Outraged, La Rebelière will use the occasion, and provisions in the *Code noir*, to have Donatien arrested on the grounds that the mulatto is an *épave* — a non-white who has no written proof to support his claim that he is a free man and who may therefore be sold at auction as a slave if no one steps forward to recover their "property."

Donatien is soon brought down to the La Rebelière plantation, where he will be held prisoner until the day of the slave auction in Saint-Pierre. Separately, both Palème and Cécile clandestinely visit Donatien in prison one night. Palème urges Donatien to flee with him via a secret passage, but Cécile makes him promise not to try to escape or kill himself. She will find a way to save him. She, Eléonore, and M. de La Rebelière then each make separate plans to purchase Donatien at the upcoming auction — the latter two via proxies. Cécile soon learns that Donatien is branded with a mark identical to her maid's, meaning that he was the property (and most likely the illegitimate son) of her late relative, M. de Rethel. She rushes off to consult the manager of the de Rethel estate and arrives in Saint-Pierre with proof of her "ownership" just as Donatien's sale to M. de La Rebelière is about to be finalized. Having turned eighteen that very day, Cécile is now able to do as she wishes and, after claiming Donatien as her property, she publicly declares her intention to free him. La Rebelière informs her, however, that the governor will never allow her to free her slave and that, as a slave, Donatien must be punished for publicly insulting a white person (La Rebelière). Cécile then announces that she will marry Donatien, since the *Code noir* automatically grants freedom to any slave married to a white woman, and that they will go to live in France.

This summary of Reybaud's tale leaves out a great deal but will at least give us a point of reference for a comparison between the short story and its adaptation as a five-act melodrama by Antier and Decomberousse. *Le Marché de Saint-Pierre* takes its name from the locus of the slave auction with which both texts dramatically conclude. However, despite that shared ending, and passages of dialogue lifted directly from the short story, the two works are in many ways dissimilar. That is, of course, not surprising. Generic (and performance) conventions shape each work according to different aesthetic traditions and different types of audience expectations. Dramatization of Reybaud's narrative will thus both change it and re-present it.

Compression, simplification, exaggeration, or clarification of both the story and its characters are generally required when narratives are reshaped as dramas, and that is certainly the case with respect to *Le Marché de Saint-Pierre*. There, in contrast to Reybaud's story, Eléonore de La Rebelière and Cécile de Kerbran are collapsed into a

Cooper   *81*

single character, Eléonore de Kerbran, the soon-to-be sixteen-year-old ward of M. de La Rebelière.[11] In accord with her uncle's dying wish, Eléonore is expected to marry her jealous, cruel, and avaricious guardian. This conflation of the two women into one reduces the complex set of relationships developed in Reybaud's tale to a conventional (dramatic) love triangle with La Rebelière, Eléonore, and Donatien in the clearly identifiable roles of villain/unworthy suitor, ingénue, and hero/deserving suitor. Such a configuration makes the outcome of the play — the announcement of Eléonore's intent to marry Donatien — both predictable and inevitable.[12]

In the place of Cécile, whose liberal (metropolitan) views on race were contrasted with both Eléonore's and La Rebelière's colonial prejudices in *Les Épaves*, *Le Marché de Saint-Pierre* introduces Mlle Hébert, a French governess whose presence is justified by Eléonore de Kerbran's younger age and unmarried status and whose enlightened beliefs about race will influence her Creole pupil. Such chaperon/teacher figures are, of course, useful substitutes for absent (deceased) mothers, and in this case Hébert may also be considered a surrogate for Mme de Maintenon, who served as an abstract source of moral education rather than an actual participant in Reybaud's tale.

The redefinition of characters and the realignment of their roles also extend to the two black men in the play: Donatien and Palème. As was made clear in Reybaud's story, the personalities and the lives of these men are very different. Those differences are exaggerated in *Le Marché de Saint-Pierre*, where Palème is given darker skin and a more prominent role as a racial antagonist bent on avenging his own and other slaves' mistreatment at the hands of whites. In the drama, Palème thus becomes a part of a triangular relationship pitting him against both his former master, La Rebelière, and against Donatien, whose moral nobility, bravery, and generosity are thrown into dra-

---

[11] The name of the character in the play, with elements borrowed from each of Reybaud's original characters, highlights this conflation. In contrast to Reybaud's text, the play insists that sixteen is the age of majority in the colonies. Just as is the case in the short story, however, in the play, the heroine comes of age on the day of the auction.

[12] Although there are differences in dramatic genre, setting, etc., these redefined relationships resemble those of Bartholo, Rosine, and Count Almaviva in Beaumarchais's *Le Barbier de Séville*.

matic relief by means of their heightened contrast to Palème's and La Rebelière's villainy.

Palème's expanded and more overtly villainous role is reflected in his frequent presence on stage (beginning with the first scenes of the play) and his physically menacing behavior. Early on, he threatens the cowardly La Rebelière with a dagger. Later, in a development not present in the short story, he will kidnap Eléonore from Donatien's home, where she has taken refuge from the same storm that interrupted her journey in Reybaud's narrative. Having had her drugged, the runaway slave carries Eléonore off into the night, in her hammock, to his *ajoupa*, where she awakens to find herself alone with him in the wilderness. Palème not only refuses to return her to Donatien's residence, but also grasps her about the legs ("genoux") to prevent her from fleeing. Their struggle, a (melo)dramatic scene of contact and constraint without direct parallel in Reybaud's more allusive, sentimental text, visually concretizes both Eléonore's virtue and Palème's role as a threat to her safety. Moreover, the scene is prominently displayed in the foreground on the left side of the frontispiece of the play's original edition. On the other side of that image, as on stage, Donatien can be seen standing on a promontory from which he looks down on their tussle. He has arrived just in time to shoot Palème in the shoulder and thereby save Eléonore's honor. As Donatien prepares to escort her back to his home, accompanied by Mlle Hébert, he orders Palème to treat the woman he loves with respect, and Palème agrees to do so. Indeed, henceforth the two men will become allies of a sort.

That Donatien is courageous, generous, and in love with Eléonore is made clear early on in the play. In contrast to Reybaud's story, where he does not appear until the women are forced to seek his hospitality during their journey to Eaux-Chaudes, Donatien figures, indirectly, in Act I of *Le Marché de Saint-Pierre*. There we learn, via a dramatic *récit* that has no precedent in *Les Épaves*, that Donatien has saved Eléonore's plantation ("héritage") from burning to the ground, thanks to his own heroic actions and his rallying of the very slaves who, in response to La Rebelière's regular mistreatment of them, had set fire to her property or were content to watch it burn. We also learn that when the fire is extinguished and the authorities are looking for slaves to punish, Donatien declares that those responsible had perished in the flames, thus sparing any surviving rebels from chastisement.

Cooper

This episode clearly highlights the contrast between Donatien and La Rebelière, whose cowardice in the face of Palème's threatened assault and whose routine cruelty to slaves frame this newly imagined *récit*.

Having shaped the audience's view of Donatien in this positive fashion, the playwrights then go on, in Act II, to introduce a monologue — the only one in the entire play — in which Donatien recalls his first sighting of Eléonore de Kerbran. The event, we are told, coincided with his return from France and, he reflects,

> Ce moment a décidé de mon sort. [... J]e l'aimais comme un fou, comme un insensé, malgré tous mes raisonnemen[t]s, tous mes efforts, au point d'oublier quelquefois les préjugés de son rang, sa fortune, ma pauvreté, bien plus... ma naissance. (II.i.7)

This instance of immediate, overwhelming emotion is, of course, absent from Reybaud's more leisurely and psychologically plausible story, as is the suggestion that Donatien had seen Eléonore on the very day he returned to Martinique. Still, the playwrights' introduction of this *coup de foudre*, a familiar form of dramatic "shorthand," not only helps to explain Donatien's previously reported efforts to save Eléonore's plantation, but also defines him as La Rebelière's (more worthy and sincere) rival for the young woman's love. It also provides an occasion for Donatien to reflect on his status in Martinican society ("[...] à la Martinique, rien ne saurait effacer la goutte de sang noir tombée dans mes veines, et je ne serai jamais aux yeux de ces insolen[t]s colons qu'un esclave qui a brisé sa chaîne..." [II.i.7]) and to congratulate himself for not having presented La Rebelière with the letter of recommendation he brought with him from France.

This letter of introduction constitutes yet another original element in the playwrights' text. Whereas in Reybaud's story, Donatien does not have any written proof of his status as a free man, here the dramatists' provide him with a document that not only attests to his freedom (manumission), but also grants him the right to collect a debt subscribed to by La Rebelière's father many years earlier. The letter in Donatien's possession leads to both new plot developments and concrete bits of stage business in the play. Donatien will finally present the document to La Rebelière, but only when he finds it necessary to justify his appearance at Eaux-Chaudes without compromising Eléonore's reputation. (She had sent Mlle Hébert to summon him for one last conversation and has no way to countermand her invitation when her jealous guardian suddenly arrives on the scene.) La Rebelière at first believes the letter Donatien hands him to be little more than a pretext for covering up a rendez-vous, then, momentarily, revises his opinion; but in the end, he reflects that the "convenient" timing of Donatien's delivery of the document justifies his worst suspicions. La Rebelière thereupon tears the letter into small pieces, erasing all proof of his father's debt and Donatien's freedom in spectacular fashion. The destruction of this letter thus not only serves as a visible sign of La Rebelière's jealousy, cruelty, and miserliness and of Donatien's chivalrous concern for Eléonore, but also leads to the mulatto's arrest as an *épave*. By dramatically underscoring the differences between the two men, the confrontation surrounding the letter helps to validate Eléonore's decision to marry Donatien at the play's conclusion. Her resolution, presented in terms of sensibility and moral and humanitarian principles in Reybaud's text, acquires a concrete, objective motive in the drama. The event also prepares the way for another confrontation between the two men in the play's final act.

Before arriving at that final scene, and in preparation for it, we must stop briefly to discuss another element of the drama that distinguishes it from Reybaud's short story: its multiple stage settings (*décors*). Whereas Reybaud provides written descriptions of the locales in which the action of her narrative takes place, the set designers offer physical representations of those sites. However stylized or clichéd they may be, the sets "transport" the viewer to Martinique, bringing a material presence and immediacy to the action in much the same way Donatien's letter of introduction and the actors' gestures did in the scene just described above. The concrete depiction of the wilderness setting in which Palème attempted his assault on Eléonore heightens the intensity of that confrontation and contributes to its dramatic power. Similarly, the multi-level set designed for Act IV, where we find Donatien imprisoned on La Rebelière's estate, allows us not only to experience the horror of the mulatto's incarceration in an underground cell, but also to observe La Rebelière's constant vigilance and the crushing weight of his political, patriarchal, and racial authority.

Cooper   **85**

The set of Act V is just as meaningful. There, we watch slaves construct a makeshift dais out of barrels and a large board upon which Donatien and the other slaves up for auction will be paraded before the bidders of Saint-Pierre. The proximity of the church and the cemetery to the platform ("[...] dans le fond, l'église du mouillage; du même côté, descendant en biais sur l'avant-scène, le mur du cimetière" [30]) symbolically points to the complicity or indifference of religious leaders to the sale of slaves and to the ultimate fate of those black men and women who will soon be sold. While the bidding proceeds on an elderly black man displayed on this stage, La Rebelière examines the other slaves up for sale who are sitting on a nearby bench. He stops in front of Donatien and insists that the mulatto walk about in front of him. Donatien refuses and a violent quarrel erupts between the two men, causing La Rebelière to threaten Donatien with a caning. The police intervene and Donatien is immediately put up on the auction block. In the end, as in Reybaud's tale, Eléonore arrives with the manager of her estate to prove that she owns Donatien and, then, to declare her intention to marry him. In the play, however, there is one last incident that was not included in *Les Épaves*. Frustrated in his pursuit of vengeance, La Rebelière draws his sword, determined to kill Donatien so that he will not escape his "just" punishment. Before the planter can attack, though, Palème stabs his former master with a dagger, killing him as the curtain falls. To be sure, this is a more dramatic, more shockingly aggressive conclusion than the announcement, in Reybaud's text, of Cécile's plan to return to France with Donatien by her side. The castigation of the villain is, however, typical of the *dénouement* of melodramas and would undoubtedly have earned warm applause from the audience at the Gaîté. It also brings full circle Palème's threat against the life of a cruel slave owner.

This brief study of Reybaud's *Les Épaves* and its dramatization by Antier and Decomberousse, *Le Marché de Saint-Pierre*, shows just how complex a matter the question of literary appropriation could be in the early decades of the nineteenth century. On the one hand, there seems to have been no legal impediment to the "borrowing" of a text, no requirement that an author grant consent for the dramatic adaptation of her work or be acknowledged or compensated for the use of her ideas, characters, etc. What is more, Mme Reybaud herself reused the Martinican setting and other elements from *Les Épaves* in another of her stories, *Marie d'Énambuc*, first published in the *Revue des Deux Mondes* in 1840, without referring readers to her earlier work.

On the other hand, it is clear from the example considered here that a text adapted for the theater — while not entirely original — is no mere reproduction of its narrative source, no matter how "dramatic" that first work might seem to be. Various types of modifications and adjustments are required to make the narrative text intelligible to a theater audience, to make it fit within the generic norms and performance conventions of drama. Moreover, those transformations are not exclusively text-based; they involve the collaboration of playwrights with stage designers, costumers, and other theater professionals, not the least of whom are the actors who embody the characters whose roles they perform. As a result of their combined efforts, the message of the original work may be refocused or re-presented in different ways or with different emphases.

Today, of course, some things are different. Films and television shows — the equivalent of the nineteenth century's popular theater — routinely include statements like: "based on the novel by" or "based on an idea by" or even "inspired by real events," and authors whose works are adapted typically receive some remuneration for the use of their text or ideas.[13] Still, this overt recognition of the practice of adaptation and the period of renewed sale of the text in print form that might follow on the heels of a film offer no guarantee that today's authors or their adapters will enjoy long-term recognition or success. As in Reybaud's time, any work, adapted or not, must resonate with audiences far beyond their original era and context if they are to enjoy perennial celebrity.

---

[13] See the article by Lutaud with its accompanying graph.

Cooper 87

Works Cited

Andersen, Hans Christian. *Mulatten: originalt romantisk drama i fem akter.* Kjøbenhavn: C. A. Reitzel, 1840.

Anon. "French Novels and Novelists." *The Dublin University Magazine* (t. 213, no. 36) Sept. 1850: 349-57.

Anon. "Théâtres." Rev. of *Cicily* etc. *L'Artiste* (t. 6, 25ᵉ livr.) 1840: 403-04.

Anon. "The Writings of Madame Charles Reybaud." *The Dublin University Magazine* (t. 40, no. 236) Aug. 1852: 234-40.

Antier, Benjamin, and Alexis Decomberousse. *Le Marché de Saint-Pierre.* Paris: Marchant, 1839. Coll. "Magasin théâtral."

Boulé, Auguste-Louis-Désiré, and Jules Chabot de Bouin. *Adriane Ritter, drame en 5 actes.* Paris: Michaud, 1838. Coll. "Musée dramatique." Based on Reybaud's *L'Avocat Loubet.*

Cochut, A. "Du projet de loi sur la propriété littéraire et la contrefaçon." *RDDM* (t. XVII) 1ᵉʳ févr. 1839: 388-402.

Cooper, Barbara T. Foreword. *Novel Stages: Drama and the Novel in Nineteenth-Century France.* Ed. Susan McCready and Pratima Prasad. Newark, DE: University of Delaware Press, 2007. 9-21.

Decomberousse, Alexis. *Le Marché de Saint-Pierre* in *Théâtre de Alexis Decomberousse.* Paris: Hachette, 1864. Vol II: 369-403.

Janin, Jules. *Histoire de la littérature dramatique.* Paris: Michel Lévy frères, 1857. Vol. V: 97-133.

Labiche, Eugène, Auguste Lefranc, and Marc Michel. *L'Avocat Loubet.* Paris: Michaud, 1838. Based on Reybaud's *L'Avocat Loubet.* Coll. "Musée dramatique."

Lefebvre, Louis, and Saint-Yves (pseud. Édouard Déaddé). *Béatrix, drame en 4 actes, imité d'une nouvelle de Mme Ch. Reybaud.* Paris: Gallet, 1839 and C. Tresse, 1840.

Luchet, Auguste. "Porte Saint-Antoine. *Céline la créole.*" *L'Artiste* (2ᵉ sér., t. I, 12ᵉ livr.) 1839: 184. Incl. reference to the adaptation of Reybaud's *L'Avocat Loubet* by Boulé et Chabot de Bouin *supra.*

Lutaud, Léna. "Ces écrivains que le cinéma s'arrache." *Le Figaro* 20 mars 2009. <http://www.lefigaro.fr/livres/2009/03/21/03005-20090321ART FIG00203-ces-ecrivains-que-le-cinema-s-arrache-.php>.

Massart, Mme. *L'Épave, drame en sept actes, en prose, d'après Mme Charles Reybaud, Mme Beecher Stowe, etc.* Bruxelles: J.-A. Lelong, 1854.

Montégut, Émile. "Romanciers et écrivains contemporains. Mme Charles Reybaud." *RDDM* (t. 35) 15 oct. 1861: 879-900.

Quérard, Joseph-Marie. *La France littéraire, ou Dictionnaire bibliographique*. Paris: L'Editeur, 1859-1864. Vol. XII: 254-57.

Renouard, Augustin-Charles. *Traité des droits d'auteur dans la littérature, les sciences et les beaux-arts*. Paris: Jules Renouard, 1838-39.

Reybaud, Mme Charles (née Henriette-Étiennette-Fanny Arnaud). "*Les Épaves*." *Revue de Paris* (t. 50) févr. 1838: 37-62. "Première Partie" and 73-101 "Seconde Partie."

———. "*Marie d'Énambuc*." *RDDM* (t. 22) 15 mai 1840: 672-700, and 1er juin 1840: 749-803, and "*Marie*." *L'Écho des feuilletons*, 13e année, 1853: 5-54.

———. *Valdepeiras*. Paris: Dumont, 1839 & Bruxelles: Société typographique belge, Ad. Wahlen et Comp., 1839.

Roosmalen, Auguste de. *Études littéraires ou recueil des chefs-d'œuvre de la littérature française*. Paris: Au bureau de l'orateur, 1845.

Scribe, Eugène. *Le Code noir*. Paris: Beck, 1842. Coll. "Répertoire dramatique des auteurs contemporains" and in *Œuvres complètes de Eugène Scribe: Opéras Comiques*. Paris: E. Dentu, 1879. Vol. IV: 277-382.

Société des auteurs et compositeurs dramatiques. *Catalogue général des œuvres dramatiques et lyriques faisant partie du répertoire de la Société des auteurs et compositeurs dramatiques*. Paris: A. Guyot & L. Peragallo, 1863.

Sollors, Werner. *Neither Black Nor White Yet Both*: *Thematic Explorations of Interracial Literature*. New York: Oxford University Press, 1997.

Vauclare, Théodore. "Théâtres de Paris. Premières Représentations. Revue dramatique." *Le Monde dramatique* 1839: 44-46.

Vigny, Alfred de. "De Mlle Sédaine et de la propriété littéraire." *RDDM* (t. 25) 15 jan. 1841: 220-52.

Travers, Seymour. *Catalogue of Nineteenth Century French Theatrical Parodies Between 1789 and 1914*. New York: King's Crown Press, 1941.

Corry Cropper

Brigham Young University

Call Me Clara: Prosper Mérimée's Hoax Ethos

Known for literary hoaxes early in his career (notably *Le Théâtre de Clara Gazul* and *La Guzla*), Mérimée seems to have formally abandoned them once his reputation was established. Yet disguises, questions of authorship, and challenges of generic conventions persist throughout Mérimée's *œuvre*. Indeed, the hoax continues to operate as an organizing principle in all his fiction. Mérimée's stories force readers to examine both their ideas concerning conventional literature and, more importantly, their perceptions of conventional values of the so-called civilized world. By centering his narratives on what might be called a hoax ethos, Mérimée questions cultural expectations of gender, morality, politics, and honor while subtly undermining dominant, hegemonic discourse in nineteenth-century France.

In perhaps the best known literary hoax in nineteenth-century French literature, Prosper Mérimée published a collection of plays in 1825 under the name of Clara Gazul, going so far as to have his own face sketched under a Spanish mantilla and above a black Spanish dress.[1] The preface to the plays suggests they were translated by one Joseph L'Estrange, a linguist who also provides significant details

---

[1] For Samuel Borton, the title of the collection, *Le Théâtre de Clara Gazul*, amounts to a second mystification, namely an anagram for one of Mérimée's friends and the artist behind the sketch of Mérimée in drag, Etienne Delécluze. It should also be noted that by signing his early works "Clara Gazul," Mérimée was able to maintain his detachment from these Romantic narratives while preserving his masculine and serious public persona. For more on Mérimée's Romantic theater, see also Barbara T. Cooper's studies.

90   *FLS, Vol. XXXVII, 2010*

regarding the work's author, Clara: her political views, her loves, and her subversive behavior. Mérimée followed this hoax up with another, more successful one in 1827 (many were not aware he authored it until more than fifteen years later). *La Guzla*, a series of Illyrian prose poems, was presented as a translation of the works of one Hyacinth Maglanovich, but it was, of course, a complete fabrication. Finally, when Mérimée published his first collection of short stories under the title *Mosaïque*, he chose to sign his work "Par l'auteur du *Théâtre de Clara Gazul.*"

Much has been written about these literary "mystifications" carried out early in Mérimée's life. Ora Avni, Jane Byers, and I have discussed Mérimée's hoaxes, offering various compelling reasons for his trickery. My objective in this article, however, is not to add another explanation of Mérimée's early subterfuge. Rather, I hope to establish that for Mérimée, even though he abandons the formalities of the literary hoax (popular in the early nineteenth century) when he becomes the serious Inspector of Historical Monuments, the hoax itself — with its accompanying disguises, plagiarisms, and obfuscations — remains central to the author's work. In fact, I hope to show that the hoax continues to operate as a primary structuring mechanism in all of Mérimée's fiction.

As a first case in point, the central narrative thread of Mérimée's most successful work, *Colomba* (1840), like a hoax, hinges on the very question of authorial identity. We learn that Colomba's father, the colonel Ghilfuccio della Rebbia, for reasons both serious and petty, is at odds with the mayor of Pietranera, Guidice Barricini. In order to get back at the colonel for defying one of his bureaucratic orders, the mayor decides to sue della Rebbia over a question of water rights. When it appears the courts will rule in favor of the colonel, Barricini produces a letter, written by a bandit named Agostini, that threatens the mayor's life, should he pursue the lawsuit further. Thanks to the letter, Barricini is able to argue that the colonel is on shaky legal ground and sought the help of bandits in order to blackmail him. But before a legal decision is reached, the bandit Agostini writes to the judge and declares that when he discovers the true author of the letter falsely attributed to him, "je le punirai exemplairement" (353).

Cropper 91

In the meantime, the colonel della Rebbia is gunned down by unknown assassins. As he lies dying, he takes a notebook from his pocket and writes down the name of his assailants. But this notebook, alas, like the fraudulent letter attributed to Agostini, ends up in the hands of the mayor. When investigators arrive and examine the notebook, they see the letters "Agosti..." scrawled on a blood-covered page and take it as clear proof that Agostini killed the colonel upon discovering that the latter had forged the bandit's signature. But upon further investigation, it is discovered that a page is missing from the notebook and that Barricini was alone with the notebook long enough to destroy the original page and forge a second document.

In this novel, a forerunner to the mystery novels that would become popular later in the century, two literary hoaxes stand at the very heart of the enigma: forgeries with legal and lethal ramifications. To add to the problem for investigators, Agostini, shortly after the colonel's murder, is himself killed in a skirmish with police. Colomba della Rebbia, however, is able to see clearly through the mystification. Her "mauvais œil" allows her to see what no one else can and, in the early stages of the investigation, she points at the mayor and resolutely declares, "Voilà l'assassin" (355).

Both Michel Crouzet and Kris Vassiler have written that two models of literature are exemplified in *Colomba*: an ancient, authentic, and "primitive" form embodied by Colomba and based on inspiration from the gods ("C'était la pythonisse sur son trépied" [398]); and a more "civilized," conventional, novelistic form embodied by Miss Lydia Nevil, who imposes her romanesque perspective on everything that surrounds her. The text parodies Lydia's clichéd perspectives while remaining respectful of Colomba's original, if occasionally violent, *ballatas*.

And if Colomba is a better poet than her British counterpart, she is also a better reader. While Lydia respects the civilized laws of the Crown and encourages Orso to do the same, Colomba sees how Barricini manipulates them and she deciphers the hidden messages surrounding her father's death. At the end of the story, a now-decrepit Barricini asks Colomba, "Cette feuille... que j'avais brûlée... comment as-tu fait *pour la lire*?" (475; my emphasis). In Mérimée's narrative, if Colomba is granted the most prominent position, if the story is named after her, it is in part because she is able to read better than anyone else, to see through the hoax and discern the hidden messages behind the falsified letters.

By "reading" the note that Barricini refers to in the above quote, Colomba is something of an archaeologist, deciphering the traces of the vanished original in the palimpsest. Seen in this light, Colomba, the decipherer of hoaxes, the reader of forgeries, is the perfect symbol of what Mérimée's readers must become in order to understand his narratives. In Mérimée's fiction the surface story is not unlike a conventional narrative with which Lydia would feel comfortable (at least it often begins that way) while Colomba represents the sinister, violent reality that is hinted at and hiding below the conventional, Romantic veneer. The real story, like the incriminating and truthful note Barracini burned, is alluded to and manifests itself in sudden, violent ways.

This is not to say simply that there are potential alternative readings of Mérimée's fiction as there are of any substantive literary text. Rather, the representation of hidden, ancient, authentic social identity is a fundamental component of all Mérimée's stories. Mérimée, an archaeologist in his own right, writes stories in which the past is preserved palimpsestically and can be inferred by a number of traces that remain in cultural practice or in archaeological evidence.

A striking example of this in *Colomba* occurs when Colomba leads her brother to the place of their father's death.

> Là s'élevait une petite pyramide de branchages, les uns verts, les autres desséchés, amoncelés à la hauteur de trois pieds environ. Du sommet on voyait percer l'extrémité d'une croix de bois peinte en noir. Dans plusieurs cantons de la Corse, surtout dans les montagnes, un usage extrêmement ancien, et qui se rattache peut-être à des superstitions du paganisme, oblige les passants à jeter une pierre ou un rameau d'arbre sur le lieu où un homme a péri de mort violente. (385)

In the above passage, although a Christian symbol physically occupies the highest position in the scene, it is the ancient, pagan "offrande" below the cross that strikes the reader as the most important. This scene reflects the tensions that weigh on Orso throughout the novel. On one hand, he is pressured to follow the French law (embodied by the Prefect), to respect the Christian doctrine of forgiveness and mercy, and to demonstrate his affection for Lydia by remaining peaceful. On the other, Orso is encouraged by Corsican tradition and by Colomba to take up arms and to take justice and revenge in his own hands.

This violent, ancient, even "pagan" culture hiding below the conventional, civilized, veneer of modernity structures all of Mérimée's narratives. The statue of Venus in "La Vénus d'Ille" — which the narrator and his host attempt to understand in modern, rationalist terms — ultimately validates the superstitions of locals when it apparently comes to life and slays the host's son. The Venus, an object that was dug up from under an olive tree, is a return of the repressed, a symbol of the past that defies modern rationality and nineteenth-century bourgeois morality.[2] Mérimée's "La Vénus" further implies that Parisian notions of modernity are themselves fraudulent, given that outside of Paris, France remained entrenched in the superstitious ideas of the past and largely rejected the Enlightenment ideas upon which the Revolution was based.[3]

The narrator of "Lokis," a reverend and scholar visiting Lithuania, is asked to perform a marriage for count Szémioth and mademoiselle Ioulka. But he is shocked to see that in this so-called Christian country, ancient practices seem more important than modern, civilized, moral ones, and he concludes, "il ne me parut plus convenable de demeurer parmi eux" (316). There are many such clues pointing to the continued, if covert, power of ancient beliefs in "Lokis": a sorceress who invokes "un dieu du paganisme" and tells the count he will become the king of the beasts (285); the ancient dance that depicts a water nymph who eats her suitors and that, according to the narrator, possesses "un caractère tout *antique*, rappelant les danses sacrées des Grecs" (294; my emphasis); the superstitious behavior of the count

---

[2] The statue, like Colomba's *ballatas*, is a symbol of antiquity. It may also be a symbol of medieval Christianity: Scott Sprenger has argued as much since, among other things, the Venus, often associated with the Virgin Mary during the middle ages, was discovered under an olive tree (a Christian symbol) and holds its fingers up in the sign of the trinity.

[3] Graham Robb's *The Discovery of France*, particularly part I, demonstrates the extent to which the French outside of Paris remained attached to their regional superstitions while rejecting, even killing, scientists sent from Paris to "civilize" them. Mérimée's "La Vénus d'Ille" can be read as a mise-en-scène of this tension and of the continued influence of regional culture.

who spits over his shoulder to ward off evil spirits "à l'exemple des *anciens* Romains" (286; my emphasis); etc. Those who believe, like the reverend, that modernity and Christianity serve as a civilizing tonic are proven wrong by the narrative's tragic dénouement: upon entering the nuptial chamber, the young bride is discovered to have been murdered by her husband who, in animal-like fashion, bit through her throat. And although the narrator describes the count as "beau" (270), endowed with a certain "galenterie chevaleresque" (313), and dressed in a civilized manner ("en robe de chambre boukhare, et tenant à la main une longue pipe turque" [270]) he, like most first-time readers, fails to perceive the significance of the other physical clues that allude to Szémioth's (and society's) hidden, primitive, animalistic — even sacrificial — nature.[4]

On a visual level, this layering of a conventional story line over the authentic primitive one recalls Delécluze's sketch of Mérimée in drag. The real author is visible — in plain sight — but the eye is first drawn to the subject's conventional vestimentary trappings. The true identity of the author comes as a surprise and provokes a second reading of the sketch. Mérimée's texts follow the same pattern: the conventional surface story is disrupted by a sudden, violent revelation and causes the reader to take a second look and reconsider all the clues pointing to the superiority of the violent, the authentic, the primitive.

Clothing, like reading, figures prominently in *Colomba*. Peter Cogman, in an article on the narrative function of dress in Mérimée, points to an insistence on clothing's potential to reveal inner impulses. "Le costume pittoresque que Colomba a préparé pour Orso, et qui le transforme, quand il le met [...] indique qu'il va céder [...] au désir de vengeance de sa sœur" (181-82). But for our study, the most significant clothing in *Colomba* may be the French dress Colomba herself puts on at the end of the narrative, replacing the black she wore when

---

[4] Scott Carpenter's article, "Supercherie et violence," studies practical jokes, particularly those found in "Lokis," and suggests that they parallel Mérimée's construction of Fantastic narratives. "The Fantastic, like the hoax or practical joke, wagers on the credulity of the reader: like the hoax, it exploits the stylistic detours of realism in order to make the reader believe the most unbelievable things; like the hoax, it leaves an aftertaste in the mouth of the reader, who knows he has been had but who takes pleasure in falling into the trap" (56).

Cropper 95

mourning her father. Speaking to her father-in-law, Colomba explains:

> N'est-ce pas que je me forme? Je prends le bras, je mets des chapeaux, des robes à la mode; j'ai des bijoux; j'apprends je ne sais combien de belles choses; je ne suis plus du tout une sauvagesse. Voyez un peu la grâce que j'ai à porter ce châle... Ce blondin, cet officier de votre régiment, qui était au mariage... mon Dieu! je ne puis pas retenir son nom; un grand frisé, que je jetterai par terre d'un coup de poing... (474)

Here, even though she is dressed in a civilized manner, the text nevertheless emphasizes her masculine, "savage" strength. The young officer may be in love with her, but she could easily throw him to the ground with one arm. And later in the same chapter, while wearing her "robe à la mode," Colomba confronts the aging Barricini and provokes him, causing him to pass out ("le vieillard poussa un cri, et sa tête tomba sur sa poitrine" [476]). Earlier in the narrative, Orso tells his sister: "La nature a eu tort de faire de toi une femme, Colomba. Tu aurais été un excellent militaire" (424). Colomba challenges conventional barriers of gender and culture by appearing more masculine than feminine, more savage than civilized. By hiding the vengeful, masculine, bellicose Colomba in fashionable dress, Mérimée calls to mind his own portrait as the Spanish playwright Clara Gazul. The last line of *Colomba* offers telling support for this reading: "Tu vois bien cette demoiselle si jolie [...] eh bien, je suis sûre qu'elle a le mauvais œil" (476). In other words, Colomba's outward trappings are a "mystification": the real Colomba is hiding under the façade.

In a similar fashion, Mérimée's Carmen is at times described as "bien déguisée" (147), hiding her violent intentions under conventional dress or behind other languages (going so far as to convince Don José that she is Basque). In one scene, she is described as "habillée superbement: un châle sur les épaules, un peigne d'or, tout en soie" (150). While in this disguise she seduces a "gros mylord" with "cheveux frisés" (recalling the young officer in love with Colomba), takes him for all he is worth before leading him to be killed. Considering Carmen as an extension of Mérimée's hoax ethos (given that her true identity hides behind another, fabricated one) causes us to equate Don José with a reader — a reader who was duped by the mystification and who did not appreciate the joke. Indeed, as Scott Carpenter

96   *FLS, Vol. XXXVII, 2010*

has pointed out, practical jokes in Mérimée's texts are never innocent
and usually hide violent impulses.

The hoax has special significance in Mérimée's *œuvre* when
transposed to the narrative, generic level as well. "Mateo Falcone," for
example, superficially adopts the appearance of a *récit de voyage*, yet
ultimately reveals itself to be something quite different. The first
paragraph of the *nouvelle* is particularly revealing in the framing of
this truly *literary* hoax.

> En sortant de Porto-Vecchio et se dirigeant au nord-ouest, vers l'intérieur de
> l'île, on voit le terrain s'élever assez rapidement, et après trois heures de
> marche par des sentiers tortueux, obstrués par de gros quartiers de rocs, et
> quelquefois coupés par des ravins, on se trouve sur le bord d'un *maquis* très
> étendu. (23)

This beginning parallels perfectly the conventions of travel literature,
employing the generic pronoun "on" to emphasize the potential for the
reader to follow the same route as the narrator. But a paragraph later,
Mérimée, with a certain detachment — even nonchalance —
introduces a clue, a bit of authenticity, into the conventional travel
narrative: "Si vous avez tué un homme, allez dans le maquis de Porto-
Vecchio, et vous y vivrez en sûreté, avec un bon fusil, de la poudre et
des balles" (23). Visit Corsican villages, enjoy a nice stroll along the
coast, visit the rugged mountains, and if you happen to kill someone,
no problem, hide in the *maquis*... Of course, the full implications of
this statement are not realized until the tale's violent and shocking
conclusion, a conclusion that causes the reader to re-evaluate the irony
of the narrative's conventional, descriptive beginning.[5]

In addition to staging what may be dubbed a generic disguise, in
"Mateo Falcone" as in "Lokis" and "Colomba," Mérimée implies that
civilization is a simple veneer over the harsh, primitive culture that
still holds sway. The story depicts the legal system (represented by the
voltigeurs who arrive on the scene in search of the bandit Sampiero)
as clearly inferior to primitive law as Mateo punishes his son for

---

[5] Mérimée further plays on the *récit de voyage* structure when he uses the
pronoun "on" again to hint at the fate awaiting Fortunato: "Un certain jour d'automne,
Mateo sortit de bonne heure [...]. Le petit Fortunato voulait l'accompagner, mais [...]
le père refusa [...]: *on* verra s'il n'eut pas lieu de s'en repentir" (25).

aiding these agents of French civilization. And even though Mateo invites his son to say his prayers before dying, he nevertheless does not leave justice to God but instead takes it into his own hands, killing his only begotten son to punish him for treason, ultimately demonstrating that the primitive beliefs are more important than the superficial beliefs of civilized Catholicism. Seen in this light, "Mateo Falcone," considered by many to be the first modern French short story,[6] is an elaborate disguise: it dresses like a conventional travel narrative but is ultimately exposed as a portrayal of the ancient, violent culture that lurks behind French-imposed legal and religious systems.

This violent and primitive "second story" (to use Armine Mortimer's term) is not limited to stories set in exotic locales. Even Mériméean narratives set in France, though they may differ by degrees from their foreign counterparts, are structured around the same idea of deception, where corruption is camouflaged by moral ethics. In "Arsène Guillot," a prostitute is taken in by the devout Mme de Piennes, who attempts to nurse her back to health and who takes it upon herself to teach religious morality to her young ward. Yet here, as in the stories set outside of France, the surface morality amounts to little more than hypocritical robes. Mme de Piennes, while teaching lessons of virtue to Arsène, is at the same time committing adultery with Arsène's former lover. And while Mme de Piennes does not shoot Arsène, her behavior aggravates Arsène's poor health and indirectly leads to the courtesan's death.

For Mérimée, then, the hoax went well beyond an early experiment with what was a fad in the 1820s. It forms a structuring concept for all of his fictional works where deception, disguise, plagiarism, and the theme of the superficial versus the authentic all figure prominently. Mérimée's hoaxes are designed to force readers to examine both their ideas concerning conventional literature and, more importantly, their perceptions of conventional values of the so-called civilized world. By centering his narratives on what might be called a hoax ethos, Mérimée questions cultural expectations of gender, morality, politics, and honor while subtly undermining dominant, hegemonic discourse in nineteenth-century France.

---

[6] See studies by Cropper, Engstrom, Sachs, and Thibaudet.

Works Cited

Avni, Ora. "Mystification de la lecture chez Mérimée: Lira bien qui rira le dernier." *Littérature* 58 (1985): 29-41.

Borton, Samuel. "A Note on Prosper Mérimée: Not de Clara Gazul but Delécluze." *Modern Language Notes* 75.4 (1960): 336-39.

Byers, Jane. "The *Théâtre de Clara Gazul* and the Spanish *Comedia*: A Case of Impudent Imitation." *Hispanófila* 27.3 (1984): 17-33.

Carpenter, Scott. "Supercherie et violence: Mérimée, ou le texte piégé." *Romantisme* 116 (2002): 49-57.

Cogman, Peter. "Exotisme et ethnologie: la fonction narrative du costume dans les nouvelles de Mérimée." *Cahiers Ivan Tourguéniev Pauline Viardot Maria Malibran* 27 (2003): 179-88.

Cooper, Barbara. "Mérimée's Romantic Theater." *Nineteenth-Century French Studies* 6 (1977-78): 72-81.

Cropper, Corry. "Revolution Under the Mantilla: Mérimée's Spanish Theatre." *Dalhousie French Studies* 66 (2004): 11-19.

_____. "Prosper Mérimée and the Evolution of the French Short Story." *Romance Notes* 40.3 (2000): 351-60.

Crouzet, Michel. "Mérimée, le roman et la nouvelle: l'exemple de *Colomba*." *Cahiers Ivan Tourguéniev* 27 (2003): 139-72.

Engstrom, Alfred G. "The Formal Short Story in France and its Development before 1850." *Studies in Philology* 42.3 (1945): 627-39.

Mérimée, Prosper. *Carmen et treize autres nouvelles*. Paris: Gallimard, 1965.

_____. *Colomba et dix autres nouvelles*. Paris: Gallimard, 1964.

Mortimer, Armine. "Second Stories." *Short Story Theory at a Crossroads*. Ed. Susan Lohafer and Jo Ellyn Clarey. Baton Rouge: Louisiana State UP, 1989. 276-98.

Sachs, Murray. "The Emergence of a Poetics." *French Literature Series* II (1975): 77-88.

Sprenger, Scott. "Consummation as Catastrophe: Failed Union in Prosper Mérimée's 'La Vénus d'Ille.'" *Dalhousie French Studies* 51 (2000): 26-36.

Thibaudet, Albert. *Histoire de la littérature française*. Paris: Éditions Stock, 1936.

Vassiler, Kris. "*Colomba*: La vengeance entre classicisme et romantisme." *Revue d'histoire littéraire de la France* 100.5 (2000): 1311-36.

Bertrand Bourgeois

The University of Melbourne

Le Muséum de Bouvard et Pécuchet:
Parodie, kitsch et ruine du musée moderne

Le musée mis en place par Bouvard et Pécuchet dans le chapitre IV du roman éponyme de Flaubert, à la fois pseudo-cabinet de curiosité et pseudo-musée moderne, s'avère en fait le lieu du kitsch où les objets sont rassemblés de façon purement hétéroclite par les deux compères dans l'impossibilité de faire signifier un monde en perte de sens. Partant, la trajectoire de la statue de saint Pierre du musée aux poubelles peut se lire comme métaphore de la mise en ruine du musée et la négation de toute transcendance signifiante pour l'homme.

> Curiosités antiques: sont toujours de fabrication moderne. (*DIR* 503)[1]

Le chapitre IV de *Bouvard et Pécuchet* commence ainsi: "Six mois plus tard, ils étaient devenus des archéologues; — et leur maison *ressemblait* à un musée" (151).[2] Derrière l'ironie du narrateur flaubertien face à l'entreprise muséale des deux bonhommes, cet *incipit* indique que leur maison est l'espace romanesque d'une réflexion sur la représentation. Cette maison qui *ressemble* à un musée suggère une

---

[1] Toutes les citations du *Dictionnaire des idées reçues* proviennent de l'édition de *Bouvard et Pécuchet* établie par Claudine Gothot-Mersch et incluant "le sottisier", "l'album de la marquise" et "le dictionnaire des idées reçues".

[2] Toutes les citations de *Bouvard et Pécuchet* proviennent de l'édition de Stéphanie Dord-Crouslé référencée en fin d'article.

100   FLS, Vol. XXXVII, 2010

triple interrogation littéraire: sur les questions de la *Mimesis*,[3] de l'imitation et de la parodie. En effet, si la maison des deux héros du roman copie un musée (c'est-à-dire un espace qui se présente comme un microcosme du réel), elle est à leur image puisque, par un mouvement circulaire, Bouvard et Pécuchet commencent par la copie et y reviennent au terme de l'échec de leur entreprise de totalisation encyclopédique de la connaissance. Ils sont en outre eux-mêmes à l'image du romancier-copiste Flaubert mourant à la tâche sans avoir pu finir cet ouvrage qui se voulait le recensement systématique, la *collection* de la totalité de la bêtise humaine.

En ce sens, il s'agit de voir comment ce muséum parodie le cabinet de curiosités, puis de s'interroger sur l'insignifiance de la collection des deux commis qui se manifeste notamment par son caractère hétéroclite et son kitsch. Partant, il semblerait que le passage d'un objet de collection, la grotesque statue de saint Pierre, du musée aux poubelles puisse se lire comme une métaphore de la mise en ruine du musée moderne et des principes qui le gouvernent.

Un pseudo-cabinet de curiosités: des raretés d'une banalité exemplaire

Dans *Collectionneurs, amateurs et curieux*, l'historien de l'art Krzysztof Pomian, spécialiste de l'ère pré-moderne et classique, parle de la curiosité dans les termes suivants:

> Incarnée dans une *Kunst- und wunderkammer*,[4] dans la bibliothèque d'un érudit, dans le laboratoire d'un chimiste, praticien de la philosophie hermétique, ou d'un physicien pour qui l'optique restait une science des miracles, exubérante, incohérente, désordonnée, travaillée par des contradictions, tirée

---

[3] Nous rejoignons le propos plus général de Claudine Gothot-Mersch à la fin de son article "Le Roman interminable: un aspect de la structure de *Bouvard et Pécuchet*" où elle souligne la présence de la notion de mimesis dans tous les niveaux du dernier roman de Flaubert: "Dans *Bouvard et Pécuchet*, on le sait, la *Mimesis* est particulièrement envahissante" (21). Pour plus de détails sur cette affirmation, on se référera également aux lignes suivantes de cet article (21-22).

[4] Pomian préfère le terme allemand, soulignant qu' "art" et "merveilles" (de la nature) se côtoient dans ces cabinets, ce que le terme plus général de "curiosités" n'exprime pas, mettant plutôt l'accent sur la passion qui pousse à constituer de tels lieux.

Bourgeois

> à hue et à dia, la curiosité a gouverné par intérim entre le règne de la théologie et celui de la science. (80)

À lire une telle analyse, il ne semble pas interdit de penser que le musée de Chavignolles soit une version tardive du cabinet de curiosités des siècles précédents. L'entreprise des deux célibataires participerait ainsi d'une épistémologie pré-moderne qui

> conçoit encore la nature comme un principe de variabilité et de diversité illimitées dont la puissance se dévoile le mieux dans ce qui est exceptionnel, singulier, voire unique. Car une nature censée être soumise à des lois toujours et partout les mêmes se manifeste vraiment dans le commun, le répétitif, le reproductible. En revanche quand on n'y voit aucune règle, les choses rares passent pour être les seules capables de la bien représenter. (63)

Le critère de la rareté ne semble à l'évidence pas étranger aux deux commis qui possèdent, parmi la diversité hétéroclite de leurs objets, "les curiosités les plus rares: la carcasse d'un bonnet de Cauchoise, deux urnes d'argile, des médailles, une fiole de verre opalin" (151) et "une hallebarde, pièce unique" (152). Cependant, ces quelques exemples indiquent immédiatement que le critère de rareté n'est pas à prendre au sérieux. Il est en effet décliné sur le mode de l'ironie flaubertienne qui joue sur des antithèses sémantiques afin de mieux dénoncer la trivialité de la collection de Bouvard et Pécuchet.

Flaubert désigne comme "les curiosités les plus rares" des objets qui sont en fait d'une grande banalité et d'un kitsch absolu. "La carcasse d'un bonnet de Cauchoise" par exemple, renvoie de façon grotesque au folklore normand; alors qu'en ce qui concerne "la hallebarde, pièce unique", Flaubert joue fort probablement sur toute l'ambiguïté sémantique de l'adjectif "unique",[5] signifiant ici peut-être moins la rareté de la hallebarde que son isolement dans la collection (c'est la seule qu'ils possèdent) et sa non-intégration au sein d'un en-

---

[5] Yvan Leclerc souligne déjà l'ambiguïté de cet adjectif dans un monde flaubertien où tout fonctionne par paire: "quand on lit à la fin de la description du musée: "une hallebarde, pièce unique", on se demande si l'adjectif doit être pris en bonne ou en mauvaise part: curiosité sans pareille ou pièce dépareillée?" (Leclerc 109). La hallebarde est bien en outre un objet ironique puisque Flaubert en fait une des entrées du *Dictionnaire des idées reçues*: "Hallebarde: Ne rime point avec "miséricorde". Quand on voit un nuage menaçant, ne pas manquer de dire: "il va tomber des hallebardes". "En Suisse, tous les hommes portent des hallebardes" (*DIR* 525).

semble d'objets médiévaux. Elle relève par ailleurs explicitement de la mode pour le Moyen Âge qui, à partir du Romantisme, a conquis tout le dix-neuvième siècle: Bouvard et Pécuchet sont victimes d'une mode qui pousse à collectionner un certain type d'objets[6] (hallebarde, cotte de mailles) dont la rareté est plus que douteuse à une époque où les objets — et partant les bibelots — deviennent reproductibles et où l'on commence à les produire en série.[7]

Le musée de *Bouvard et Pécuchet* ne serait donc qu'un pseudo-cabinet de curiosités puisque les objets qui le composent ne sont pas d'une rareté et d'une exemplarité exprimant la diversité d'un cosmos signifiant. Leur rareté plus que douteuse les pose plutôt comme les débris insignifiants d'un monde incohérent et grotesque qu'il est désormais impossible de faire signifier comme totalité. Quatre aspects fortement problématiques de cette collection d'objets méritent d'être notés: son caractère hétéroclite, son désordre organisationnel, son impossibilité à renvoyer à l'invisible et finalement sa fragmentation irréductible. Ces quatre caractéristiques inviteraient à définir ce rassemblement d'objets moins comme une collection que comme un

---

[6] Flaubert le souligne explicitement dans la suite de ce chapitre: "Le goût des bibelots leur était venu, puis l'amour du Moyen Âge". Soulignons d'ailleurs que l'on trouve des hallebardes dans la salle gothique de la "maison-musée" de Pierre Loti à Rochefort. Cette salle gothique recrée une ambiance médiévale alors qu'il n'y a quasiment aucun objet authentique du Moyen Âge. Elle pose donc, comme le musée de Bouvard et Pécuchet, le problème du simulacre, de la copie et du kitsch.

[7] Reproductibilité et production en série des bibelots dont Flaubert est pleinement conscient, le personnage d'Arnoux et sa fabrique de céramiques dans *L'Éducation sentimentale* en sont la preuve: "Pour le [Frédéric] distraire d'abord par quelque chose d'amusant, elle [Madame Arnoux] lui fit voir l'espèce de musée qui décorait l'escalier. Les spécimens accrochés contre les murs ou posés sur des planchettes attestaient les efforts et les engouements successifs d'Arnoux. Après avoir cherché le rouge des cuivres des Chinois, il avait voulu faire des majoliques, des faënza, de l'étrusque, de l'oriental, tentés enfin quelques-uns des perfectionnements réalisés plus tard. Aussi remarquait-on, dans la série, de gros vases couverts de mandarins, des écuelles d'un mordoré chatoyant, des pots rehaussés d'écritures arabes, des buires dans le goût de la Renaissance, et de larges assiettes avec deux personnages, qui étaient comme dessinés à la sanguine, d'une façon mignarde et vaporeuse. Il fabriquait maintenant des lettres d'enseignes, des étiquettes à vin; mais son intelligence n'était pas assez haute pour atteindre jusqu'à l'Art, ni assez bourgeoise pour viser exclusivement au profit, si bien que, sans contenter personne, il se ruinait" (222). Ce petit musée annonce déjà à plusieurs égards celui de Bouvard et Pécuchet.

Bourgeois

"amas d'objets indigestes" (*BP* 125)[8] pour parodier la définition ironique du chocolat proposée dans le chapitre III du roman.

Une collection insignifiante: hétéroclite, kitsch et ruines

Le caractère hétéroclite des objets rassemblés frappe immédiatement le lecteur à la découverte du musée de Bouvard et Pécuchet: contrairement au principe de cohérence qui veut que toute collection repose sur la sélection d'objets à partir d'au moins un (et le plus souvent plusieurs) point(s) commun(s) justifiant leur rassemblement et permettant déjà d'établir des correspondances entre ces objets et de les faire signifier comme un tout; les objets rassemblés par Bouvard et Pécuchet n'ont aucun point commun et sont juxtaposés dans une syntaxe flaubertienne sans subordination et qui réduit la coordination au minimum (marques de ponctuation, "et", "puis"). Franc Schuerewegen est sans doute le premier à avoir noté le caractère fondamentalement hétéroclite de cette collection, son incohérence irréductible:

> Dans ce ramassis de curiosités qui ne sont réunies, semble-t-il, que parce qu'elles ne peuvent tenir ensemble, on chercherait en vain un principe de cohérence quelconque. [...] Toute opération d'assemblage ici serait inutile, en ce qu'elle ne pourrait jamais cacher l'incohérence fondamentale marquant cette collection. (43)

Un des seuls points communs que l'on pourrait trouver entre ces objets serait l'impossibilité de "tenir ensemble", c'est-à-dire de n'avoir aucun point commun, sinon un caractère grotesque et un mauvais goût certain comme l'a suggéré Normand Lalonde.[9]

Le seul véritable point commun de ces objets serait selon nous d'être *kitsch*, au sens où Abraham A. Moles et Eberhard Wahl entendent ce mot dans leur célèbre article "Kitsch et objet". Dans cet article, ils identifient la première grande époque du kitsch comme "celle de la prospérité des grands magasins, entre 1880 et 1914" (107), data-

---

[8] Alors que Bouvard et Pécuchet s'intéressent à la médecine, Flaubert incorpore une citation du *Manuel théorique et pratique d'hygiène ou l'art de conserver sa santé* du docteur Joseph Morin, qui définit ainsi le chocolat.

[9] "[...] malgré le caractère relativement noble de certaines de ses pièces, dans leur ensemble, en tant que collection, les objets réunis dans le 'Muséum' sont tout à fait grotesques et du plus mauvais goût" (455).

tion qui fait ainsi coïncider la parution de *Bouvard et Pécuchet* (1881) avec les débuts de l'ère kitsch. Notons toutefois immédiatement que faire du "kitsch" le point commun de ces objets ne constitue pas un principe unificateur car il renvoie justement à l'hétéroclite et l'incohérence qui lui sont inhérents. De plus, et c'est d'ailleurs l'un des modes du kitsch, certains objets de cette collection ne sont pas kitsch en tant que tels, mais plutôt par leur proximité avec d'autres objets avec lesquels ils contrastent violemment et composent un "ensemble" kitsch: "la figure au pastel d'une dame en costume Louis XV" fait, par exemple, "pendant au portrait du père Bouvard" (152), les deux tableaux formant ainsi un couple pictural plutôt déroutant. Ce caractère hétéroclite s'accompagne d'un désordre et d'un encombrement tout aussi caractéristiques du kitsch:[10] les objets saturent l'espace, ils gênent la circulation ("les spécimens de géologie encombraient l'escalier"; "on se heurtait à une auge de pierre" [151]). Et, comme l'a souligné Schuerewegen, un certain nombre d'objets servant habituellement à lier, à organiser, à joindre les choses entre elles ("une chaîne énorme"; "deux chenets"; "des serrures, des boulons, des écrous" [151]) se retrouvent hors d'usage: ils participent au désordre en même temps qu'ils soulignent l'impossibilité de tout ordre.

Ces objets hétéroclites expriment également l'impossibilité de tout sens: ce sont des serrures (pour reprendre métaphoriquement un objet du texte) hors d'usage dont ni Bouvard, ni Pécuchet, ni le lecteur n'ont la clef. Une clef qui serait de toute façon inutile puisque les serrures sont hors d'usage. Pomian a insisté sur le fait que la collection, qu'elle soit pré-moderne ou moderne, renvoie toujours à l'invisible, que chaque objet de la collection fonctionne comme un *sémiophore*[11] et que la collection peut être pensée comme un système de signes qui renvoie moins à la réalité matérielle des objets qu'à une réalité absente (le sacré ou le passé, par exemple) que les objets désignent et que la collection rend signifiante. Or, les objets de la collection de Bouvard et Pécuchet ne renvoient à rien d'autre qu'à eux-mêmes ou tout au

---

[10] Désordre et encombrement renvoient au "principe de cumulation" que Moles et Wahl définissent comme l'un des principes caractéristiques du kitsch.

[11] Pour reprendre le terme employé par Pomian. Pour sa définition, voir *Sur l'histoire* (167-215). Il affirme en particulier que "c'est le traitement d'une chose de façon à en faire une image, en l'exposant au regard et en empêchant qu'on s'en serve, qui transforme cette chose en sémiophore" (167).

Bourgeois   *105*

mieux à un exotisme de pacotille (les noix de coco de Pécuchet, le sombrero), à un historicisme suspect ("une auge de pierre [un sarcophage gallo-romain])" (151), "l'arbre généalogique de la famille Croixmare" (152) ou encore à un terroir dérisoire ("une monstrueuse galoche, pleine de feuilles, les restes d'un nid"; "un tonneau de faïence que chevauchait un paysan" [152]), trois *pseudo-ailleurs* caractéristiques des objets kitsch.

Les objets ne renvoient à aucun invisible et la collection n'a aucun sens[12] (si ce n'est justement celui de signifier le non-sens comme y insiste Schuerewegen): même si certains objets racontent une histoire, celle-ci n'est qu'à l'image de leur matérialité insignifiante, comme ce décime dont on ignore l'époque d'origine et dont on sait seulement qu'il a été "rendu par un canard" (152). Même l'objet principal du musée, la statue de saint Pierre, que l'ironie de Flaubert présente à l'aide du style indirect libre comme l'objet "le plus beau" (152) du musée, est dépourvu de toute valeur *sémiophorique*.

Comme le soulignent Moles et Wahl, l'objet religieux "est perpétuellement menacé par le kitsch" (111) car il cherche à récupérer l'émotion esthétique à son profit et à faire appel au plus grand nombre. Or, la description de la statue de saint Pierre proposée par Flaubert fait bien de cet objet une incarnation du kitsch en même temps qu'elle le dépossède de toute valeur sacrée. Elle ne renvoie pas à la divinité, mais seulement à la médiocrité de son exécution matérielle: contraste violent des couleurs (vert, bleu, jaune); désacralisation de la "clef du Paradis", "vert pomme", et de "la tiare", "pointue comme une pagode", réduites ainsi à des sortes de gadgets mièvres; apparence clownesque ("joues fardées, de gros yeux ronds, la bouche béante, le nez de travers et en trompette") du visage du saint et, enfin, *trivialisation* des éléments d'ornements et de la signature de la statue: "et à ses pieds comme une colonne se levait **un pot à beurre**, portant ces mots en **lettres blanches sur fond chocolat**" (152).[13]

---

[12] Normand Lalonde suggère similairement que l'invisible que désignent les objets du Muséum de Bouvard et Pécuchet serait "peut-être simplement le danger qu'il y a, toujours, de dire une sottise lorsqu'on parle ou qu'on écrit […]; l'invisible, c'est ce fond de bêtise où s'alimente nécessairement l'intelligence, cette part insaisissable de sottise qu'il y a dans le fait de *vouloir* être intelligent" (462).

[13] Je souligne.

Le seul invisible vers lesquels feraient signe les objets de l'étrange muséum de Bouvard et Pécuchet serait un invisible par défaut, un invisible inaccessible, celui du musée, dont on n'aurait ici que le spectre et dont tous ces objets ne seraient que les ruines, montrant ainsi l'impossibilité de tout musée, de toute organisation des objets dans un monde où ceux-ci triomphent désormais de l'homme en l'envahissant de leur profusion hétérogène et en le réduisant lui-même au statut d'objet. La plupart des objets du musée des deux copistes sont des débris, des restes d'objets, de simples morceaux épars. Ils sont, en outre, les sujets de tous les verbes alors que la voix d'un sujet connaissant s'efface au profit de la voix passive et d'un "on" indéterminé: "les yeux étaient frappés par de la quincaillerie", "on voyait [...] des serrures, des boulons, des écrous", "le sol disparaissait sous des tessons de tuiles rouges", "la carcasse d'un bonnet de Cauchoise", ou encore "un morceau de cottes de mailles ornait la cloison à droite" (151). Ces objets désignent en fait l'objet manquant, le reste de la cotte de mailles par exemple, mais aussi le sujet manquant, c'est-à-dire le *cogito* qui pourrait mettre de l'ordre dans tout cela, un *cogito* dont le dédoublement du collectionneur en deux bonhommes incapables de classification exprime déjà le vacillement[14].

Derrière cette prolifération de ruines, c'est le vide d'une collection impossible qui est désigné. Il est métaphorisé par le "triangle de guipure" puisqu'il s'agit selon la définition du Robert d'une "dentelle sans fond dont les motifs sont séparés par de grands vides" et exprimé encore plus explicitement par l'absence du bahut Renaissance: "Une place demeurait vide en face de la cotte de mailles, celle du bahut Renaissance" (153). La description des objets se termine sur ce vide doublement significatif puisqu'il ne sera jamais rempli (le bahut, inachevé, sera finalement détruit par Gorgu) et puisque ce meuble fait signe vers la collection traditionnelle d'objets d'art de valeur et d'ensembles décoratifs de la Renaissance (mobiliers, peinture, etc.) comme on peut encore en trouver chez de grands collectionneurs du XIXe siècle à la même époque.[15] Le texte souligne d'ailleurs l'incapacité des deux commis à constituer de tels ensembles: "pour avoir

---

[14] Pour plus de détails sur cette question du dédoublement, voir l'ouvrage d'Yvan Leclerc référencé en fin d'article.

[15] Par exemple dans la maison-musée mise en place par le couple Jacquemart-André à Paris dès 1868.

Bourgeois

des morceaux dans le genre du meuble, Bouvard et Pécuchet s'étaient mis en campagne. Ce qu'ils rapportaient ne convenait pas" (153).

Cette mise en ruines du cabinet de curiosités autant que du musée moderne, c'est-à-dire le constat de l'impossibilité de toute collection totalisante, quelle que soit l'épistémologie qui la gouverne, peut enfin, à notre sens, se lire métaphoriquement dans la fin tragique de la pièce principale du musée, la statue de saint Pierre. Cette fin survient au chapitre VIII alors que les deux bonhommes se préoccupent de métaphysique et de philosophie. Au cours de cette recherche d'une totalité abstraite dont s'enorgueillissent d'abord Bouvard et Pécuchet, le narrateur constate: "À présent le muséum les dégoûtait. Ils n'auraient pas mieux demandé que d'en vendre les bibelots. — Et ils passèrent au chapitre deuxième: des facultés de l'âme" (285).

Du musée aux poubelles: l'exemple de la statue de saint Pierre

Qu'est-ce qui les dégoûte finalement dans le muséum qu'ils ont eux-mêmes constitué? En premier lieu, sans doute son impossibilité de fonctionner comme totalité: il désigne leur échec d'une compréhension globale du monde que la métaphysique semble leur promettre (même si une fois de plus cette tentative échoue, Bouvard et Pécuchet s'embrouillant dans la diversité des systèmes entre lesquels ils ne peuvent choisir). L'épisode où ils décident de se débarrasser de la statue de saint Pierre alors qu'ils discutent philosophie dans le muséum confirmerait une telle interprétation:

> le saint Pierre, vu de profil, étalait au plafond la silhouette de son nez, *pareille à un monstrueux cor de chasse.*
>
> On avait peine à circuler entre les objets et souvent Bouvard, n'y prenant garde, se cognait à la statue. Avec *ses gros yeux, sa lippe tombante et son air d'ivrogne,*[16] elle gênait aussi Pécuchet. Depuis longtemps, ils voulaient s'en défaire, mais par négligence, remettaient cela de jour en jour.
>
> Un soir, **au milieu d'une dispute sur la monade**, Bouvard **se frappa l'orteil au pouce de saint Pierre** — et tournant contre lui son irritation:

---

[16] Les italiques sont de nous et soulignent le grotesque monstrueux de cette statue. La statue de saint Pierre, dans son esthétique autant que dans son parcours romanesque participe à l'évidence à la poétique du "grotesque triste" de *Bouvard et Pécuchet* dégagée par Michel Crouzet dans son célèbre article "Sur le grotesque triste dans *Bouvard et Pécuchet*".

108   FLS, Vol. XXXVII, 2010

"Il m'embête ce coco-là, flanquons-le dehors!"

C'était difficile par l'escalier. Ils ouvrirent la fenêtre, et l'inclinèrent sur le bord doucement. Pécuchet à genoux tâcha de soulever ses talons, pendant que Bouvard pesait sur ses épaules. Le bonhomme de pierre ne branlait pas. Ils durent **recourir à la hallebarde comme levier** — et arrivèrent enfin à l'étendre tout droit. Alors, ayant basculé, **il piqua dans le vide, la tiare en avant**. Un bruit mat retentit; — et le lendemain, ils le trouvèrent **cassé en douze morceaux, dans l'ancien trou aux composts**.[17] (291)

Le contexte dans lequel survient cet événement est celui d'"une dispute sur la monade". Or, la monade n'est rien d'autre, d'un point de vue théorique, que la pièce de collection parfaite, l'élément qui représente à la fois l'unité et la totalité, l'unité parfaite. Bref, elle représente une connaissance du monde pleine et harmonieuse[18] devenue impossible pour les deux commis en ce milieu du XIXe siècle. Or, cette notion parfaite contraste dans la pratique avec le saint Pierre hétéroclite où Bouvard se cogne le pied, contraste signifiant, de façon comique et presque littérale, l'impossibilité de concilier la théorie avec la pratique de la réalité quotidienne.

Bouvard décide par conséquent de jeter la statue. La chute du saint Pierre, renversant symboliquement son caractère pseudo-sacré, favorisée elle-même par une autre pièce du musée (l'ironique hallebarde!), puis le fait qu'il se brise en douze morceaux (autre ironie flaubertienne: la précision quantifiable[19] des débris), représentent métaphoriquement, semble-t-il, la ruine du musée qui finit en morceaux épars ne constituant plus aucune totalité même corporelle mais de simples détritus qui trouvent logiquement leur place dans "l'ancien trou aux composts" (291).

---

[17] Je souligne.

[18] La réflexion repose sur la définition rapide que donne le dictionnaire Robert de cette complexe notion philosophique: "Chez les pythagoriciens, unité parfaite qui est le principe des choses matérielles et spirituelles. — (Fin XVIIe) Chez Leibniz, substance simple, inétendue, indivisible, active, qui constitue l'élément dernier des choses et qui est douée de désir, de volonté et de perception".

[19] De plus, le choix par Flaubert du "religieux" chiffre "douze" (évoquant les apôtres du Christ) n'est sans doute pas anodin. Nous retrouvons ici ce que dit Michel Crouzet sur "le comique numérique" dans *Bouvard Pécuchet* : "Un bon exemple du grotesque triste est le comique numérique; l'anthropomorphisme multiplie les comptabilités exactes […], c'est-à-dire les coupures arbitraires pratiquées sur le Tout, avec une précision et un aplomb parfaitement bouffons. Le chiffre, et le chiffre rond, est l'exemple même de l'illusoire appropriation des choses au savoir" (Crouzet 64).

Bourgeois 109

En outre, le musée en tant que tel cesse peu après d'exister pour marquer le triomphe du kitsch religieux. Bouvard et Pécuchet échangent en effet avec un "négociant en articles de piété" (308) une partie de leurs objets (dont la hallebarde) contre des bibelots religieux tous plus kitsch les uns que les autres pour décorer leur maison:

> Il en déballa quelques-uns, enfermés dans des boites sous le hangar: croix, médailles et chapelets de toutes les dimensions, candélabres pour oratoires, autels portatifs, bouquets de clinquant — et des sacrés cœurs en carton bleu, des saint Joseph à barbe rouge, des calvaires de porcelaines. Pécuchet les convoita. Le prix seul l'arrêtait.
>
> Goutman ne demandait pas d'argent. Il préférait les échanges, et monté dans le muséum, il offrit, contre les vieux fers et tous ses plombs, un stock de ses marchandises. (308)

Un tel kitsch religieux n'est d'ailleurs pas sans rappeler celui de la décoration que Félicité met en place dans sa chambre où le perroquet empaillé Loulou est élevé en incarnation grotesque et triviale du Saint-Esprit[20] comparable au saint Pierre à l'"air d'ivrogne" des deux bonshommes.

---

[20] "Cet endroit où elle admettait peu de monde, avait l'air tout à la fois d'une chapelle et d'un bazar, tant il contenait d'objets religieux et de choses hétéroclites. [...]. On voyait contre le mur: des chapelets, des médailles, plusieurs bonnes Vierges, un bénitier en noix de coco; sur la commode, couverte d'un drap comme un autel, la boîte de coquillages que lui avait donnée Victor; puis un arrosoir et un ballon, des cahiers d'écritures, la géographie en estampes, une paire de bottines; et au clou du miroir, accroché par ses rubans, le petit chapeau de peluche! Félicité poussait même ce genre de respect si loin qu'elle conservait une des redingotes de Monsieur. Toutes les vieilleries dont ne voulait plus Madame Aubain, elle les prenait pour sa chambre. C'est ainsi qu'il y avait des fleurs artificielles au bord de la commode, et le portrait du comte d'Artois dans l'enfoncement de la lucarne.

Au moyen d'une planchette, Loulou fut établi sur un corps de cheminée qui avançait dans l'appartement. [...].

À l'église, elle contemplait toujours le Saint-Esprit, et observa qu'il avait quelque chose du perroquet. Sa ressemblance lui parut encore plus manifeste sur une image d'Epinal, représentant le baptême de Notre-Seigneur. Avec ses ailes de pourpre et son corps d'émeraude, c'était vraiment le portrait de Loulou.

L'ayant acheté, elle le suspendit à la place du comte d'Artois, — de sorte que, du même coup d'œil, elle les voyait ensemble. Ils s'associèrent dans sa pensée, le perroquet se trouvant sanctifié par ce rapport au Saint-Esprit, qui devenait plus vivant à ses yeux et plus intelligible. Le Père, pour s'énoncer, n'avait pu choisir une colombe, puisque ces bêtes-là n'ont pas de voix, mais plutôt un des ancêtres de Loulou. Et Féli-

110 FLS, Vol. XXXVII, 2010

En guise de conclusion, notons que selon Pécuchet, le saint Pierre, réduit en miettes dans la fosse aux composts, est paradoxalement la pièce manquante dans ce musée du kitsch religieux qu'est désormais leur maison de Chavignolles:

> Leurs acquisitions furent distribuées dans tous les appartements. Une crèche remplie de foins et une cathédrale de liège décorèrent le muséum. Il y eut sur la cheminée de Pécuchet, un saint Jean-Baptiste en cire, le long du corridor les portraits des gloires épiscopales, et au bas de l'escalier, sous une lampe à chaînettes, une sainte Vierge en manteau d'azur et couronnée d'étoiles. Marcel nettoyait ces splendeurs, n'imaginant au paradis rien de plus beau.
>
> Quel dommage que le saint Pierre fût brisé et comme il aurait fait bien dans le vestibule! Pécuchet s'arrêtait parfois devant l'ancienne fosse aux composts, où l'on reconnaissait la tiare, une sandale, un bout d'oreille, lâchait des soupirs puis continuait à jardiner. (309)

Cette ultime ironie flaubertienne laisse peu de doutes sur la signification de la transformation finale du musée: l'entreprise de totalisation du musée moderne que le musée de Bouvard et Pécuchet imite en vain ne peut finir qu'aux poubelles, de la même manière que toute transcendance religieuse est désormais impossible et réduite à une prolifération matérialiste d'objets kitsch produits en série et destinés à satisfaire des individus en train de se transformer en consommateurs crédules.

---

cité priait en regardant l'image, mais de temps à autre, se tournait un peu vers l'oiseau." (*Trois contes* 72-73)

Bourgeois

Ouvrages cités

Crouzet, Michel. "Sur le grotesque triste dans *Bouvard et Pécuchet*". *Flaubert et le comble de l'art. Nouvelles recherches sur Bouvard et Pécuchet*. Paris: Sedes, 1981. 49-74.

Flaubert, Gustave. *Bouvard et Pécuchet*. Éd. Claudine Gothot-Mersch. Paris: Gallimard, 1979. [1880]

_____. *Bouvard et Pécuchet. Dictionnaire des idées reçues*. Éd. Stéphanie Dord-Crouslé. Paris: Flammarion, 1999. [1880]

_____. *L'Éducation sentimentale*. Paris: Flammarion, 1969. [1869]

_____. *Trois contes*. Paris: Flammarion, 1986. [1877]

Gothot-Mersch, Claudine. "Le Roman interminable: un aspect de la structure de *Bouvard et Pécuchet*". *Flaubert et le comble de l'art. Nouvelles recherches sur Bouvard et Pécuchet*. Paris: Sedes, 1981. 9-22.

Lalonde, Normand. "La Collection curieuse de *Bouvard et Pécuchet*". *Romanic Review* 83.4 (1992): 445-66.

Leclerc, Yvan. *La Spirale et le monument. Essai sur* Bouvard et Pécuchet *de* Gustave Flaubert. Paris: Sedes, 1988.

Moles, Abraham A., et Eberhard Wahl. "Kitsch et objet". *Communications* 13 (1969): 105-29.

Pomian, Krzysztof. *Collectionneurs, amateurs et curieux. Paris, Venise: XVIᵉ-XVIIIᵉ siècle*. Paris: Gallimard, 1987.

_____. *Sur l'histoire*. Paris: Gallimard, 1999.

Schuerewegen, Franc. "Muséum ou Croutéum? Pons, Bouvard, Pécuchet et la collection". *Romantisme* 55 (1987): 41-54.

FLS, Volume XXXVII, 2010

Paola Scarpini

University of Sheffield

Quand les *topoi* ne sont plus les mêmes: le cas d'*Ipomédon* de Hue de Rotelande

Ipomédon, le premier roman de Hue de Rotelande, est une œuvre étonnante et pleine d'humour qui ne cesse de fasciner. Tout en restant fidèle à la tradition littéraire qui la précède, Hue de Rotelande réussit à créer un roman original, non seulement en parodiant les principaux textes courtois du XIIe siècle mais aussi en véhiculant un message qui va à l'encontre des valeurs courtoises présentes dans ces textes. Dans son roman, Hue s'attaque aussi aux *topoi* narratifs, en les renversant à sa guise pour créer une histoire qui sort de l'ordinaire. Cet article examine certains de ces *topoi* et essaie de mettre en valeur le travail que le poète a effectué dans le double dessein de déstabiliser ses lecteurs et les amener à réfléchir.

Hue de Rotelande est un auteur qui est encore peu connu du grand public, bien que son œuvre principale *Ipomédon* ait déjà suscité l'intérêt de certains spécialistes. Depuis les travaux de A. J. Holden, plusieurs études ont été publiées, notamment sur l'ironie et la misogynie de Hue de Rotelande, traits distinctifs d'un style qui veut souligner sa distance vis-à-vis des œuvres chevaleresques de son époque. Peu d'informations nous sont parvenues sur cet auteur, et la plupart de celles-ci ont été fournies par le poète lui-même, au fil de ses vers. Nous savons qu'il était gallois et contemporain de Gautier Map (qui était l'auteur du *De Nugis Curialium* et juge itinérant pour le roi Henri II), et qu'il a écrit son deuxième roman, *Prothéselaüs*, pour Gilbert

Fitz-Baderon,[1] quatrième seigneur de Monmouth, avant 1191 (Holden, *Ipomédon* 7). Ce sont donc ses œuvres qui parlent pour lui et elles nous révèlent un poète qui possédait une profonde connaissance des textes courtois de son époque, fussent-ils liés à la matière antique comme le *Roman de Thèbes* ou à la tradition celtique comme le *Tristan*, et qui a su faire preuve d'originalité en attaquant avec son ironie les romans en langue vernaculaire du XIIe siècle.

Comme d'autres poètes de Grande Bretagne qui vivaient à cette époque, Hue ne partageait pas entièrement les valeurs courtoises liées aux œuvres chevaleresques écrites en France; sans les dénigrer pour autant, il ne les avait pas adoptées telles quelles mais plutôt adaptées à la vision de la vie et de la société dans laquelle il vivait. S. Crane explique que "the insular poets of love at first resist[ed] much in courtly convention, then gradually accept[ed] it more fully while adapting it to suit insular literary purposes and social ideals" (Crane 135-36). Il existait donc un réel contraste entre la littérature chevaleresque écrite en France et celle produite en Angleterre au cours du XIIe siècle; si celle-ci s'opposait fermement à des normes banales et rigides (Crane 137), c'était surtout parce que les poètes anglais ne partageaient plus la même vision de la *fin'amor* et des idéaux chevaleresques. Dans l'Angleterre de cette fin de XIIe siècle, ces conventions étaient moins respectées, peut-être aussi parce que la société anglaise était "less rigidly divided by class than continental society" (Crane 140). Hue de Rotelande faisait donc partie de ce genre de poètes et, comme eux, il a su utiliser des motifs appartenant au registre *classique* de la littérature chevaleresque pour écrire un roman (*Ipomédon*) complètement nouveau, où le rire et la parodie ne sont pratiquement jamais absents. Tout aussi remarquable est le fait qu'un auteur gallois, si proche du monde celtique et de ses mythes, ait écrit une œuvre chevaleresque sans inclure la *merveille*, motif littéraire qui avait séduit plusieurs écrivains contemporains. On dirait que Hue puise dans la réalité pour mieux la parodier par la suite: les dialogues, les quiproquos créés par le héros lors de ses multiples déguisements, les parodies d'autres textes célèbres et le cynisme du narrateur créent un sublime effet de burlesque qui s'écarte de la norme: il sait amuser, il sait dérouter, mais souvent

---

[1] "Hugue se tait et se repose; / De cest livre fait finement, / Al plus haut baron le present / E al meillour desus la nwe: / C'est ly gentils de Monemwe, / Gilbert le fiutz Badeloun" (Prothéselaus, ll. 12696-701).

Scarpini 115

tout cela cache une âpre critique envers les (fausses) valeurs de son époque.

Ipomédon est le héros éponyme d'une histoire qui, bien qu'elle n'ait pas le mérite de posséder une intrigue complexe, présente au moins l'avantage d'être insolite. Le canevas proposé est celui de la majorité des romans chevaleresques, c'est-à-dire l'histoire des aventures d'un vaillant chevalier qui grâce à ses prouesses obtient la main de la dame qu'il aime, mais c'est la structure de chaque épisode qui va à l'encontre des conventions littéraires. Le roman apparaît, au premier abord, comme un ensemble d'épisodes parodiques et burlesques; il suffit de citer le thème du tournoi, qui ne conduit pas au mariage des protagonistes suite à la fuite du héros, pour comprendre que l'auteur ne se souciait guère de la tradition romanesque. Néanmoins, le travail de Hue se révèle comme quelque chose de plus qu'une histoire chevaleresque affublée de quelques épisodes burlesques, et il suffit d'analyser quelques *topoi* littéraires pour apprécier le travail poétique de l'auteur.

Dans *Ipomédon*, Hue de Rotelande se moque des conventions romanesques qui, jusqu'à ce moment-là, avaient été largement respectées par les écrivains contemporains. Eley décrit avec précision ce à quoi les lecteurs de ce récit chevaleresque doivent faire face: l'histoire abonde en diversions, volontairement placées pour déjouer les attentes du public et pour le pousser à réfléchir sur l'importance réelle des conventions littéraires (Eley 98). Dès le début, les personnages comme les lecteurs ont affaire à de faux indices qui introduisent dans les esprits des associations qui se révéleront erronées.

L'histoire commence avec un court portrait des personnages principaux, dont le roi de Sicile, Méléagre, qui est sans enfant; son neveu, plein de vertus, est son héritier:

> Mes tant ot de mesaventure
> Ke onques ne fist engendreüre,
> De grant joie fust for partiz
> Ke unques ne ot filie ne fiz;
> Mes un son neveu pruz aveit
> Ke sun heir apres lui esteit.
> Mult esteit prisé e amez
> E as armes mult alosez,

> Mult esteit sage pur vérité
> E de plusors mult honuré,
> Beas iert e fiers, de grand vertu,
> Capaneus apelé fu; [...]. (ll. 69-80)

Ici Hue vient d'introduire un autre couple "roi et neveu" comme Arthur et Gauvain, le roi Marc et Tristan ou bien le roi Clovis et Partonopeu. Le jeune homme, qui s'appelle Capaneüs, est *pruz* (vaillant) à tel point que le roi l'a désigné comme son héritier; il est très *prisé e amez* (apprécié et aimé) et il a toutes les qualités requises pour être un chevalier honorable (beauté, fierté, force, sagesse). Après cette description très élogieuse de Capaneüs, Hue termine en disant "ore lerroms de li atant / assez en orrez an avant" (ll. 85-86), laissant croire à ses lecteurs que ce jeune, beau, et valeureux garçon peut être le héros de son récit. D'ailleurs cela serait logique, puisque non seulement ce neveu de roi correspond fidèlement au héros chevaleresque typique, mais en plus le portrait de Capaneüs suit celui de La Fière, l'héroïne du roman. Pourtant, Capaneüs disparaît au vers 86, et il ne paraîtra pas avant deux mille vers, revêtant un rôle secondaire jusqu'à la fin du poème et laissant ainsi le lecteur déconcerté devant ce premier changement brutal dans les schémas narratifs.

Peu de temps après, le public extradiégétique est confronté à un autre épisode hilarant et déconcertant à la fois: lorsqu'Ipomédon confie à son maître Tholomeu son intention d'aller parfaire son éducation ailleurs, le jeune homme prie Tholomeu de défendre sa cause auprès de ses parents, car il craint une réponse négative:

> Ypomedon mult ly mercie
> E après luy requiert e prie
> Ke il prene congé del roi,
> Ke il ne coruce vers soi,
> E da mere, la reÿne,
> De servir la Fiere Meschine. (ll. 291-96)

Le public s'attend donc à un échange dialectique serré entre le maître d'Ipomédon et ses parents prêts à défendre leurs positions avant de céder à la requête de leur fils. La tradition littéraire antérieure avait habitué les lecteurs à des situations précises lors du départ du héros vers le monde de l'errance aventureuse. Dans *Cligès*, Chrétien de Troyes nous raconte en détail la façon dont les parents d'Alexandre

Scarpini 117

le Grand réagissent à sa décision de partir quérir aventure et gloire en Grande Bretagne, auprès du roi Arthur (ll. 169-253). Le père d'Alexandre apprend la nouvelle avec "joie et pesance" (l. 170) et fait à son fils un long discours de trente-cinq vers sur les qualités dont il devra se servir une fois qu'il sera en Grande Bretagne. C'est le discours d'un souverain mais aussi d'un père qui souhaite voir son fils accomplir son rêve de devenir un chevalier de la cour du roi Arthur. Après cet épisode, Chrétien insiste (pendant vingt-sept vers) sur le chagrin de la mère d'Alexandre, l'impératrice. L'épisode, qui commence avec "Molt fu l'empererriz dolente" (l. 222) et se termine avec "Au congié de l'empereriz / Qui le cuer ot dolente el ventre, / Del batel en la nef d'en entre" (ll. 248-50), met l'accent sur la douleur de l'impératrice en nuançant, cependant, le ton dramatique par des mots de bienveillance et de compréhension: malgré la souffrance de voir partir son fils, elle ne fait rien pour le retenir car elle sait que ce voyage est justifié. Cligès aussi, quand il décide de quitter la Grèce pour la Grande Bretagne, doit se confronter avec son oncle Alis pour lui demander la permission de partir (ll. 4164-4224). Au début, Alis refuse de lui octroyer ce droit (ll. 4168-78) et Cligès doit plaider sa cause avec plus de conviction pour obtenir de lui ce qu'il souhaite au-dessus de tout.

Il paraît donc que quand un jeune homme noble quitte son pays pour aller chercher aventure et gloire ailleurs, il est normal que son entourage le plus proche (père, mère ou oncle dans le cas d'un orphelin) oppose une certaine résistance, soit par le biais d'un sentiment de détresse, soit par un refus clair (mais pas forcément définitif). Est-ce un *topos*? Partonopeu, le héros de *Partonopeu de Blois*, avait dû faire face à trois situations similaires dans la première moitié du poème: deux fois sa mère complote à son insu pour l'éloigner de Mélior, la femme qu'il aime, dans le but de pouvoir le garder à la cour du roi de France avec elle:

> Plorant en vient al roi de France
> En lui a ele sa fiance
> De son fil od soi retenir. (ll. 3927-29)

Ensuite Mélior aussi essaie de le persuader de ne pas la quitter, de peur qu'une fois retourné auprès des siens, il serait poussé à commettre quelques folies qui pourraient les séparer (ll. 4204-78).

Il semblerait donc qu'il existe bien un modèle narratif associé au départ du héros, et si tel est le cas, Hue de Rotelande a volontairement eu recours aux mêmes prémisses quand Ipomédon a quitté le royaume d'Apulie pour créer auprès de son public extradiégétique les mêmes attentes. Cependant, dans *Ipomédon*, non seulement le roi n'oppose aucune résistance au départ de son fils mais en plus, aux longues préoccupations d'Ipomédon (ll. 237-66), il répond avec un seul vers (l. 300: *Ly roi l'otrie bonement*), écrit en plus en discours indirect. Hue a réduit ce débat à quatre vers, dont un seulement dédié aux paroles du roi. Les six vers qui suivent sont réservés aux sentiments contradictoires de la reine, qui toutefois ne donnent naissance à aucune discussion:

> A la reÿne mut pesa.
> Mout a envis luy graanta
> Ke sis fiz deüst esloigner;
> El n'ot for ly sul, si l'ot cher,
> Mes quant li mestres le loeit,
> Si granta ceo qu'il voleit. (ll. 297-306)

La crainte d'Ipomédon est ridiculisée, puisque le contraste entre sa longue plaidoirie et la réponse de ses parents crée un effet de burlesque; à ceci s'ajoute le fait que les attentes du lecteur aussi sont tournées en ridicule, en aplatissant complètement l'effet dramatique qui aurait pu résulter de la situation initiale. Nous sommes placés face à un renversement total des attentes du public: le débat, les lamentations de la reine, la défense de la part de son maître, tout est réduit à néant, montrant encore une fois que les conventions du genre chevaleresque ne s'appliquent pas selon la norme.

Dès l'arrivée d'Ipomédon à la cour de La Fière, les publics intradiégétique et extradiégétique sont confrontés à un héros insolite. Bien que l'auteur nous l'ait décrit comme un *beau juvenceus* (l. 183), *curteys et vaillant et mult bien lettrez* (l. 204), qui *de tuz [se fet] prisez e loer* (l. 516), nous apprenons que malgré ses nombreuses qualités, il a un horrible défaut: *par semblant trop cuars esteit* (l. 521), c'est-à-dire qu'il est lâche. Comme nous venons de le voir, c'est de son propre gré qu'Ipomédon voulait aller à la cour de La Fière pour améliorer son éducation (ll. 237-66) et ceci, comme le dit Eley, "immediately suggests an engagement with the chivalry topos" (103): le lecteur s'at-

Scarpini **119**

tend, par conséquent, à ce qu'Ipomédon agisse selon les *topoi* che-valeresques et qu'il montre sa valeur à la cour de La Fière. Or, il se comporte tout autrement et il se tache de cette épithète déshonorante de *cuars*, lâche. On commence donc à douter de la bonne suite de l'histoire: est-ce qu'Ipomédon se révélera un excellent chevalier au cours de l'histoire, de sorte que le roman deviendra un panégyrique des vertus chevaleresques? Ou bien, est-ce que La Fière, subjuguée par la beauté et la courtoisie d'Ipomédon, changera d'avis et oubliera son vœu, en montrant aux lecteurs que les valeurs chevaleresques sont désormais dépassées (Eley 103)? Le roman ne prendra pas une seule direction, mais plusieurs, adoptant les deux théories à la fois: Ipomédon est bien un chevalier vaillant, mais les valeurs chevaleresques sont désormais dépassées. Nous verrons par la suite comment Hue va représenter ces valeurs de façon à amener subtilement le public extra-diégétique à arriver à cette conclusion.

Quand Ipomédon arrive en Sicile, il le fait en grande pompe en se faisant ainsi remarquer par le roi Méléagre et son neveu, Capaneüs (ll. 2714-52). Le roi, attiré par la magnificence d'Ipomédon, accepte la demande de ce dernier de lui octroyer un *don en blanc*. La requête qui suivra sera singulière et déroutante pour le lecteur: Ipomédon demande et obtient du roi de devenir le favori de la reine et de pouvoir lui donner un baiser, chaque soir, en l'accompagnant à sa chambre. Un parallèle ironique avec Tristan s'impose: lui, qui était le favori caché de la reine Iseut et qui devait dissimuler au roi Marc son amour pour elle, a été démasqué dans la chambre de la reine. Ipomédon, par contre, obtient avec une ruse subtile tout ce que Tristan n'a jamais eu et ceci avec l'accord du roi. Hue de Rotelande cherche-t-il à souligner la ruse de son héros et à faire passer Tristan pour un sot? Quoi qu'il en soit, l'auteur d'*Ipomédon* semble faire glisser dans l'esprit du lecteur l'idée que si Tristan avait été aussi rusé qu'Ipomédon, il aurait peut-être pu "approcher" la reine Yseut sans devoir se cacher. Mis à part cette parodie tristanienne, il y a dans l'épisode du don contraignant un autre détail à souligner, c'est-à-dire le bouleversement même de ce *topos*. Ce motif, qui normalement avait une fonction littéraire assez précise,[2] revêt ici un rôle narratif nouveau: ici *le don en blanc* ne

---

[2] À ce sujet, voir les études de Philippe Ménard, Jean Frappier et Corinne Cooper-Deniau.

déclenche pas l'aventure,[3] il n'annonce pas un changement ou un événement dramatique,[4] et il n'est pas utilisé par le héros pour franchir un obstacle ou résoudre un problème.[5] Le *topos* du don contraignant se retrouve dans tous les romans breton de Chrétien de Troyes (Frappier 240) et il constitue donc un schéma bien connu par les lecteurs de Hue De Rotelande. Dans notre texte, Ipomédon arrive en Sicile après une période où il avait traversé la France en gagnant prestige et honneurs (ll. 1771-1800), laissant supposer qu'il était prêt à montrer sa valeur également à la cour du roi Méléagre. Le motif du don contraignant néanmoins ne suit pas les schémas habituels car Ipomédon utilise ce don pour une requête absurde qui, apparemment, n'a aucune fonction outre celle de parodier Tristan. Au niveau diégétique, ce comportement encourage les "deux publics" à croire à la couardise du héros, bien que le lecteur soupçonne déjà qu'elle soit feinte. Il faudra attendre le tournoi de trois jours pour que ce doute soit dissipé complètement.

Lors de ce tournoi, Ipomédon démontre au public extradiégétique qu'il n'est pas un lâche, et il fait preuve d'intelligence pour éviter que son jeu soit démasqué. Le tournoi, qui a pour but de trouver un mari à La Fière, correspond souvent à des attentes littéraires bien précises: dans les poèmes chevaleresques, le tournoi permet de faire connaître les vertus du héros qui, après être passé par une série d'épreuves édifiantes, manifeste de façon remarquable sa réelle valeur. Comme le souligne H. Martin, souvent le tournoi suit une période d'obscurité pour le héros, après laquelle il a "une épiphanie éclatante" (301). La littérature qui précède l'œuvre de Hue nous fournit de nombreux cas. Par exemple, dans *Partenopeu de Blois*, le héros est laissé pour mort avant d'être secouru par Urraque et armé pour participer au tournoi des trois jours; Lancelot se laisse couvrir d'infamie avant de gagner le tournoi et être acclamé comme le meilleur. Ces exemples et ces schémas étaient bien présents dans l'esprit des lecteurs, puisqu'il s'agissait

---

[3] Voir, par exemple, l'épisode initial de *Le Chevalier à la charrette* (ll. 173-79, éd. Méla), la requête d'Yvain à Laudine dans *Le Chevalier au Lion* (ll.2547-78, éd. Hult), la demande d'Alexandre à son père dans *Cligès* (ll. 86-91, éd. Méla-Collet).

[4] Voir, par exemple, l'épisode d'Hypsipyle, avant l'arrivée d'Adraste et de son armée sous les murs de Thèbes (*Roman de Thèbes*, ll. 2545-60).

[5] Voir, par exemple, l'épisode de la demande du clerc Bernard au duc Richard de Normandie dans le Roman de Rou (vol. I, ll. 2103-24).

Scarpini 121

de textes ayant une grande renommée; c'est précisément sur ces textes que Hue a bâti son œuvre et, en la mettant en parallèle avec *Tristan*, *Partonopeu de Blois*, *Cligés* et *Le chevalier de la charrette*, il a créé des attentes précises chez son public extradiégétique, attentes qui, pour lui, étaient assez simples à transformer. Non seulement Ipomédon n'a vécu aucune épreuve qui lui aurait permis d'exhiber sa prouesse avant le tournoi, mais en plus il part à la fin sans réclamer la main de La Fière, la laissant sans mari et sans prétendants, puisque tous les autres avaient été vaincus par Ipomédon. Notre héros ne répond aux expectatives de... personne: ni à celles du public extradiégétique, ni à celles du public intradiégétique.

Les deux, en effet, s'attendaient à un mariage après la fin du tournoi ou du moins à un quelconque aboutissement, pas à la fuite du héros et à la déception de l'héroïne. Si ce tournoi est l'étalage des prouesses chevaleresques d'Ipomédon, il est aussi la parade de l'incontinence émotionnelle de La Fière. Fidèle jusqu'au fanatisme à son vœu, La Fière tombe amoureuse à chaque fois que le chevalier inconnu, toujours différent à ses yeux à cause de son armure, gagne les joutes du jour. Le jour suivant, elle se promet d'être fidèle à son cœur et à son amour pour Ipomédon, mais face à la bravoure et la hardiesse du nouveau chevalier, dont elle ignore l'identité, ses sentiments changent et elle est prête à se donner à ce potentiel amant. Selon l'analyse de Roberta Kruger,

> Ipomédon's [...] deception playfully inverts the topos of love service and ironizes female desire. Rather than striving to make his worth known to his beloved lady [...], Ipomédon tricks [her] and provokes consternation and disappointment in [his] female public. (*Misogyny* 400).

Par conséquent, si d'un côté le tournoi est pour Hue l'occasion de montrer que son héros rentre dans les *topoi* chevaleresques, de l'autre il sort de tous les schémas de la *fin'amor* et dénonce l'inconstance et les caprices des femmes. La Fière est incapable de rester fidèle à l'homme qu'elle dit aimer mais peut-être ce n'est pas entièrement de sa faute; Hue dénonce ici l'absurdité du *topos* de la *fin'amor*, qui voudrait que l'amour de la dame soit déclenché par le courage, la vigueur et la noblesse d'esprit du chevalier. Notre pauvre héroïne est, dès lors, *obligée* de changer ses sentiments chaque jour, c'est-à-dire quand les joutes sont gagnées par un chevalier plus vaillant et plus courageux que le précédent. Bien évidemment, ce que La Fière ignore, le public extradiégétique le connaît dès le début: ces trois chevaliers sont la seule et même personne, Ipomédon. À ce moment, le lecteur se trouve face à un dilemme, comme Eley l'a démontré brillamment (103), et dont l'analyse peut se résumer à ceci: La Fière à chaque fois est attirée par un homme différent, montrant à tout le monde sa frivolité. Ceci va à l'encontre du *topos* de la *fin'amor*, qui voudrait la femme ferme dans ses sentiments; mais le lecteur sait que ces trois chevaliers sont la même personne (Ipomédon) qu'elle aime malgré sa feinte couardise. Faut-il donc en déduire que la femme est attirée par les hommes vaillants sans le savoir? Et que la *fin'amor* conduit la femme toujours vers le même homme? Hue ne nous donne pas de réponse précise, il laisse au lecteur le soin de tirer ses conclusions. Par contre, le texte révèle clairement une critique de ces valeurs qui se basent plus sur un jugement superficiel qu'une analyse approfondie de la nature humaine. La Fière et les gens de la cour jugent Ipomédon pour ce qu'il paraît être, sans se soucier de voir au-delà de ses prouesses cynégétiques. Pourtant, lors de la battue de chasse organisée par La Fière, Ipomédon ne montre pas seulement du courage et du savoir-faire mais aussi une habilité particulière dans le dressage des chiens — attributs qui rappellent beaucoup le chasseur par antono-mase, Tristan. Un moment en particulier mérite d'être retenu, la capture et le dépeçage d'un cerf qui évoquent indubitablement l'arrivée de Tristan en Cornouailles et à la cour du roi Marc.[6] La Fière, sous le charme d'Ipomédon, confesse à elle-même qu'*il est curteis et vaillant* (l. 664) et que son cœur pourrait l'aimer. Spensley reconnaît que "it is fitting that La Fière's feeling towards him [Ipomédon] should reach crisis point during a hunting expedition. Her prolonged view of him as he demonstrates his courtly skills as a hunter, stirs her to passion" (346). Hue exploite ici le *topos* de la chasse comme synonyme de la passion, et il fait en sorte de glisser le doute dans l'esprit des lecteurs: il leur laisse supposer qu'une scène d'amour pourrait suivre, d'autant plus qu'ici nous sommes en présence d'une chasse au cerf, animal

---

[6] Cet episode nous est parvenu seulement dans les traductions allemandes et norroise: Tristan et Yseut, la saga norroise, épisodes 20 et 21 et aussi Gottfried Von Strassburg, Tristan, trad. par A. T. Hatto, ch. 4: "The Hunt".

Scarpini 123

riche en symbolisme.[7] Puisque Ipomédon nous est présenté comme un autre Tristan, on pourrait penser que La Fière soit son Yseut et que la chasse ait la fonction d'un philtre d'amour. Cependant, même si tous les éléments sont présents, rien de tout cela ne se produit. La Fière voit cette passion comme une *folie* (l. 687) et elle réussit à ne pas céder à ce sentiment qui la vouerait à être *honie* par tout le monde (l. 681), car Ipomédon n'est pas le chevalier *pruz* (l. 682) qu'elle voudrait. Le lecteur est doublement déçu: non seulement tout le monde se moque du manque de courage d'Ipomédon et ne voit pas en lui les mêmes qualités de Tristan, mais en plus La Fière se montre une véritable "orgueilleuse d'amour," freinant toute passion.

Les apparences jouent aussi un rôle trompeur lors du tournoi: La Fière se fie plus à ses yeux qu'à son cœur et personne n'arrive à faire le rapprochement entre les trois chevaliers inconnus. Capaneüs, non plus, n'arrive pas à voir au-delà des apparences: lui, qui avait précédemment vu et admiré les trois différents chevaux d'Ipomédon lors de son arrivée en Sicile (ll. 2645-94), ne réussit pas à les reconnaître pendant le tournoi. Les gens, et surtout les femmes, de la cour du roi Méléagre croient qu'Ipomédon part à la chasse chaque matin et eux aussi sont victimes des apparences et de la ruse du héros. Tout ceci se passe dans la première partie du roman, et bien que les aventures ne soient pas encore terminées, le lecteur a déjà compris qu'il est en train de lire un poème qui se déjoue de tout: des conventions, des grands mythes littéraires et aussi de son public. Comment ne pas remarquer les apparents manques de vraisemblance que l'auteur nous impose? Le plus éclatant est la révélation de la mère d'Ipomédon concernant ce demi-frère inconnu: comme Eley l'a relevé, cette nouvelle tombe au beau milieu du récit et elle se présente comme une parenthèse sans aucun lien avec le reste de l'histoire (99). Ipomédon ne pose aucune question à sa mère à propos de ce demi-frère, ni son nom, ni pourquoi il a été caché jusqu'à ce moment-là; le seul indice est une bague qui permettra à Ipomédon d'être reconnu par son frère. Le narrateur non plus ne prend pas le soin de donner davantage de détails à son public extradiégétique, et cet épisode se conclut en laissant les lecteurs avec une multitude de questions. À ceci il faut ajouter qu'Ipomédon ne

---

[7] Sur le symbolisme du cerf, voir Paolo Galloni, Il cervo e il lupo. Caccia e cultura nobiliare nel Medioevo; Thiébaux Marcelle, The stag of love: the chase in medieval literature; Beryl Rowland, Animals with human faces.

mentionnera plus le demi-frère dans le texte: on serait presque tenté de l'oublier, mais voilà que l'auteur l'utilise à la fin du poème comme un *deus ex machina* pour terminer son récit. Si la recherche d'un frère perdu n'est pas un *topos* littéraire très récurrent, la reconnaissance par le biais d'une bague était très répandue dans la littérature vernaculaire du XIIe siècle. Dans l'épisode final de la bataille entre Enéas et Turnus (ll. 9835-50, éd. Petit), dans le lai de Milun (ll. 429-80) et surtout dans les deux épisodes des *Folies* Tristan, la bague a toujours été un objet chargé de symboles et d'une valeur cognitive très précise. Le *topos* est presque respecté, puisque la rencontre d'Ipomédon avec son demi-frère Capaneüs permet de mettre un terme aux aventures d'Ipomédon, de le réunir avec son demi-frère, d'épouser La Fière et de devenir roi d'Apulie.[8] Alors peut-on affirmer que "tout est bien qui finit bien"? Sûrement, mais il faut souligner aussi que Hue s'est bien moqué de ses lecteurs: Ipomédon avait déjà la bague au doigt quand il est arrivé en Sicile et il a rencontré Capaneüs. Il ne l'a jamais ôtée pendant son séjour à la cour du roi Méléagre où Capaneüs était toujours présent, mais il a fallu un combat corps à corps, pendant lequel les deux chevaliers revêtaient une armure, pour que Capaneüs s'aperçoive de la bague d'Ipomédon. Le *topos* de la reconnaissance par le biais de la bague a été modifié et adapté aux fins diégétiques tout en nous donnant l'illusion que dans cet épisode les conventions littéraires avaient été respectées. Cette modification créatrice opérée par le bouleversement des *topoi* littéraires, nous montre l'habilité de Hue à manipuler les textes connus, les conventions littéraires, la rhétorique et aussi ses lecteurs, qui ne se rendent pas compte qu'ils sont ses pantins,[9] exactement comme les personnages de son roman. L'auteur pointe son doigt contre ces valeurs désormais lointaines et absurdes qui n'avaient plus rien de réel et qui n'étaient qu'apparence.

Tout le roman se base sur un contraste permanent entre l'*être* et le *paraître*, la présence de la parodie tristanienne renforce cette

---

[8] La résolution d'Ipomédon à ne jamais révéler son identité, son goût pour les déguisements et le parallèle très marqué avec Tristan (dans certains épisodes Ipomédon revêt même le masque de Tristan; voir ll. 7757-7936) nous laissent croire que tout le récit est une quête identitaire d'Ipomédon.

[9] "narrator's puppets": expression reprise à Eley (100).

dichotomie[10] et le motif du bouleversement des conventions joue un rôle prédominant dans ce souci extrême des apparences. Toutefois, ce n'est pas le seul message que recèle ce roman: en faisant une parodie du roman courtois, Hue conteste la notion de *fin'amor* héritée des troubadours et remet en question la chevalerie élaborée par Chrétien de Troyes. L'auteur réussit à atteindre, malgré la situation burlesque et chaotique initiale, "un équilibre dans la complexe dialectique de la prouesse chevaleresque et de la *fin'amor*" (Chênerie, *Récits d'amour* [Intro. et notes] 39); c'est, en effet, pour ridiculiser ces deux idéaux courtois que Hue crée un héros qui cache volontairement son courage aux yeux de tout le monde et une héroïne inconstante dans son amour, incapable de reconnaître la valeur d'un homme, car trop soucieuse des apparences. Mais tout en faisant cela, Hue nous offre un héros qui, grâce à son *engin*,[11] arrive à se faire aimer par trois femmes de sang royal, à ne pas être victime de la séduction féminine, à se venger de leurs moqueries, et tout ceci sans jamais perdre son caractère courtois. Bref, Ipomédon triomphe à chaque occasion et toujours par inversion de la *fin'amor*: les femmes montrent toujours leur superficialité, leur inconstance, leur déloyauté tandis qu'Ipomédon, même dans les situations les plus humiliantes, ne perd jamais son caractère courtois, son élégance et sa bonne éducation (Chênerie, *Le chevalier errant* 40; Krueger, "Misogyny" 400-02). Grâce à une grande adresse poétique et un style mordant, Hue de Rotelande a su transformer les conventions littéraires et sociales de son époque, les placer dans un contexte qui, sans être tout à fait original, se présente comme "différent" et se distancie de la littérature à laquelle son public était habitué. On peut donc affirmer que Hue a repris certains *topoi* de la littérature courtoise et qu'il les a adaptés à une vision satirique des normes littéraires en vigueur à son époque. De plus, il a fait en sorte de créer un double lien avec le public extradiégétique. Ce dernier est souvent amené à réfléchir sur la situation paradoxale vécue par Ipomédon, à prendre ses distances pour pouvoir mieux juger les valeurs transmises par la société, et tout ceci sans se rendre compte que c'est toujours l'auteur qui dirige cette interprétation. Hue, tout en faisant rire son public,

---

[10] Dans l'histoire de Tristan l'écart entre illusion et réalité est évident et présent sur plusieurs plans narratifs. Le jeu entre semblance et senefience régit toute l'histoire tristanienne.

[11] Sa ruse, son intelligence.

l'entraîne là où il le veut par le biais de son style dynamique et innovateur; sachant déjouer les modes littéraires et les idéologies, il a su ajouter une note de réalisme à un courant littéraire qui semblait perdu dans ses propres mythes.

Ouvrages cités et consultés

Benoît de Sainte-Maure. *Le Roman de Troie.* Éd. Léopold Constans. Paris: Firmin Didot, 1904-1912. D'après la version de gallica.bnf.fr.

Beryl, Rowland. *Animals with human faces.* Knoxville : University of Tennessee Press, 1973.

Calin, William. "The Exaltation and Undermining of Romance: *Ipomedon*". *The Legacy of Chrétien de Troyes.* Vol. 2. Éd. Norris J. Lacy, Douglas Kelly, and Keith Busby. Amsterdam: Rodopi, 1988. 111-24.

Chênerie, Marie-Luce. *Le chevalier errant dans les romans arthuriens en vers des XIIe et XIIIe siècles.* Genève: Librairie Droz, 1986.

_____. Intro. et notes. *Récits d'amour et de chevalerie, XIIe au XVe siècle.* Éd. Danielle Régnier-Bohler. Paris: Robert Laffont, 2000.

Chrétien de Troyes. *Cligès.* Édition critique d'après le ms. B.N. fr. 12560. Éd. Charles Méla et Olivier Collet. Paris: Livre de Poche, 1994. Lettres Gothiques.

Chrétien de Troyes. *Le Chevalier au Lion.* Édition critique d'après le ms. B. N. fr. 1433. Éd. David F. Hult. Paris: Livre de Poche, 1994. Lettres Gothiques.

Chrétien de Troyes. *Le Chevalier de la Charrette.* Édition critique d'après tous les manuscrits existants. Éd. Charles Méla. Paris: Livre de Poche, 1992. Lettres Gothiques.

Cooper-Deniau, Corinne. "Culture cléricale et motif du 'don contraignant.' Contre-enquête sur la théorie de l'origine celtique de ce motif dans la littérature française du XIIe siècle et dans les romans arthuriens". *Le Moyen Âge* 111.1 (2005): 9-39.

Crane, Susan. *Insular Romance: Politics, Faith and Culture in Anglo-Norman and Middle English Literature.* Berkeley: University of California Press, 1986.

Eley, Penny. "The Subversion of Meaning in Hue de Rotelande's *Ipomedon*". *Reading Medieval Studies* 26 (2000): 97-112.

Frappier, Jean. "Le motif du 'don contraignant' dans la littérature du Moyen Âge". Travaux de linguistique et littérature 7 (1969): 7-46. Réimpr. dans *Amour courtois et Table Ronde.* Genève: Droz, 1973.

Scarpini

Galloni, Paolo. *Il cervo e il lupo. Caccia e cultura nobiliare nel Medioevo.* Bari: Laterza, 1993.

Hanning, Robert W. "*Engin* in Twelfth-Century Romance: an Examination of the *Roman d'Enéas* and Hue de Rotelande's *Ipomedon*". *Yale French Studies* 51 (1974): 82-101.

Hue de Rotelande. *Ipomedon*. Éd. A. J. Holden. Paris: Klincksieck, 1979.

_____. *Ipomedon*. Intro. et notes de Marie-Luce Chênerie, éd. Danielle Régnier-Bohler. *Récits d'amour et de chevalerie, XIIe au XVe siècle.* Paris: Robert Laffont, 2000.

Krueger, Roberta L. "Misogyny, Manipulation, and the Female Reader in Hue de Rotelande's *Ipomédon*". *Courtly Literature. Culture and context.* Éd. K. Busby et E. Kooper. Amsterdam-Philadelphia: John Benjamins Publishing, 1990. 395-409.

_____. "Women Readers and the Ideology of Gender in Old French Verse Romance". Cambridge: Cambridge University Press, 1993.

Legge, Dominica. "Anglo-Norman Literature and its Background". Oxford: Clarendon, 1963.

Martin, Hervé. *Mentalités médiévales, XI-XV siècles.* Paris: PUF, 1996.

Ménard, Philippe. "Le don en blanc qui lie le donateur: réflexions sur un motif de conte". *An Arthurian Tapestry: Essays in Memory of Lewis Thorpe.* Éd. Kenneth Varty. Glasgow: Published on Behalf of the British Branch of the International Arthurian Society at the French Department of the University of Glasgow, 1981. 163-73.

Partonopeu de Blois. Éd., trad. et intro. de O. Collet et P.-M. Jauris. Paris: Livre de Poche, 2005. Lettres Gothiques.

Spensley, Ronald M. "The Structure of Hue de Rotelande's *Ipomedon*". *Romania* 95 (1974): 341-51.

Thiebaux, Marcelle. *The Stag of Love: The Chase in Medieval Literature.* Ithaca: Cornell University Press, 1974.

Tristan et Iseut. Les poèmes français. La saga norroise. Éd. D. Lacroix et P. Walter. Paris: Le Livre de Poche, 1989. Lettres Gothiques.

Wace. *Le Roman de Rou.* Éd. A. J. Holden. Paris: A. & J. Picard, 1970.

FLS, Volume XXXVII, 2010 — Stealing the Fire

Nora Cottille-Foley

Georgia Institute of Technology

Un texte en cache-t-il un autre?
Le palimpseste chez Marie Darrieussecq

> À deux reprises Marie Darrieussecq a été accusée de plagiat. Tout
> d'abord en 1998 par Marie NDiaye, qui l'accuse d'avoir "singé" son
> écriture dans *Naissance des fantômes*, puis par Camille Laurens en
> 2007, qui reconnaît ses propres récits autobiographiques dans *Tom est
> mort*. Les réactions de la presse révèlent une conception idéalisatrice de
> l'œuvre littéraire. Afin d'éviter les nombreux écueils qui entourent la
> question du plagiat — le jugement éthico-juridique, la douleur psycho-
> logique de l'écrivain plagié, le concept historiquement fluctuant de
> l'originalité artistique — l'article fait appel à la terminologie de Genette
> pour analyser les rapports de l'hypertexte *La naissance des fantômes*
> aux textes de Marie NDiaye, qui l'ont précédé.

———

> J'ai eu le sentiment, en le lisant, que *Tom
> est mort* avait été écrit dans ma chambre,
> le cul sur ma chaise ou vautrée dans mon
> lit de douleur. Marie Darrieussecq s'est
> invitée chez moi, elle squatte. (Laurens,
> "Syndrome" 7)

Comme le remarque Bernard Géniès dans *Le Nouvel Observateur*, la rentrée littéraire 2007 a eu son lot de scandales (Géniès). La
violence des mots cités ci-dessus rend compte de la colère de l'écrivain Camille Laurens contre un autre écrivain, Marie Darrieussecq,
qu'elle accuse de "plagiat psychique" ("Syndrome" 4). Laurens lui

reproche de s'être largement inspirée de ses propres récits autobiographiques exprimant la douleur ressentie à la mort de son enfant — *Philippe* et *Cet absent-là* — dans la rédaction d'un ouvrage de fiction que Darrieussecq fait publier en 2007, *Tom est mort*. Selon Laurens, qui entreprend de dresser l'inventaire des emprunts illégitimes, il s'agirait d'une "usurpation d'identité" ("Syndrome" 4). Les emprunts seraient nombreux et relèveraient non seulement de phrases, idées, scènes ou situations retravaillées — jamais reprises exactement — mais encore du rythme lui-même et de la syntaxe. Laurens affirme que, malgré les légères modifications opérées par Darrieussecq, l'inspiration est manifeste ("Syndrome" 4-5). Plutôt que de se concentrer uniquement sur la réalité tangible des emprunts à son texte, Laurens fait l'erreur de multiplier les accusations et ainsi de déplacer involontairement la controverse en avançant qu'un auteur ne devrait pas écrire au sujet de la mort d'un enfant à moins d'avoir vécu ce deuil. Cette maladresse lui est fatale. Les journalistes s'en emparent et ironisent sur la naïveté de ses propos et sur l'ineptie des interdits qu'elle entendrait faire respecter. Dans ce débat par journaux interposés à l'interstice de la réflexion métalittéraire et de la presse People, Darrieussecq devient la victime des calomnies d'une rivale égarée par la douleur, voire de la jalousie que susciteraient ses succès de librairie (Kéchichian, "*Tom est mort*, la polémique").

Mais cette polémique en réveille une autre, lui fait écho en quelque sorte puisque, neuf ans plus tôt, à l'occasion de la publication de *Naissance des fantômes*, c'est la très respectée Marie NDiaye qui avait accusé Darrieussecq, non pas de l'avoir plagiée, mais plutôt "singée":

> Au fil des pages [de *Naissance des fantômes*], je me retrouve [écrit NDiaye] dans la position inconfortable et ridicule de qui reconnaît, transformées, triturées, remâchées, certaines choses qu'il a écrites. Aucune phrase, rien de précis: on n'est pas dans le plagiat, mais dans la singerie. (Kéchichian, "Darrieussecq")

Là encore, les journalistes ont exprimé leur gêne face aux accusations. Parce que les emprunts remarqués par Laurens et NDiaye sont de nature fluide, leur existence semble échapper à l'attention des journalistes. Mais les commentaires des journalistes indiquent également, en filigrane, une conception idéalisatrice d'une littérature pure, éternelle et intrinsèquement au-dessus de tout soupçon. Pour Patrick Kechichian, journaliste au *Monde*, il s'agit là d'une "de ces querelles de clochers parisiens qui semblent être faites pour distraire méchamment, pour faire accroire que la littérature est d'abord affaire de mesquineries, de médisances" (Kéchichian, "Darrieussecq"). Pire encore, selon le même journaliste, NDiaye accuserait Darrieussecq de plagiat pour "être dans l'air du temps". Il s'agirait d'une "agitation malsaine" entraînant perversement "l'oubli même de la littérature" (Kechichian, "La littérature"). Pour qui a suivi le parcours littéraire de NDiaye, la référence à l'air du temps est inepte. Les critiques s'accordent à remarquer la distance que l'écrivain préfère entretenir entre son écriture et le milieu parisien de l'édition.[1] Non seulement a-t-elle vécu aux quatre coins du monde mais encore, lors de ses séjours en France, semble-t-elle préférer les coins retirés à la capitale. En fonction de sa réticence face aux évènements médiatiques, les journalistes anxieux de l'interviewer racontent avec amusement les périples géographiques qu'ils ont dû entreprendre pour parvenir à leurs fins. Dans ce contexte, les références de Kechichian manquent de fondement. Si ces références sont injustifiées quant à la biographie de NDiaye, il est à soupçonner qu'elles sont révélatrices des schèmes de pensée du journaliste et de confrères exprimant les mêmes idées. Les expressions utilisées par Kechichian témoignent toutes d'une forte répugnance à considérer le façonnage d'une œuvre romanesque. Il semblerait que l'écrivain doive être un artiste et non pas un artisan. Le choix des termes — particulièrement les reproches aux querelles de clocher, à la distraction et à l'air du temps — indique à quel point le journaliste privilégie l'abstraction éthérée d'un art littéraire universel et intemporel. Il n'est pas question de considérer l'ici et le maintenant auxquels ramène insidieusement la réalité corporelle de l'écriture mais plutôt de s'adonner à l'immortalité d'une valeur artistique supérieure dont la transcendance ne saurait souffrir d'être remise en question. Les accusations de plagiat de la part de Marie NDiaye puis de Camille Laurens sont taboues car elles touchent à un écrivain dont la valeur littéraire a été reconnue et que, par conséquent, elles remettent en question la valeur transcendantale de la littérature elle-même.

---

[1] Voir par exemple la réflexion humoristique de Michel Braudeau: "Marie NDiaye, par exemple, est très talentueuse et respectée. Elle n'a pas eu besoin de crier pour se faire entendre, elle. Sans bouger de sa campagne" (24).

Pour comprendre la gêne et la distanciation hautaine, parfois méprisante, qui entourent les accusations de plagiat, il est nécessaire de situer le débat dans une dimension historique. Comme le rappelle Christian Vanderdorpe, une esthétique de l'imitation parcourt non seulement les œuvres des Anciens mais également la production du Moyen Âge et celle de la Renaissance, "à la condition que l'écrivain améliore la matière empruntée et qu'il l'intègre à un projet original" ("Le plagiat"). La situation change au XIXe siècle. L'idée de progrès entérine le mythe du génie de l'écrivain. La modernité célèbre l'esthétique de l'originalité tandis que la critique institutionnelle se lance dans une chasse au plagiat ("Le plagiat"). Mais dès le XXe siècle, la possibilité même d'une originalité absolue est remise en question dans le champ de la narratologie. Ainsi, Julia Kristéva indique la relation inévitable d'un auteur au contexte textuel qui a formé sa pensée et sa sensibilité littéraire: "Tout texte, nous dit-elle, se construit comme une mosaïque de citations, tout texte est absorption et transformation d'un autre texte" (15). Il s'agit, selon le terme de Kristéva, d'un processus d'intertextualité. Gérard Genette reprend et développe cette terminologie dans *Palimpsestes*, le palimpseste étant un texte que l'on a inscrit sur un parchemin dont on a auparavant effacé l'écriture précédente, laquelle peut cependant encore se deviner sous le nouveau texte. Genette utilise cette métaphore pour désigner "cinq types de relations transtextuelles" dont l'intertextualité ne serait que la plus basique et recouvrirait les processus de citation, plagiat et allusion. Le plagiat serait caractérisé par "la présence effective d'un texte dans un autre" (8). Bien qu'il n'y ait pas de véritable frontière entre ces catégories, ou du moins qu'elles demeurent poreuses, Genette distingue l'intertextualité de l'hypertextualité. Cette dernière se situe entre la transformation et l'imitation par un texte — l'hypertexte — d'un texte précédent — l'hypotexte. Cette distinction permet d'adopter un nouvel angle d'étude pour les phénomènes d'emprunt décriés par NDiaye et Laurens.

Dans sa lettre accusatoire contre Darrieussecq, Laurens pressent l'ambiguïté du statut du plagiat. Elle prédit qu'on lui avancera que "tous les artistes pratiquant en outre couramment la citation, le collage, le sampling, l'allusion, l'intertextualité, le mixage, on doit admettre que tout est public, que tout circule" ("Syndrome" 7). Comme sa lettre le prouve, l'étymologie du terme plagiat — rapt textuel —

Cottille-Foley 133

décrit adéquatement la crainte de l'auteur "de se voir trahi, singé, moqué, pompé, vampirisé" (13). Les termes utilisés par Laurens traduisent une réalité psychologique complexe découlant en partie de l'importance accordée à l'originalité artistique dans nos sociétés. Mais l'aspect émotionnel de sa réaction ne devrait pas invalider sa plainte. Comme l'indique David Goldblatt, la contribution artistique d'un individu dans la sphère publique détermine son identité. De plus, l'originalité de son style est probablement sa contribution artistique la plus importante, elle est garante de sa singularité (72-73). Si l'inspiration des générations précédentes est inévitable, voire même désirable, les emprunts à des œuvres contemporaines menacent à la fois l'identité artistique et la singularité de leur auteur dont ils risquent de déprécier et d'obscurcir l'originalité par leur propre succès de librairie. Charles Nodier l'affirme dès 1828 lorsqu'il remarque que "le plagiat commis sur les auteurs modernes, de quelque pays qu'ils soient, a déjà un degré d'innocence de moins que le plagiat commis sur les anciens, et beaucoup d'écrivains d'une délicatesse reconnue l'ont désapprouvé" (3). Le pays est également important pour Nodier, qui ajoute ailleurs que le délit de plagiat est aggravé lorsque l'auteur plagié est "moderne et national" (35). On pressent déjà ici l'importance de l'économie de marché, qui sanctionne la place respective des écrivains dans un créneau particulier. D'où le sentiment peut-être pour Laurens que sa place est usurpée et que Darrieussecq a écrit *Tom est mort* dans sa chambre à elle et sur sa chaise à elle, Laurens.

D'après leurs lettres et leurs commentaires, il est évident que Laurens et NDiaye se sont posé la question de la catégorie dans laquelle ranger les emprunts faits par Darrieussecq à leurs récits. Toutes deux semblent écarter la catégorie de "pastiche involontaire" identifiée par Genette. Laurens, dressant une longue liste des emprunts qu'elle a observés, remarque amèrement: "c'est terrible mais je vois Marie Darrieussecq rayant au fur et à mesure sur une liste les 'scènes à faire'" ("Syndrome" 5). NDiaye remarque le même phénomène et parle quant à elle de "bricolage" et d'un "système de montage copier-coller" (Assouline). Dans le contexte d'une ambiguïté fondamentale quant au rôle de l'originalité artistique et afin d'éviter l'aspect éthico-juridique du terme "plagiat", on utilisera ici le concept d'hyper-textualité pour approcher les textes concernés. Parce que *Tom est mort* se complique d'un débat sur l'autobiographie fictive, on se concentrera sur les rapports de l'hypertexte *La Naissance des fantômes* de Darrieussecq aux textes de Marie NDiaye qui l'ont précédé. Il s'agira, non pas de faire un procès, mais plutôt de dégager les modalités d'un processus de palimpseste où les textes de NDiaye se donnent à lire entre les lignes. Comme l'indique Philippe Carrard dans son extension de la métaphore, la possibilité de déchiffrer la première inscription devrait contribuer à la lecture correcte du texte le plus récent (Carrard 205). Parce que les auteurs sont contemporains, on poursuivra l'extension de Carrard en supposant que l'hypertexte peut à son tour influencer les romans ultérieurs de l'auteur de l'hypotexte. À travers l'étude du traitement des fantômes dans les textes concernés — étude forcément limitée dans le cadre de cet essai — on cherchera à dégager les apports d'une étude intertextuelle à l'analyse littéraire et à la compréhension de l'évolution des œuvres.

Le thème principal de *La Naissance des fantômes* (1998) concerne la disparition d'un époux. Deux textes de Marie NDiaye se penchent sur cette situation. Dans *Un Temps de saison* (1994), Herman, un professeur de mathématiques parisien en villégiature, constate la disparition de son fils et de sa femme. L'enquête qu'il mène auprès des habitants du village lui apprend peu à peu que sa femme et son fils se sont transformés en présences fantomales et ont élu résidence dans un grenier. Au cours de sa quête, Herman se liquéfie progressivement dans l'atmosphère pluvieuse du village. Dans *La Sorcière* (1996), à la suite d'un abandon par son mari du domicile conjugal, une femme s'engage dans une quête au cours de laquelle elle se désintègre peu à peu. Le processus de désintégration physique, psychique et matérielle du personnage principal est récurrent dans les romans de NDiaye. Il caractérise l'ensemble de sa production artistique de 1989 à 2001. Dans *La Femme changée en bûche* (1989), la voix de la narratrice se dilue progressivement jusqu'à disparaître dans une cacophonie de dialogues simultanés. Dans *En Famille* (1990), une jeune fille métisse, tentant de correspondre au modèle ethnique que lui impose sa famille, en vient à perdre toute consistance corporelle (Cottille-Foley). Tuée à deux reprises dans le texte, elle se dissout dans une présence fantomale de plus en plus affaiblie. Dans *Rosie Carpe* (2001), le personnage principal, vampirisé par sa propre famille, devient l'ombre d'elle-même, une présence dont toute volonté semble avoir disparu. D'autres œuvres content respectivement la mort progressive d'une

Cottille-Foley

jeune fille dont la conscience sombre au fur et à mesure des ravages de l'anorexie dont elle souffre, la perte de sa maison et de son enfant par une femme transformée en diablesse, et enfin, la vampirisation psychologique d'une femme de ménage par son employeuse.[2] Ce thème si récurrent peut être considéré comme une signature stylistique de NDiaye durant cette période. À travers ce processus qui la positionne entre le réalisme, le merveilleux et le fantastique, NDiaye dépasse les clichés littéraires. Elle transcende la banalité du quotidien pour en représenter les phénomènes d'aliénation de façon novatrice, créant un genre à part qui ne saurait se résumer au réalisme magique.

Chez Darrieussecq aussi les fantômes abondent. Cependant, leur première apparition date de *Naissance des fantômes*. Il s'agit ici non seulement de l'apparition progressive du fantôme du mari, laquelle n'a après tout rien de surprenant, mais également de la vaporisation, de la perte de volonté et de la vampirisation dont la narratrice elle-même se sent être l'objet. Tout comme NDiaye, Darrieussecq utilise ici la désintégration comme représentation littéraire de l'aliénation. La narratrice se vaporise après la mort de son époux tout comme Herman se liquéfie après la disparition de sa femme et de son enfant (*Un Temps de saison*), ou encore comme Lucie qui perd toute consistance identitaire après l'abandon de son mari (*La Sorcière*). Peu après la disparition de son époux, la narratrice de *Naissance des fantômes* remarque, "Ce soir-là, ce fut la dernière fois, à mon souvenir, que je réussis à me percevoir comme entière, pleine et ramassée; ensuite, je me suis diffusée comme les galaxies, vaporisée très loin comme les géantes rouges" (13). Si le même adjectif de "vaporeuse" est utilisé dans *Un Temps de saison* (103), c'est surtout l'idée de la désintégration du personnage et de sa volonté qui rapproche ces textes. Dans le texte de NDiaye, Herman se dilue dans l'hostilité d'un climat pluvieux et froid. Il sent son être fondre peu à peu et perdre toute consistance face à la force revêche et menaçante des villageois, lesquels n'acceptent jamais entièrement sa présence. Si la liquéfaction caractérise Herman, parallèlement, dans le texte de Darrieussecq, la mer s'impose peu à peu comme l'image même de cette dissolution. L'écume des rouleaux des vagues évoque en la narratrice la représentation de son propre cerveau:

---

[2] Respectivement dans la nouvelle "Le jour du président", dans le conte pour enfants *La Diablesse et son enfant* et enfin dans la pièce de théâtre *Hilda*.

> J'imaginais ainsi mon propre cerveau, soumis à la pression et vaporisé, toutes les connexions de mon cerveau peu à peu défaites, brumeuses et floues (une maille effilochée, une mantille de poussière ne retenant même plus les propres atomes de sa dispersion), et ma pensée se vaporisait à son tour en cherchant à s'épandre à la mesure de ce qui lui manquait, épousant le corps creux, vide et volatil de mon mari. (66-67)

Si la mer n'apparaît pas dans le premier roman de Darrieussecq, elle caractérise son œuvre à partir de *Naissance des fantômes*. Il semblerait que l'idée première de désintégration, vaporisation et liquéfaction ait libéré un autre registre métaphorique pour cet auteur originaire du Pays Basque, un registre infiniment riche, infiniment profond, celui de l'océan. Le thème est amplement repris et exploré dans deux écrits subséquents: *Le Mal de mer* et *Précision sur les vagues*. Dans *Naissance des fantômes* s'annonce un autre thème lié ici à l'océan et que l'on retrouvera jusqu'à *Tom est mort:* la présence fantasmatique d'un cadavre dans l'imaginaire des personnages (ici et plus tard dans *Bref séjour chez les vivants*, un corps noyé déformé), laquelle présence répond sourdement, en abyme, à l'idée plus aérienne de vaporisation et de présences fantomales.

Si le thème de la dissolution progressive du protagoniste semble être emprunté à NDiaye à la fois dans sa forme métaphorique (la vaporisation, la liquéfaction et la vampirisation) et dans sa signification (l'aliénation due à la perte du conjoint), la gestion narratologique de cette métaphore est cependant différente. Chez NDiaye, la métaphore, comme chez Kafka, devient littérale. La femme et l'enfant d'Herman sont littéralement devenus des présences vaporeuses résidant au village. Les filles de Lucie se transforment véritablement en oiseaux dans *La Sorcière*, laissant quelques plumes incriminantes sur leur passage. Quelques témoignages semblent l'indiquer, toujours de façon ambiguë, faisant flotter le texte entre merveilleux et réalisme, ambiguïté qui, selon Todorov, est la définition même du fantastique. Cependant, le but affiché du texte ne semble pas résider dans l'effet du fantastique sur le lecteur — en tout cas pas dans cette délicieuse frayeur superstitieuse qu'un texte de Poe ou de Maupassant peut déclencher — mais plutôt dans l'expression d'une réalité sociale du protagoniste. C'est bien l'aliénation au sein de la famille et de la communauté que NDiaye dénonce dans chacun de ses romans depuis *La Femme changée en bûche* jusqu'à *Rosie Carpe*. Le protagoniste devient le témoin involontaire de sa propre disparition. Sa passiveté face aux évènements qui l'accablent, sa léthargie et sa paralysie progressive évoquent non seulement l'enlisement propre au cauchemar — ingrédient supplémentaire de l'inquiétante étrangeté caractérisant le fantastique — mais également le déterminisme de sa situation sociale — élément du réalisme.

Naissance des fantômes fait une place différente à l'image des fantômes et à la volonté du protagoniste. Nous sommes dans le domaine de la comparaison. Les expressions comparatives abondent dans le roman, en particulier l'expression "comme si". Elles indiquent que les métaphores et les comparaisons sont une façon pour la narratrice de mettre en image ce qu'elle ressent. Lorsqu'elle indique que, chaque jour, "il fallait se lever et faire comme si" (59), l'expression désigne alors la norme plutôt que l'image. Ce renversement de la comparaison indique que la narratrice est passée de l'autre côté du miroir, que sa réalité est désormais alternative et que son point de vue narratif est subjectif. C'est donc depuis l'angle de son imaginaire qu'il faut interpréter sa rencontre du fantôme de son mari. L'hésitation interprétative n'est pas véritablement possible. Le récit se donne à lire dans la subjectivité d'une conscience en souffrance. Contrairement à l'incompréhension hébétée des protagonistes NDiayens, spectateurs involontaires et impuissants de leur propre éradication sociale, la narratrice de *Naissance des fantômes* contrôle l'interprétation des évènements, elle dirige le récit. C'est elle qui choisit le champ lexical des comparaisons et la fabula, clémente, lui laisse tout le loisir de l'auto-observation. Nul empressement — elle ne travaille pas, nulle inquiétude financière — elle découvre que l'argent continue à arriver sur son compte en banque grâce aux activités antérieures de son mari, nulle turpitude sociale — sa mère et sa meilleure amie cherchent à l'aider — ne vient troubler les étapes du deuil. Le récit est raconté depuis la perspective de sa guérison, après qu'elle ait pu communier avec la nébuleuse pailletée de son fantôme de mari. Le roman de Darrieussecq s'apparente à une étude psychologique du deuil alors que ceux de NDiaye expriment l'aliénation sociale et familiale. Leurs fantômes respectifs ne sont pas de même nature.

Si l'œuvre de NDiaye a pu servir d'inspiration et de déclencheur d'images dans *Naissance des fantômes*, la frustration éprouvée par NDiaye devant la récupération de ce qui fait son originalité a elle-même servi de déclencheur dans les textes suivants: les images d'imitation vampirique viennent les hanter. Dans la pièce de théâtre *Hilda* (1999), une propriétaire bourgeoise exploite la servante qu'elle veut imiter et remplacer auprès de l'époux de celle-ci. Dans le roman *Mon Cœur à l'étroit* (2007), la question du plagiat est traitée de façon plus directe. L'un des personnages, ironiquement prénommé Ange et soupçonné d'on ne sait d'abord quel crime, reçoit une blessure que s'ingénie à triturer un voisin, Noget, lequel s'avère être un écrivain reconnu et respecté dont on apprendra plus tard qu'Ange a plagié les œuvres. Ange s'attire le mépris des voisins de son immeuble quand, lors d'une fête, il parodie une jeune étudiante chinoise qui avait l'habitude de se promener nue derrière une fenêtre face à son appartement. Alors que la jeune fille est pure, humble et innocente dans sa nudité, Ange est odieux dans son imitation de sa démarche (95-96). La narratrice remarque, "nous ne savons qu'être hideux en voulant la railler" (96). Le plagiaire est ici non seulement un usurpateur (il s'arroge les lauriers d'une gloire dont il n'est pas la véritable source, son prénom même est en contradiction avec son identité), mais encore, il est hideux dans la déformation parodique qu'il impose à l'objet imité — déformation qui ne va pas sans rappeler le terme de "singerie" que NDiaye utilisa dans la controverse qui l'opposa à Darrieussecq. Noget, l'écrivain dont on ne connaît pas les motifs, le guérira en le nourrissant de plats trop riches qui l'écœurent et font suinter sa blessure. Loin d'être un roman vindicatif, *Mon Cœur à l'étroit* semble marquer un tournant dans l'œuvre romanesque de NDiaye. Les marasmes identitaires de la narratrice trouvent une résolution tandis que le noyau familial parvient à se reconstituer.

Comme cette brève analyse a pu le démontrer, la lecture de l'hypotexte permet de mieux comprendre la genèse de l'hypertexte et, au-delà, le développement artistique de deux écrivains contemporains, NDiaye et Darrieussecq. Afin de s'autoriser la possibilité d'une telle analyse, il faut dépasser le culte de l'originalité et enfreindre les tabous relatifs à l'imitation. L'œuvre artistique vacille nécessairement entre ces deux pôles. Tout roman charrie en son cours les textes qui l'ont précédé, mais l'œuvre d'art transmute les matériaux qu'elle emporte en son lit. L'écrivain est un alchimiste et, loin des disputes éditoriales, c'est cette alchimie qui nous intéresse.

Ouvrages cités

Assouline, Pierre. "Les vérités de Marie NDiaye". 19 novembre 2007. <http://passouline.blog.lemonde.fr/2007/11/19/les-verites-de-marie-ndiaye/>.

Braudeau, Michel, Lakis Proguidis, Jean-Pierre Salgas, et Dominique Viart. *Le Roman français contemporain*. Paris: adpf, 2002.

Carrard, Philippe. "*Palimpsestes: La littérature au second degré* by Gérard Genette". *Poetics Today* 5.1 (1984): 205-08.

Cottille-Foley, Nora. "Les mots pour ne pas le dire ou encore l'indicibilité d'une visibilité frottée de fantastique dans les œuvres de Marie NDiaye". *Revue des Sciences Humaines* 293 (2009): 13-23.

Darrieussecq, Marie. *Bref séjour chez les vivants*. Paris: POL, 2001.

———. *Le Mal de mer*. Paris: POL, 1999.

———. *La Naissance des fantômes*. Paris: POL, 1998.

———. *Précision sur les vagues*. Paris: POL, 1999.

———. *Tom est mort*. Paris: POL, 2007.

Genette, Gérard. *Palimpsestes*. Paris: Seuil, 1992. Points Essais.

Géniès, Bernard. "Celles par qui le scandale arrive". *Le Nouvel Observateur* 2234 (30 août 2007). <http://hebdo.nouvelobs.com>.

Goldblatt, David. "Self-plagiarism". *The Journal of Aesthetics and Art Criticism* 43.1 (1984): 71-77.

Kechichian, Patrick. "Darrieussecq a-t-elle 'singé' Marie NDiaye?" *Le Monde* 4 mars 1998. <http://abonnes.lemonde.fr>.

———. "La littérature en proie à ses fantômes". *Le Monde* 13 mars 1998. <http://abonnes.lemonde.fr>.

———. "*Tom est mort*, la polémique". *Le Monde* 24 août 2007. <http://abonnes.lemonde.fr>.

Kristéva, Julia. *Sémiotikè, recherches pour une sémanalyse*. Paris: Seuil, 1978.

Laurens, Camille. *Cet Absent-là*. Paris: Léo Scheer, 2004.

———. "Marie Darrieussecq ou le syndrome du coucou". *La Revue littéraire* 32 septembre 2007. <http://himmelweg.blog.lemonde.fr/files/2007/09/laurens_camille-controverse.1190797020.pdf>.

———. *Philippe*. Paris: POL, 1995.

NDiaye, Marie. *La Diablesse et son enfant.* Paris: L'Ecole des loisirs, 2000.

———. *La Femme changée en bûche*. Paris: Minuit, 1989.

———. *Hilda.* Paris: Minuit, 1999.

_____. "Le jour du président". *La Nouvelle Revue Française* 537 octobre 1997: 51-67.

_____. *Mon Cœur à l'étroit*. Paris: Minuit, 2007.

_____. *Rosie Carpe*. Paris: Minuit, 2001.

_____. *La Sorcière*. Paris: Minuit, 1996.

_____. *Un Temps de saison. Paris*: Minuit, 1994.

Nodier, Charles. *Questions de littérature légale. Du Plagiat, de la supposition d'auteurs, des supercheries qui ont rapport aux livres.* Paris: Droz, 2003.

Todorov, Tzvetan. *Introduction à la littérature fantastique.* Paris: Seuil, 1971.

Vandendorpe, Christian. "Le plagiat". <http://www.lettres.uottawa.ca/vanden/plagiat.htm>. 5 janvier 2009.

Trae DeLellis

University of Miami

Copycat, Copycat:
The Anxiety of Influence in *Irma Vep*

> Remakes, long considered the refuge of cinematic hacks and thieves, get a revision in Olivier Assayas's *Irma Vep*. While Harold Bloom once claimed that "The French have never valued originality" (xv), Assayas's retake on the remake squarely examines and transcends the conventional conceptions of influence and originality.

For its sixtieth anniversary celebration, the Cannes Film Festival commissioned over thirty internationally renowned filmmakers to submit a short film expressing their own feelings about the cinema to form the omnibus film, *Chacun son cinéma* (2007). Each filmmaker embarked on the project with a stringent time limit of three to four minutes and the condition that the film would take place in a cinema. Among this group of celebrated filmmakers, Olivier Assayas contributed *Recrudescence*, which commences with an unnamed man (George Babluani) and focuses on a young woman (Deniz Gamze Ergüven) who is entering a multiplex to meet her date (Lionel Dray). The couple, unaware of the man watching them, purchase tickets and "childish" candy before entering their screening. While the couple succumb to the desires aroused by a darkened theater, the man, who has been intently following them, silently filches the woman's purse. After the screening, the woman calls her own phone, which the thief answers, "Yes, it's me." Indicative of the ambiguity for which Assayas has been celebrated and derided, *Recrudescence* offers little explanation to character motivation or personal histories. Despite its lack of resolution, this vignette encapsulates the issue at hand, one of supreme importance to Assayas: a cinematic theft.

Property and, specifically, intellectual property, artistic and commercial, serves as a concurrent theme throughout Assayas's work. *Fin août, début septembre* (*Late August, Early September* 1998) abounds with property issues, including the apartment shared by Gabriel and Jenny, the clothing designs of Anne, and the texts of Adrien. Likewise, *Les Destinées sentimentales* (2000) deals in great depth with the production of porcelain and brandy in the face of international competition. These ideas of property rights and competition have only intensified in works of Assayas's such as *demonlover* (2002) and *Clean* (2004). *demonlover* revolves around a corporate war over distribution rights for pornographic Japanese anime, while *Clean* centers on the ownership and marketing of a deceased musician's back catalogue. *Boarding Gate* (2007), a quasi-continuation of the international corporate world of *demonlover*, even features a DVD piracy operation run out of China. Assayas's latest film, *L'heure d'été* (*Summer Hours* 2008) deals with a French family, as they settle the estate and property issues raised by their mother's death. Despite these various forays into intellectual property ownership, Assayas's greatest meditation on the creative process and collision of art and commerce comes in the form of *Irma Vep* (1996), the film that cemented Assayas's international reputation as one of France's most interesting filmmakers.

With *Irma Vep*, Assayas challenges Harold Bloom's claim that "the French have never valued originality," by engaging directly with Bloom's concept, "the anxiety of influence" from his seminal text, *The Anxiety of Influence: A Theory of Poetry* (xv). Addressing the postmodern axiom that "everything has been done before," Bloom proposes a theory of poetic and literary influence that examines an artist's relationship to previous artists and works of art. Bloom posits that artists find inspiration to create art through a predecessor's works, and in order to avoid a weak, derivative version of the forerunner's ideas, the new artist must address his or her own anxiety of influence (5). In cinematic terms, Bloom's argument finds no greater validity than in the process of the remake.

Despite Bloom's claim about the French and originality, the remake in French cinema is a site of great contention, particularly its relationship to American cinema. In *Encore Hollywood: Remaking French Cinema*, Lucy Mazdon examines the ongoing trend of Hollywood studios remaking French films, and the resulting connotations of "cultural imperialism" (19).[1] The cultural tensions between France and the United States in regards to cinema infuse the discussion and context of *Irma Vep*. In the film, Assayas engages with the anxiety of influence by creating a film about a film crew remaking yet another film. *Irma Vep* is a film about remaking, essentially a meta-remake. In their own study of remakes, Andrew Horton and Stuart Y. McDougal frame their examination around two interesting questions: "What exactly are the boundaries of a remake? At what point does similarity become simply a question of influence?" (1). As a meta-remake, *Irma Vep* centralizes and deconstructs the boundaries between influence and theft at the heart of remake studies.

The three films — the film we are watching, the film being made, and the original film — feed off one another. Studies of remakes often pit the original against its remake, usually dismissed as inferior or a thoughtless copy. *Irma Vep* challenges this binary by following René Vidal (Jean-Pierre Léaud), a fledgling director, as he attempts to remake Louis Feuillade's 1915 serial film *Les vampires* for French television with Hong Kong action star Maggie Cheung, who plays a version of herself in the lead role. Assayas challenges the relationship between original and remade text through the anxiety of influence to create a third text outside and beyond the binary division of original and copy. *Irma Vep*, as the third text, addresses Bloom's concepts of anxiety of influence and the "horror of contamination," a fear of unoriginality and repeating previous works (xxiv). Assayas's film calls artistic integrity, appropriation, and originality into question and be-

---

[1] In Franco-American film relationships, there have been two court cases regarding charges of theft and plagiarism between the producers of René Clair's *À nous la liberté* (1931) and Charlie Chaplin's *Modern Times* (1936) and the estate of Henri-Georges Clouzot's *Les diaboliques* (1955), when Jeremiah S. Chechik remade the film in 1996 as *Diabolique*. See David Robinson's examination of the *Modern Times* scandal on the Criterion DVD of *À nous la liberté* and Susan Hayward's *Les Diaboliques* for a detailed examination of the controversy surrounding Chechik's remake.

gins a search for something new, something outside the illusive and limited definition of originality.[2]

Inevitably, *Irma Vep* has been compared to other remakes, such as François Truffaut's *La Nuit américaine* (*Day for Night* 1973; see Sutton) and *Les Misérables* (see Metz). In point of fact, Assayas's concern for the conflicts of filmmaking more closely resembles Rainer Werner Fassbinder's *Warnung vor einer heiligen Nutte* (*Beware of a Holy Whore* 1971).[3] Truffaut's film is a romantic and comic "valentine to the filmmaking process," as Armond White put it, whereas Fassbinder offers a nightmare version full of sadomasochistic mind games and egotistical power trips. This distinction becomes paramount in an analysis of Assayas's film, which falls somewhere in between the extreme versions of Truffaut and Fassbinder, and the effects from the anxiety of influence.

---

[2] Ironically, Assayas's film has spawned a pair of additional meta-remakes involving the production of a remake such as Abel Ferrera's *The Blackout* (1997), in which director Mickey Wayne (Dennis Hopper) attempts to remake Christian-Jaque's *Nana* (1955), and Nobuhiro Suwa's *H Story* (2001), which follows the director's attempt to remake Alain Resnais's *Hiroshima, mon amour* (1959). In addition, Hsiao-hsien Hou's *Le voyage du ballon rouge* (*The Flight of the Red Balloon* 2007) includes a Chinese film student studying in France and filming a remake of Albert Lamorisse's *Le ballon rouge* (*The Red Balloon* 1956). Also of note, Lars Von Trier's *De fem benspaend* (*The Five Obstructions* 2003) documents the remaking process when he challenges Jørgen Leth to remake Leth's film *Det perfekte menneske* (*The Perfect Human* 1967) five times with various restrictions.

[3] Sutton and Metz emphasize the relationship between Assayas and Truffaut's films because of Assayas's past work with *Cahiers du cinema* and the casting of Léaud. It is important to note that neither article mentions the casting of Lou Castel, who plays José Mirano, the director who replaces René. Sutton and Metz overlook Castel's own cinematic past, which includes his role as the director in Fassbinder's *Beware of a Holy Whore*. In the recent re-release of *Irma Vep* on DVD, Assays stated: "When I was writing *Irma Vep*, *Beware of a Holy Whore* was a very important reference in many ways. At that time I felt that the one movie about modern film making was *Beware of a Holy Whore*. Much more than *La Nuit américaine*, which is a movie I love. […] But it has very little to do with modern film making. Whereas in the modern independent film making where *Beware of a Holy Whore* is pretty much it, you know; it was the blueprint for [Wenders's] *State of Things*. It's a movie that was much more present for me at that time than *La Nuit américaine* which is the film *Irma Vep* is always compared to. But I think it's very misleading."

DeLellis
145

In their respective studies, Sutton and Metz emphasize certain aspects of *Irma Vep* at the risk of overlooking the relationship between the anxiety of influence and authorial control in the film.[4] Assayas uses *Irma Vep* to explore the issues of influence, originality, and their effect on the relationship between director and star. The significance of the director-star relationship arises early when René and Maggie meet for the first time and expose their shared anxiety of influence, which will dominate the remaining narrative of *Irma Vep*. Before a dialogue between director and star begins, Assayas introduces images of Maggie from *Dung fong saam hap* (*The Heroic Trio* 1993) by Johnny To. Rather than utilizing a more traditional frame-within-a-frame construction, Assayas allows To's film to overtake the frame of *Irma Vep*. Throughout *Irma Vep*, outside texts invade and overtake Assayas's frame and give weight to the overwhelming, sometimes suffocating power of outside influences and their threat to originality.

Assayas cuts to René holding a remote control, a symbol of his directorial power, and we see that he and Maggie have been watching this action film. René explains his hesitation over remaking *Les vampires* and his championing of Maggie in the role of Irma Vep. Maggie learns that René stipulated his participation in the remake on the condition that he could cast Maggie in the role. This revelation cements the bond between director and star throughout the filmmaking process. René concludes that a French actress playing Irma Vep after Musidora, the original star, would be "blasphemy." The addition of a "Chinese Irma Vep" convinces René that he has an original contribution to Feuillade's legacy: Maggie functions as René's muse and symbol of originality.

During this time, Maggie flips through a pile of videos and laserdiscs of her past films scattered across René's floor. The images of these outside texts layered upon one another illustrate the intricate web of influences that feeds René and Maggie's shared anxieties. These films influence René in the casting of Maggie and, at the same time, they tie Maggie to her past roles while forming her star-image. These past influences and roles will eventually restrict both director

---

[4] Sutton examines *Irma Vep* as an example of "spectorial remaking" instead of authorial remaking (69). Metz focuses on the use of Léaud as an intertextual reference to evoke the *nouvelle vague* (66).

and star as they try to achieve originality through the act of remaking. Assayas ends the scene with another outside text conquering the frame: Feuillade's *Les vampires*. At this pivotal moment, director and star confront Feuillade's original film as well as Musidora, the original Irma Vep. As they remake *Les vampires*, René and Maggie will be continually haunted by these figures and influences.

During the following day, Assayas demonstrates the contagiousness of influence-anxiety when Maggie arrives for a costume fitting. In a Parisian sex shop, Maggie expresses concern about her costume to Zoé (Nathalie Richard), the costume designer: "It's not what I expected. Is this what René wanted?" Zoé quickly assures Maggie by offering photographic evidence of René's vision for the costume. In yet another example of an outside influence, Zoé offers a magazine clipping of Michelle Pfeiffer as Catwoman from Tim Burton's *Batman Returns* (1992). This exchange confirms the contamination and spread of unoriginality. At lunch, Zoé explains her own reservations about remaking and becomes the voice of originality in *Irma Vep*. Zoé vehemently opposes remakes and asks a central question to Assayas's film: "Why are we doing what's already been done?" Once considered a promising and innovative director, Zoé suggests that René has lost his authorial voice because of "other things on his mind." These "things" remain unidentified, but it seems logical that the constant intrusion of and reliance on outside texts have inhibited René's originality. Zoé's cryptic comment suggests that René has already succumbed to his own anxiety of influence by remaking *Les vampires*.

On set, the differences and similarities between Feuillade and René emerge. During this time, René attempts to battle his own anxiety of influence. René's sequence re-films the scene from *Les vampires*, in which Moreno drugs and replaces Irma Vep with a doppelganger in his quest to become the Grand Vampire. René's scene follows the earlier sequence shown to Maggie in their first meeting. Both René and Feuillade, in addition to Assayas, practice the major tenet of French cinema, "the integrity of the shot," explored by Alan Williams (126). Despite their similarities, each director accomplishes this shared ambition through different means. Whereas Feuillade relies on camera placement and depth of field to preserve shot unity, René utilizes camera movement. Both approaches, placement and movement, aim to capture as much action as possible without the in-

DeLellis 147

trusion of or reliance on montage.[5] René's reliance on camera movement (he attempts over twenty takes) over camera placement signals a visual originality outside of Feuillade's past approach. It is important to note that René is not attempting a shot-for-shot remake of Feuillade's film; he wants both to celebrate Feuillade's work and to distance himself from it.

Despite noble effort toward an original approach, Assayas quashes René's hope for originality when the cast and crew attend a screening of the daily rushes. After a second filming sequence on René's set, Assayas makes an abrupt cut from the filming of the images to the images filmed.[6] Again an additional text, this time René's own, overtakes the frame of Assayas's film. Interestingly, René's film is in black and white, like Feuillade's original, in opposition to the common policy of remaking black and white films in color.[7] From René's silent black and white images, Assayas cuts to the cast and crew in uncertain silence as the rushes end. Markus (Bernard Nissile), René's cinematographer, breaks the heavy silence by demanding the director's response. René launches into a tirade and announces, "It sucks! It's shit!" The outburst, reminiscent of the director in *Beware*

---

[5] Both scenes focus on three distinct areas: Irma Vep, the trunk holding her doppelganger, and the window where Moreno signals to his gang. In addition to his stationary camera and carefully composed shot, Feuillade implements editing. On the other hand, René offers a greater proximity to the action and forgoes editing through the use of camera movement. Of course, since René is currently filming and unable to edit, it is possible that he may decide to cut later on, but the fact that the crew has filmed the scene more than twenty-four times suggests that he desires a continuous take. Through camera movement, René captures the same action in a single shot that takes Feuillade ten shots. In addition, René's emphasis on movement and lengthy take echoes Assayas's own style.

[6] The second filming sequence picks up where the first left off. It is both a continuation of René's film and the sequence from *Les vampires*. In the scene, Irma Vep is carried past her double and thrown out the window. The way Assayas films the sequence allows a glimpse at the trickery of filmmaking when Maggie exits and a stunt woman enters René's frame. Interestingly, we then see three versions of Irma Vep: Maggie, the doppelganger, and the stuntwoman — a version of a version of a version.

[7] Like René's version of *Les vampires*, Suwa's *H Story* also makes the interesting choice to maintain the original's use of black and white cinematography, in contrast to more popular remakes such as Gus Van Sant's *Pscyho* (1998) or Chechik's *Diabolique*, which actually includes a self-referential joke about the then-popular colorization of cinematic classics.

of a Holy Whore or the producer in Jean-Luc Godard's *Le mépris* (*Contempt* 1963), registers the intensity of René's anxiety of influence. The continual filming only exacerbates René's anxiety, eliciting increasingly erratic and violent behavior from the director.

René's anxiety and disturbing conduct become the topic of discussion during the following scene. After the screening, the cast and crew disperse. Maggie is nearly left behind until she runs into Zoé, who takes Maggie to a dinner party at Markus's apartment. At the dinner table, in René's absence, Markus informs his guests that he warned René against remaking *Les vampires* and calls the project "a trap." Markus concludes that, on some level, all "directors thrive on hypocrisy," but offers no further explanation. Such an ambiguous and loaded statement calls out for interpretation. In one sense, Markus might be referring to the difficulty of creating anything original in a postmodern context, a difficulty that aggravates René's anxiety of influence. The process of remaking is by nature contradictory: an attempt to create something new from something old.

A musical sequence follows when a party guest turns on the stereo. Neither Sutton nor Metz comments on this sequence, but it is paramount for understanding both Assayas's observations and the interplay of originality and influence. The song playing, "Bonnie and Clyde" by Luna, represents a remake itself. The song parallels the themes of influence and originality in *Irma Vep*. The song is a cover by an English-speaking indie-band, performed in French, of a duet between Serge Gainsbourg and Brigitte Bardot, recorded 28 years prior, which in turn was inspired by a poem, "The Trail's End," by Bonnie Parker, herself. In a film about a filmmaker remaking another film, the song — a version of an interpretation of an original source — echoes the omnipresent issues of originality, influence, appropriation, and reproduction found throughout *Irma Vep*. The song's significance is underscored when it reappears over the end credits of Assayas's film; the song serves as a succinct conclusion and summary of the complexity of remaking as explored in *Irma Vep*.

René makes up for his absence when Maggie, returning to her hotel from the party, receives a bombardment of frantic messages from her director. Maggie returns to René's home, where they first met, in the wake of an unseen and unheard domestic dispute between René and his wife. In his weak state, René expresses regret over

DeLellis   149

committing to the remake project; he confesses, "Feuillade had the right eye," and concludes, "Images of images [are] worthless." In an attempt to assuage her director's concerns and anxieties, Maggie claims they are doing something different, something "1996," but fails to convince René and perhaps herself. At the exact moment when the director and star engage in a fruitful discussion, just as it appears that René may have a handle on the project and a fresh point of view or original approach to the film, he begins to feel the effect of the sleeping pills he has been given by the police. Ironically, this anti-anxiety medication prevents René from escaping his anxiety of influence and dooms his remake of *Les vampires*.

As René sleeps, the narrative of *Irma Vep* shifts from director to star. Assayas turns to Maggie's own anxiety of influence, which has been developing throughout the film of René's remake. During their final on-screen discussion, René challenges Maggie to discover her character. When she describes her approach as a "fantasy" and "game," René violently objects: "No! It is very important!" Despite this directness from the director, during the production René offers conflicting instructions to his star, which increases Maggie's own anxiety of influence. In fact, Maggie, unlike René, must battle two figures of influence: René, her director, and Musidora, the original Irma Vep. This dual influencing is first shown while René screens the sequence from *Les vampires* for Maggie during their initial meeting. As the original film plays, René provides his own commentary on the film, Musidora, and Irma Vep, and this unduly influences Maggie's own interpretation of her character.

During the filmmaking process, René instructs Maggie to be herself, but at the same time he continually evokes the memory of Musidora as inspiration. René's continued reference to and reverence for Musidora takes a toll on Maggie and heightens her anxieties of replaying the role of Irma Vep. Undermining the relationship between director and star is miscommunication, or what Bloom might call "mis-reading," caused by their language barrier (xii). At one point, René informs his colleague, "I'm not sure she understands everything I say." The miscommunication between director and star leaves Maggie confused, unsure, and anxious. It is only after their final conversation that Maggie is able to confront her own anxieties in order to enter the role of Irma Vep. As René succumbs to his drug-induced sleep,

Maggie exits the ground floor window and returns to her hotel as Sonic Youth plays over the soundtrack.

The source of this music is identified as Maggie's hotel room. While listening to the angst-ridden and trance-inducing sounds of Sonic Youth, Maggie restlessly circles her room as Assayas's camera strains to keep pace. The camera moves across the room in search of its subject and discovers various influential artifacts. Magazines, CDs, posters, and advertisements cover Maggie's room. The overlap of influential imagery, reminiscent of René's video collection, signifies the proliferation of influences on Maggie's psyche as she creates the character of Irma Vep. Assayas even goes so far as to drift over a television screen featuring picture-in-picture, a literal visualization of overlapping texts. However, in contrast to René, Assayas suggests that these textual influences and images, far from distracting Maggie, actually help her become her character — a 1996 version of Irma Vep.

Now in character, in a trance-like state, Maggie exits her room as Irma Vep and stalks the hotel halls looking for an adventure. She enters the room of another guest, where a naked woman speaks to her absent lover on the phone. Maggie, the star watched by the audience, becomes a voyeur. In the bathroom, Maggie takes method acting a step further when she mimics Musidora's Irma Vep by stealing a necklace. Similar to Feuillade's original film, Maggie makes an exciting exit out a window into the rain where she suddenly awakes from her somnambulist state and drops the jewels into the hotel courtyard.[8] Unlike René, who fails to become his own original version of Feuillade, Maggie becomes her own new version of Irma Vep.

---

[8] Feuillade's lingering influence on Assays's work can be found in other films such as *demonlover* and *Boarding Gate*, both of which feature a female protagonist who enters and exits windows like Musidora in *Les vampires*.

DeLellis 151

Despite Maggie's astonishing breakthrough, the film under production continues to unravel. The final day of shooting begins without the film's director and star: René has disappeared and Maggie overslept. The mutual absence of director and star cements their bond through their shared anxiety of influence. Maggie arrives only to be told during a rehearsal that the film is a wrap; René's film remains incomplete.

At the conclusion of *Irma Vep*, René and Maggie have been replaced by a new director and star. Assayas ends his film, *Irma Vep*, with a screening of René's unfinished project. The cast and crew, minus Maggie and René, gather to watch the remnants of René's film. This final screening scene echoes the previous screening in which René implodes; the juxtaposition of these two scenes intensifies René's absence. For the last time, a text outside of Assayas's film overtakes the frame. This final additional text is by far the most disjointed, abstract, and avant-garde of the texts offered throughout *Irma Vep*. René offers a shocking and unconventional interpretation of Feuillade's source material. René's completed film, composed of silent black and white close-ups of Maggie, features etches and scratches across the celluloid.

This exceptional decision inspired a debate between Metz and Sutton over the question of influence. Although René's decision may at first appear startlingly original, both scholars attribute a different filmmaker as an influence on René. Metz calls René's film "at once both profoundly radical and nihilistically hollow" by appearing avant-garde while remaining tainted by past influences (66). Sutton and Metz debate the original influence of René's film, the former arguing for the Lettrist filmmaker Isidore Isou and his infamous *Traité de bave et d'éternité* (*Venom and Eternity* 1951), and the latter locating René's inspiration, or appropriation, in the work of American avant-garde filmmaker Stan Brakhage.

René's failed attempt at originality suggests the possibility that originality as a concept is nonexistent, a falsity, an unachievable goal, one that is, as Metz puts it, "hollow." However, it would be a grave mistake simply to dismiss René's film as unoriginal or empty of meaning; after all, *Irma Vep* revolves around the production of René's film. It is possible to read René's film and its scratches as a defensive maneuver. By destroying the celluloid of his film, René prevents the possibility of a new director appropriating the material to finish the film. Ironically, in this reading, René attempts to prevent the use of his images in another film while himself using Feuillade's film as inspiration.

The greatest significance of René's film parallels Assayas's interest in the director-star relationship and the issue of influence.[9] The placement of celluloid scratches throughout René's film simultaneously acknowledges and restricts Maggie's influence as star. At times the etchings deny or restrict Maggie's own vision, while at others the scratching extends and concentrates her vision. René comments on his power struggle with Maggie through his film: she is his friend and his foe. His fear and fascination with his star, combined with their shared anxiety of influence, leads to the abandonment of their project.

Toward the end of *Irma Vep*, Maggie reveals that she has seen René after his breakdown and that he seems at peace. Maggie tells Zoé that she now "understands" René. Maggie's understanding arises from her acknowledgment of her own anxiety of influence that she shares with René. Unfortunately, Maggie and René are unable to reconcile their anxieties in time to save the film. At the same time, both seem pleased, or at least relieved, that they have escaped their anxieties by abandoning the project. Maggie interprets René's breakdown as "a way out" of remaking Feuillade's film and in turn frees her from portraying Irma Vep.

Assayas ends *Irma Vep* without answering the question of influence in René's film. On the other hand, Assayas's film offers a new interpretation of originality. Although numerous reviewers cite *Irma Vep* as a "postmodern" film, Assayas reaches beyond this ambiguous and conflicted term. In a film about remaking a film, Assayas challenges the conceptions of originality at the core of the postmodern discourse. In this challenge arises a new approach expressed by Mikhail N. Epstein, who proposes that "post-modernism announced an

---

[9] *Irma Vep*'s interest in the director-star relationship is even more intriguing when read along with Assayas and Cheung's relationship outside of the film. Assayas, who wrote the part for Cheung, would eventually marry the actress. Ironically, the two signed their divorce papers while working together for the second time in *Clean*, another film written with Cheung in mind.

DeLellis 153

'end of time,' but any end serves to open at least a crack in time for what is to come after, and thus, indicates the self-irony of finality, which turns into another beginning" (*After the Future* 329). Assayas's ending for *Irma Vep*, with Maggie and René leaving the project, becomes a beginning when a new actress and director are recruited to remake Feuillade's film. The conclusion of *Irma Vep* showcases Assayas's general distaste for resolution in favor of ambiguity that carries over into many of his films, especially *demonlover* and *Boarding Gate*.

By framing *Irma Vep* as a meta-remake with an open ending, Assayas confronts many of the tenets of the remake as a cinematic mode: originality and predictability. The self-awareness and reflexivity of *Irma Vep* and its place as a "postmodern" film beckons for what Epstein calls an "end of time," and supports his concept of a new period defined by the prefix "trans-":

> In considering the names that might possibly be used to designate the new era following "postmodernism," one finds that the prefix "trans" stands out in a special way. The last third of the 20th century developed under the sign of "post," which signaled the demise of such concepts of modernity as "truth" and "objectivity" [...]; "primary origin" and "originality" [...] are now becoming reborn in the form of "trans-subjectivity" [and] "trans-originality." ("Place of Post-Modernism" 222)

Perhaps the most obvious aspect of this new era can be found in *Irma Vep* and Assayas's investment in transnationalism. The first meeting between René and Maggie abounds with breakdowns of national boundaries. The scene consists of a René, a French director, speaking with Maggie, a Chinese, English-educated action star, about Hong Kong action films he had seen in Marrakech over German beers. Not incidentally, Maggie's shirt is a single garment composed of various national flags. Transnationalism is a constant part of Assayas's cinema as seen in an early short such as *Laissé inachevé à Tokyo* (1982), which follows two writers working in Japan, and his more recent films, *demonlover*, *Clean*, and *Boarding Gate*, which feature globe-jumping narratives.

In the embracement of "trans-" as an alternative to the conception of postmodernism, Epstein urges the re-evaluation of originality. With *Irma Vep*, Assayas offers a meditation on the reality of originality in relation to reproduction, cinema, and the remake. Assayas's approach, greatly influenced by his documented affinity for punk music, dismantles conventional understandings of originality destroying the traditional remake in favor of a meta-remake. In its movement beyond originality, *Irma Vep* creates a new beginning from a dead end and contrives, paradoxically, a new form of originality by confronting the anxiety of influence in the remake process. *Irma Vep* acknowledges the fluidity of texts and their influential power, which cannot be escaped, and epitomizes Bloom's theory of the anxiety of influence.

Assayas's film and its relationship to René's film and Feuillade's original suggests that influence need not be a source of anxiety, but a welcome conversation between texts and artists. The deconstruction of *Les vampires* in René and Assayas's films constitutes a move beyond conventional adaptations and remakes toward a new understanding. The texts are no longer locked in a relationship of ambivalence, competition, and contradiction; they become complementary and interconnected. By dismantling and remaking the remake through a confrontation of the anxiety of influence, Assayas creates something at once completely unoriginal and entirely original.

Works Cited

Bloom, Harold. *The Anxiety of Influence: A Theory of Poetry*. 2nd ed. New York: Oxford University Press, 1997.

Epstein, Mikhail N. *After the Future: The Paradoxes of Postmodernism and Contemporary Russian Culture*. Trans. Anesa Miller-Pogacar. Amherst: The University of Massachusetts Press, 1995.

_____. "The Place of Postmodernism in Postmodernity." Trans. Slobodanka Vladiv-Glover. *Russian Postmodernism: New Perspectives on Late Soviet and Post-Soviet Culture*. Ed. Thomas Epstein. Providence: Berghahn Books, 1998.

Horton, Andrew, and Stuart Y. McDougal, eds. *Play It Again, Sam: Retakes on Remakes*. Berkley: University of California Press, 1998.

Mazdon, Lucy. *Encore Hollywood: Remaking French Cinema*. London: British Film Institute Publishing, 2000.

Metz, Walter. "From Jean-Paul Belmondo to Stan Brakhage: Romanticism and Intertextuality in *Irma Vep* and *Les Misérables*." *Film Criticism* 27.1 (Fall 2002): 66-84.

DeLellis 155

Sutton, Paul. "Remaking the Remake: Olivier Assayas's *Irma Vep* (1996)." *French Cinema in the 1990s: Continuity and Difference*. Ed. Phil Powrie. Oxford: Oxford University Press, 1999. 69-80.

Williams, Alan. *Republic of Images: A History of French Filmmaking*. Cambridge: Harvard University Press, 1992.

White, Armond. *Truffaut's Changing Times: The Last Metro*. http://www.criterion.com/current/posts/1044.

Films

Batman Returns. Dir.Tim Burton. Warner Brothers, 1992.

Boarding Gate. Dir. Olivier Assayas. Zeitgeist Films, 2007.

Chacun son cinéma ou ce petit coup au cœur quand la lumière s'éteint et que le film commence. Dir. Theodoros Angelopoulos, Olivier Assayas, et al. Pyramide distribution, 2007.

Clean. Dir. Olivier Assayas. Palm Pictures, 2004.

demonlover. Dir. Olivier Assayas. Palm Pictures, 2002.

Les Destinées sentimentales. Dir. Olivier Assayas. Pathé Distribution International, 2000.

Dung fong saam hap. Dir. Johnnie To.Various distributors, 1993.

Fin août, début septembre. Dir. Olivier Assayas. PolyGram Film Distribution, 1998.

L'heure d'été. Dir. Olivier Assayas. IFC Films, 2008.

Irma Vep. Dir. Olivier Assayas. Zeitgeist Films, 1996.

Les misérables. Dir. Claude Lelouch. Warner Brothers Pictures Distributors, 1995.

La Nuit américaine. Dir. François Truffaut. Columbia Pictures, 1973.

Recrudescence. Dir. Olivier Assayas. Part of *Chacun son cinéma ou ce petit coup au cœur quand la lumière s'éteint et que le film commence*. Pyramide distribution, 2007.

Les vampires. Dir. Louis Feuillade. Gaumont, 1915.

Warnung for einer heiligen Nutte (*Beware of a Holy Whore*). Dir. Rainer Werner Fassbinder. New Yorker Films, 1971.

Patricia Reynaud

Georgetown University, School of Foreign Service, Doha, Qatar

Le goût des autres d'Agnès Jaoui: de l'adaptation de P. Bourdieu au cinéma à sa subversion

> En juxtaposant deux moments de la théorie sociologique et en séparant "critique sociale" et "critique artiste" on dévoilera, dans une première partie, le discours bourdieusien tel qu'il est à l'œuvre dans le film d'Agnès Jaoui. Bourdieu prépare le terrain à un second type d'analyse en termes de fluctuations des espaces sociaux. La seconde partie vient subvertir la perspective de Bourdieu et suggère que la critique artiste sait mieux que quiconque adapter ses goûts à ses intérêts financiers. Une fois dévoilée, la supercherie des artistes permet de constituer un nouvel état post-bourdieusien du champ artistique qui révèle certains enjeux du néolibéralisme.

Si l'on en croit Pierre Bourdieu, le monde social s'organise autour de luttes pour la domination des espaces sociaux, luttes qui sont le plus souvent euphémisées dès lors que les stratégies de domination sont cachées et parfois même inconscientes. Dans son film *Le goût des autres* sorti en 2000, la réalisatrice Agnès Jaoui a mis en images, à travers l'histoire d'une impossible relation amoureuse, les rapports entre deux personnages qui exemplifient, à un niveau social plus englobant, les rapports de leur classe respective ou, pour être plus précis, de leur fraction de classe.

Les deux espaces qui nous sont proposés n'ont, au départ, rien en commun et ceci va se traduire par le manque de compréhension réciproque entre M. Castella, le patron d'une petite usine située à Rouen et Clara Deveaux, comédienne de théâtre classique et d'avant-garde ainsi qu'intermittente du spectacle qui, pour "joindre les deux bouts" donne des cours d'anglais à Castella. Pour dire les choses simplement, leurs goûts sont tellement incompatibles que tout les sépare, du moins au début. Castela est bouleversé par Clara lorsqu'il la voit interpréter le rôle principal de Bérénice dans la tragédie de Racine. Au théâtre où il est venu par hasard pour voir sa nièce jouer dans un rôle secondaire, il s'opère en lui une catharsis alors qu'il voit Clara pour la première fois. Certes pas la dernière: ce sera pour lui l'occasion d'un long apprentissage et de la fréquentation assidue du théâtre pour lequel il se découvre un goût insoupçonné. Son existence chavire alors qu'il subit de plein fouet l'effet inespéré de la transfiguration esthétique. On pourrait ajouter que sa situation de petit patron riche mais peu épanoui va l'inciter à se tourner d'autant vers le monde du spectacle, fasciné qu'il est par le groupe d'artistes. Sa vie est un long fleuve tranquille prodigieusement ennuyeux aux côtés d'une épouse[1] à l'intelligence déficiente, aux goûts conventionnels et tape-à-l'œil, dans un intérieur cossu mais sans légitimité, qu'elle a décoré elle-même[2] et qu'il qualifiera négativement plus avant dans le film de "bonbonnière" en raison de l'abus du rose et des motifs floraux.[3]

---

[1] Elle se prénomme Angélique, ce qui n'est pas dénué d'humour. Si, dans la suite de cet exposé, nous nous référerons à la bêtise de l'intelligence comme forme sublimée de bêtise, le film nous convie aussi à réfléchir sur "la bêtise de l'ignorance" émanant de la personne d'Angélique précisément. Elle a la double fonction "d'ange exterminateur" et de femme castratrice! Ses limitations nous amènent à soulever la question de l'élitisme latent du film, puisque son mauvais goût sert de repoussoir pour un public "averti". La différence entre Angélique et Castella, et ultérieurement peut-être la raison structurelle de leur séparation finale, est que Castella, malgré ses bévues, apprend de ses erreurs et devient, toute proportion gardée, un peu plus subtil à la fin du film. Par contraste, elle semble incapable d'évoluer.

[2] En sa qualité de décoratrice, elle participe directement de ces nouvelles professions de la bourgeoisie en ascension sociale qui, par la place qu'elles font au sens artistique peuvent donner l'illusion à tout détenteur de s'adonner à une véritable carrière d'artiste. L'apparition de ces métiers a eu pour résultat de banaliser la représentation de l'artiste.

[3] La scène prend place après que Castella ait disposé le tableau abstrait dans leur salon. Elle remarque, horrifiée, le changement. C'est un des rares moments où il fait preuve d'autorité envers Angélique, sa femme: "[...] pour une fois que j'aime quelque chose, tu peux pas me le laisser? Tu crois que je suis bien dans cette bonbonnière, là! Je peux plus les voir, moi, ces murs roses, ces petits oiseaux, ces fleurs partout".

Reynaud 159

Pour pouvoir aborder la notion de légitimité des goûts et couleurs, il s'avère nécessaire de faire un bref rappel historique sur la constitution des espaces sociaux qui sont aussi des espaces de goûts. Depuis le XVIIIᵉ siècle, les lettrés ont toujours vu dans la bourgeoisie l'incarnation de la trivialité et de l'affairisme.[4] Mais si la critique artiste — romantiques en tête — s'est ainsi structurée en opposition à la normalité et au manque d'originalité bourgeoise, cette critique, défendant l'imagination et l'individualisme, s'est opposée également à la société industrielle qui était l'emblème du règne bourgeois car le philistin sans envergure se délecte de sa réussite matérielle. On sait d'autre part que la révolution de 1848, surnommée et pour cause "la sociale", va aussi permettre à un autre type de critique, la critique sociale, de s'élaborer contre la société non seulement bourgeoise mais capitaliste. Ces deux critiques de la bourgeoisie ne se recoupent pourtant pas car leur buts ont souvent été opposés: à une critique socialo-marxiste insistant sur la dimension politique des phénomènes révolutionnaires, la critique artiste restera souvent esthétique et libertaire sans nécessairement remettre en question les fondements libéraux (au sens du libéralisme économique) de la société post- révolutionnaire et les rapports de classe inégaux. Se sentant victimes d'une société obtuse, Flaubert[5] et Baudelaire traceront un portrait sans pitié du bourgeois de leur époque mais sans pour autant compatir aux misères d'une classe ouvrière, qu'en tant qu'aristocrates de l'art ils dédaignent autant que les philistins. Après tout, les deux classes ne partagent-elles pas une vulgarité crasse et la même bêtise, puisqu'il leur est impossible de s'élever au-delà de l'utilitarisme? L'imbrication entre ce double registre de critiques permettra en partie d'expliquer les glissements et la "flexibilité"[6] des espaces sociaux dans le film de Jaoui.

---

[4] À l'époque prémoderne les artistes étaient redevables envers leurs mécènes, et, de ce fait, soumis à leur censure. Cependant les mécènes, exceptions mises à part, ne cherchaient pas à être cultivés eux-mêmes. Dans le film, nous verrons que Castella, le "néo-manager" fortuné met un point d'honneur à se cultiver: il semble qu'il veuille comprendre artistiquement ce qu'il achète et ne point passer pour un inculte.

[5] Il est intéressant de souligner que Rouen est la ville natale de Flaubert, ville du nord qui, si l'on en croit le film, ne connaît pas de minorités et ne reflète aucunement toute la diversité de la population française.

[6] J'entends ici par "flexibilité" les nouveaux modes d'organisation du travail mis en place par l'économie néolibérale depuis le milieu des années 80, qui préconisent la mouvance, le changement, le nomadisme.

160 FLS, Vol. XXXVII, 2010

Ce film reprend bien, et prolonge l'histoire de la constitution du champ artistique: celle du scénario bourdieusien bien connu de la critique artiste contre les puissances de l'argent. Cette fois il décrit la déliquescence de ce scénario, dans une société devenue postindustrielle et néolibérale. Il se situe, mais non exclusivement comme nous verrons, dans l'espace des classes dominantes que Bourdieu a schématisé dans son ouvrage *La distinction* et dont il a affiné les analyses dans *Les règles de l'art*, livres dans lesquels deux espèces de capital s'entrechoquent: le capital culturel dont les artistes sont bien pourvus et le capital économique, l'apanage de Castella et des siens.

1. Une adaptation réussie de la théorie de Bourdieu au cinéma

Les artistes et intellectuels, ces dominés de la classe dominante font de nécessité vertu: ils compensent leur manque de capital économique par une vision hautaine de la culture et des goûts légitimes qu'ils parviennent à imposer à cet illégitime de la culture qu'est Castella au point de le rendre littéralement dysfonctionnel dans son travail: il en oublie le rendez-vous qui aurait permis la signature de l'important contrat avec les Iraniens. Il se fait vertement tancer par son directeur Weber qui a perdu un mois de travail et doit reprendre les discussions avec les clients. Dans ces deux fractions de la classe dominante, l'une détient le capital économique, pouvoir temporel s'il en est, et l'autre le pouvoir symbolique, réplique athée du pouvoir spirituel, qui consiste en l'art de manipuler la définition des goûts légitimes. Ces fractions se partagent toutes deux le travail de domination. Ce sont pourtant les artistes qui, dans un premier temps, parviennent à leurs fins et imposent leur vision aux "autres" dont, comme le suggère le titre du film, les goûts sont problématiques. Ils emploient tour à tour des stratégies de subversion et des coups de force symbolique. Avant tout, ils manient le mépris avec beaucoup d'élégance et de distinction faisant presque oublier leur intolérance sous une forme euphémisée et donc méconnaissable en tant que "racisme de l'intelligence".[7] Ces

---

[7] Cette expression de Bourdieu est une des formes de la violence symbolique qui consiste à culpabiliser ceux qui n'ont pas les goûts légitimes et à leur inculquer une sorte de honte de soi. Jaoui a réussi ce tour de force de montrer les préjugés et l'exclusion à travers le prisme des artistes, supposés, selon un lieu commun opératif, être tolérant et jouir d'une grande ouverture d'esprit. Dans une interview, A. Jaoui disait en substance que J.P. Bacri et elle-même avaient envie de parler du sectarisme et du fait que les gens se groupent par référence culturelle, chacun croyant détenir

Reynaud   161

artistes s'en prennent aux valeurs dominantes en niant un quelconque intérêt pour l'argent, l'art n'ayant pas de prix comme chacun sait, mais en soutirant en fin de compte un fructueux contrat auprès de Castella.[8] S'ils avaient l'honnêteté de mettre leurs actes en accord avec leur parole, ils devraient pouvoir se passer de la prébende de Castella.

En célébrant le fétiche qu'est l'œuvre d'art, comme art transcendant et universel et en octroyant au tableau d'avant-garde une surenchère distinctive, le vernissage d'Antoine offre l'occasion de renforcer le caractère sacré du jeu des dominants et les valeurs du champ artistique. La note dissonante, parmi tout ce beau monde des artistes et intellectuels surtout intéressés par les mondanités d'usage, est que le seul à s'intéresser sincèrement aux tableaux est... ce béotien de Castella! Par son habitus[9] de dominé (son père est émigré d'origine espagnole), tout le portait à incorporer en lui les goûts de la culture populaire dont il est issu et dont il est le produit (indigne). C'est ce que le film démontre bien lorsqu'il regarde les feuilletons télévisés américains avec sa femme ou dans sa façon de s'habiller terne[10] et frôlant

---

dans son clan la vérité. Elle ajoutait qu'ils avaient envie de parler de l'exclusion et du fait que les gens étaient si méprisants les uns envers les autres à partir du moment où ils n'avaient pas les mêmes références.

[8] La mesquinerie de ces comportements pourrait s'expliquer par ce que l'on nomme en sociologie sociale "la misère de position" qui doit être distinguée de la "misère de condition"; c'est-à-dire de la pauvreté matérielle et de l'exclusion. La première est le fait d'agents qui occupent une position dominée dans l'espace social mais qui sont situés assez hauts dans la hiérarchie. Ils sont à la fois des dominants-complices et des dominés-victimes qui souffrent psychologiquement de leur position et dont la vengeance inconsciente contre un ordre social qui, pensent-ils, les brime et les sous-estime, se fait sur le mode du ressentiment.

[9] L'habitus est le social fait corps ou incorporé. Bourdieu définit les habitus comme "des principes générateurs de pratiques distinctes et distinctives [...] des principes de classement, [...] de vision et de division, des goûts différents. Ils font des différences entre ce qui est distingué et ce qui est vulgaire [...]. Ainsi le même comportement peut paraître distingué à l'un, prétentieux ou m'as-tu-vu à l'autre, vulgaire au troisième" (*Raisons pratiques* 23).

[10] Ce caractère terne, sans brio du vêtement est rendu, cinématographiquement, à travers ses expressions faciales, maussades elles aussi, que l'on voit poindre sur son visage sans jamais l'éclairer. Le seul instant où il s'illumine, moment où l'émotion théâtrale le submerge au point que les larmes lui montent aux yeux, la caméra capte son visage en gros plan, mais, dans la pénombre du lieu, et cerné qu'il est par la rangée des spectateurs, cet instant d'éblouissement semble relativisé, et perdre de l'éclat qui aurait dû le caractériser. En fin de compte, Castella ne sort pas embelli

l'hypercorrection qui connote l'autodidacte élevé dans l'échelle sociale par sa réussite financière et son mariage, non par des diplômes ou une pratique de la culture livresque, théâtrale et musicale (dont il ne maîtrise aucunement les codes).[11] Il est mis à rude épreuve par les artistes qui, se rendant compte du genre de bévues et du manque de goût dont il est capable, le transforment en souffre-douleur sans qu'il lui soit toujours possible de comprendre précisément ce qu'il a dit ou fait de malséant. Castella possède néanmoins cette bonne volonté culturelle de celui qui a réussi. Grâce à cela, lorsqu'il s'essaye sans complexe à la poésie et qu'il propose la lecture de son poème à Clara, son échec retentissant est l'une des scènes les plus pénibles à soutenir visuellement. Y est mis à nu le mal-être du poète improvisé devant son indignité et le peu de charité et de compréhension dont elle fait preuve face à sa "déclaration d'amour".[12] Il n'est pas question dans cet exposé de juger des goûts mais d'indiquer que le système dans lequel ces goûts s'insèrent dépend d'un arbitraire culturel parmi d'autres — arbitraire que les aléas de l'histoire n'ont pas rendus normatifs.

---

physiquement par cette expérience. D'une manière plus générale, les prises de vue sur lui sont statiques alors que celles qui concernent Clara sont fluides et dynamiques; elles la suivent dans son jeu de scène, qui se veut sublime, et dans la rue où elle marche toujours d'un pas vif, seule ou en compagnie des autres artistes. L'idée sous-jacente est que l'artiste doit savoir s'adapter à son rôle (rester en état d'apesanteur) et vaincre les pesanteurs du succès matériel qui, seul, ne vaut pas grand-chose.

[11] Le costume-cravate est un signe de pouvoir et un signe de la morale bourgeoise qu'il ne peut encore dépasser. La possession le possède et, si l'on peut utiliser cette image, l'alourdit. La moustache peut se lire aussi comme signe de conventionnalisme. Seulement lorsqu'il la rase, pour faire plaisir à Clara, qui n'aime pas les hommes à moustaches, elle ne s'aperçoit nullement du changement. Elle a si bien internalisée une image conventionnelle de lui que, lorsqu'il la dépasse, à petites doses puisque l'habitus est, somme toute, une structure "structurante", donc difficile à modifier, elle continue à le voir et à le percevoir de la même manière qu'auparavant. Seule Manie saura remarquer le changement: c'est le seul personnage du film qui sache dépasser les préjugés de classe.

[12] Comme il l'a faite sans retenue et en n'y mettant pas les formes, elle ne pouvait l'accepter car, chez elle, tout est affaire de maîtrise et de mesure. De plus, lue dans un mauvais anglais et dans un genre, la poésie, dont les règles lui sont étrangères, l'échec n'en est que plus retentissant alors qu'elle a totalement sous-estimé la charge humaine, émotionnelle, affective qu'il avait placée dans son poème, au départ une rédaction assignée par Clara.

Reynaud   *163*

Formellement, cette idée est rendue avec un génie tout artistique par le choix du lieu dans lequel Castella récite son poème: le Salon de Thé ou "English Tea Room", lieu social par excellence "neutre" puisqu'il renvoie à l'imaginaire anglais et que, ce faisant, il défamiliarise. Il fut d'ailleurs choisi par les deux protagonistes pour le cours particulier d'anglais qui offre à Castella un cadre moins perturbant que le bureau de son usine où il se voit, "management" oblige, en permanence dérangé.[13] Pour elle, c'est un endroit agréable où elle exerce son activité de subsistance, étrangère à sa pratique artistique qui, seule, donne un sens à sa vie. Cet environnement relativement neutre permet de dégager à l'état brut et de donner à voir la notion d'arbitraire qui, lorsqu'elle est prise dans un réseau de relations fortement codifiées (au bureau, au théâtre, dans la galerie d'art), passe plus facilement inaperçue.[14] Voici mis à jour tout le travail de la violence symbolique[15] qui évacue la force brute pour la remplacer par des rapports sociaux euphémisés. Les protagonistes qui la subissent sont le plus souvent incapables de la percevoir comme une forme de violence. Ainsi, Castella éprouve l'affront du refus. Il ne comprend cependant pas encore que, en remettant son poème à sa place — celle de produit culturel illégitime — Clara lui a signifié la supériorité de ses propres goûts, elle qui est obligée au même moment de lui vendre des cours d'anglais pour survivre. L'épisode permet enfin de voir s'affronter deux habitus contradictoires détenus par les agents dont le capital culturel est antinomique et qui luttent ici sur le marché du bien

---

[13] Le bureau est également doté d'un sens symbolique à l'instar de la cravate et de la moustache. Il représente un signe supplémentaire de son ancrage dans une appartenance hiérarchique, stable, pesante et peu mobile. Acceptant de se déplacer dans un autre lieu pour son cours d'anglais, le geste peut signifier que, dans ce territoire sans ancrage explicite et où il n'a pas le pouvoir, il s'expose directement au verdict implacable de Clara. Dominant dans son univers, l'entreprise, il est dominé ailleurs, car il fait alors partie d'un autre champ.

[14] Le salon de thé exerce un "effet de contexte". L'environnement augmente ou diminue l'intensité de la motivation artistique. Il aurait dû être plus propice que le bureau au cours d'anglais mais voilà, la poésie en langue étrangère n'est pas pour les novices, et un travail de longue haleine eût été nécessaire pour que puisse être reconnu à son devoir le statut de poème légitime.

[15] Cette violence est à l'œuvre dans tout mécanisme de légitimation: reconnaître les dominants comme légitimes équivaut aussi à ignorer le caractère arbitraire de leur domination reposant sur une violence euphémisée.

164   FLS, Vol. XXXVII, 2010

symbolique qu'est la prise de parole,[16] révélant au public les enjeux importants de ce champ.[17] À la fin de cette scène morose, il est aisé de se rendre compte combien la domination doit à l'assentiment des dominés. Castella se fait le complice consentant à sa propre dépossession et Clara préserve, pour un moment encore, l'illusion de l'autonomie du champ intellectuel et artistique dont Flaubert et Baudelaire s'étaient faits les défenseurs au temps plus glorieux de sa constitution.

Il ne semble cependant pas que cette poésie frappée d'indignité puisse rendre compte du processus plus pernicieux encore "d'involution" dont Bourdieu fait mention dans *Contre-feux* (83) et qui consiste à rabattre l'œuvre vers le produit pour servir à des fins commerciales, en utilisant les prévisions des spécialistes de marketing. Dans le domaine de la poésie, c'est ce que Jacques Roubaud a surnommé "la poésie muesli" et qui constitue une toute autre déviation. Bourdieu le cite même directement:

> [Il s'agit] de productions culturelles en simili, qui peuvent aller jusqu'à mimer les recherches de l'avant-garde tout en jouant des ressorts les plus traditionnels des productions commerciales et qui, du fait de leur ambiguïté peuvent tromper les critiques et les consommateurs à prétentions moderniste. (83)

Le "produit final" de Castella, si l'on peut le qualifier ainsi, est une poésie naïve, voire simpliste, libérée des contraintes du genre, utilisant certes des images conventionnelles ("rain" rime avec "brain", "sun" avec "fun" et "song" avec "strong") mais d'une certaine manière authentique (ou se voulant telle).[18] Mais on serait en droit de se de-

---

[16] Cet acte "de prise de parole" au niveau de Castella se révèle constituer un échec, puisque le message ne passe pas. Acte performatif, il fonctionne souvent mieux au plan collectif sur le mode de la revendication. Rappelons que *Mai 68* avait symboliquement représenté une prise de parole par les dominés, qui avaient alors réussi leurs objectifs. Nous renvoyons à un autre ouvrage de Bourdieu sur ces questions: *Ce que parler veut dire*.

[17] Les champs sont des microcosmes relativement homogènes et autonomes. Il en existe de nombreux: le champ artistique, universitaire, politique. Ce sont des espaces de concurrence et de lutte.

[18] On peut qualifier son inspiration de populiste, ce qui la stigmatise au regard des normes légitimes. Il aurait fallu, pour plaire à Clara, que ce populisme soit dissimulé donc transfiguré et ennobli par une combinaison avec des formes plus savantes.

mander si ce processus "d'involution" ne sera pas ultérieurement à l'œuvre en ce qui concerne la fresque d'usine que Castella commande aux artistes vers la fin du film. Sa réalisation, dont nous n'apercevons que les plans, pourra-t-elle, alors, être qualifiée de produit "en simili" à valeur commerciale ou de réel produit artistique? Jaoui laisse habilement cette question en suspens dès lors que le film se clôt avant que la fresque ne soit effectivement réalisée. De même, toute l'ambiguïté du film consiste à ce qu'Antoine ne réponde qu'évasivement à la question de Clara quand elle lui demande s'il ne trouve pas gênant le projet qu'ils ont ensemble et s'il n'a pas de scrupules. Elle, en tout cas, a l'impression que Benoît et lui profitent de l'argent de Castella. La discussion se clôt sur la question de savoir qui a eu l'idée de la fresque et dès lors que ce n'est pas lui, il semble que Clara ait vu juste quant aux buts inavoués ou, au mieux, inconscients, de ses amis. L'ironie dramatique du film se marque ici, car le spectateur voit plus et plus avant que les personnages eux-mêmes. Cette double perspective s'inscrit dans l'épisode du poème et de son contrepoint, la création industrielle que représente la fresque murale.

Il apparaît donc que la question de la valeur des productions culturelles — indépendamment des goûts de classe qu'elles expriment et véhiculent — soit posée dans ce film, avec, en arrière plan, le problème réel déjà soulevé par Bourdieu et qui s'applique tout autant au roman et au cinéma. Nous faisons allusion ici à ces "univers autonomes" de production, associant auteurs, réalisateurs, producteurs et critiques (dont Jaoui elle-même est une digne représentante[19]) qui

---

[19] Agnès Jaoui est d'abord la réalisatrice de ce film. Par une mise en abyme, elle joue elle-même le personnage central de Manie, le point de mire de tous les regards. Un an avant ce film, Jean Pierre Bacri et elle avaient écrit le scénario du film *Un air de famille* (1999) dans lequel les deux scénaristes jouaient déjà un rôle dans leur propre création. Il revient en force en 2000 pour interpréter celui de Castella dans *Le Goût des autres*. Mentionnons aussi que, dans la vie, Jaoui et Bacri forment un couple. Plus probant encore que ces jeux de rôle démultipliés (la réalisatrice est aussi l'actrice qui est aussi la compagne du personnage principal masculin dans la vie…): cette complexité renvoie à un univers social qui évoque formellement l'illusion théâtrale: les artistes ne sont pas ce qu'ils prétendent être. Il existe un décalage entre leurs prétentions et l'importance qui leur est effectivement reconnue dans le monde social. Ils font de leur vie une mise en scène permanente sur le mode négatif de la retenue et de la tension.

doivent être conservés coûte que coûte, car leurs œuvres, même lorsqu'elles ont la chance de connaître un succès commercial, résistent aussi à la commercialisation. Un second danger, que l'on peut qualifier d'insidieux, se situe à un autre niveau: les artistes, nourris d'avant-garde, sont désormais capables de constituer

> une demande marchande de produits étiquetés comme "transgressifs" même si les "tabous" mis en cause n'ont plus que de lointains rapports avec le contenu réel des censures, des non-dits et des interdits qui pèsent aujourd'hui sur la faculté de penser et de parler. (Boltanski 400)

Pour parer à ce danger il faudrait étudier les conséquences des événements de Mai 68: on verrait comment les revendications de liberté, authenticité, libération ont été incorporées dans la critique artiste pour devenir normes quelques dix ans plus tard. C'est ce qui a permis d'institutionnaliser la révolte en la subventionnant et de récupérer parallèlement la subversion, selon l'heureuse formule citée par Ève Chiapello (225).

Imaginons un instant que les rapports sociaux aient été autres. Si Castella était un patron d'industrie issu, comme c'est souvent le cas, d'une fraction dominante de la bourgeoisie ou haute bourgeoisie, sa culture serait pareillement dominante et on ne rencontrerait pas ou peu cette allodoxie[20] qui fait le charme grinçant de tous les quiproquos du film. La conséquence de son parcours atypique rend son profil culturel dissonant c'est à dire qu'il combine des activités culturelles légitimes (il va au théâtre et pleure devant Bérénice, il apprécie l'art contemporain) et des activités peu légitimes (il regarde les feuilletons télévisés et ne lit pas). Un parfait exemple d'allodoxie dans le film est insinué lorsque Castella fait des remarques enthousiastes sur la pièce de Molière *Le malade imaginaire* qu'il a fort apprécié mais que, pour des

---

[20] L'allodoxie est une erreur d'identification, une forme de fausse reconnaissance. Voici ce qu'en dit A. Accardo: "Cet écart entre la reconnaissance et la connaissance est à l'origine de ces erreurs d'identification, ces bévues qui font parfois croire aux dominés que l'opérette c'est de la grande musique [...] et, d'une façon générale, prendre pour des pratiques distinguées, rares, raffinées, propres aux dominants, des pratiques qui sont, en fait, aux yeux des dominants encore et toujours des pratiques vulgaires, communes, grossières, propres à des dominés. Ces erreurs trahissent l'incompétence des dominés, c'est-à-dire leur incapacité à mettre en œuvre des critères de goût, des principes d'évaluation qu'ils n'ont jamais pu intérioriser puisqu'ils n'appartiennent pas à leur monde" (189).

raisons de mise en scène, ils ont détesté. Il s'enfonce plus avant et propose à Clara de faire du comique parce que cela marche bien auprès du public.... Consternés d'abord, les artistes le prennent au mot et en rajoutent: avec Ibsen, il peut mourir de rire. Dès lors que Castella ne peut manifestement connaître Ibsen, ils lui présentent comme une sorte de comique norvégien. Ils continuent à se jouer de son ignorance avec ironie, invoquant comme soi-disant comiques d'autres dramaturges d'avant garde.

Tout dirigeant d'entreprise, dominant s'il en est, se doit de maîtriser l'usage spécifique du langage, ne serait-ce que pour donner des ordres à ses subordonnés. Castella n'a aucune élégance dans cette tâche dont dépend pourtant le succès de sa fonction, et c'est ce que son le polytechnicien Weber lui reproche, sans avoir bien vu l'origine des limitations de son patron.[21] Les comédiens, Clara en tête, possèdent éminemment cette maîtrise symbolique du langage: mieux que quiconque, ils savent traduire en mots l'émotion esthétique suscitée par le sublime du jeu racinien ou ibsénien. L'éloquence de Clara, son exceptionnelle diction, son hexis corporelle impeccable hors-de-scène bien dissimulée sous l'apparence d'une mise savamment négligée attestent bien, quelle que soit la circonstance, qu'elle reste maîtresse de ses émotions sans que jamais un style "relâché" ne puisse la caractériser, puisque c'est la mise en scène pointilleuse qui prédomine chez elle.[22]

---

[21] Notons que Weber est le seul dominant dominant du film pourvu abondamment à la fois en capital culturel et en capital économique. Même Castella est un dominant dominé, car il manque de capital culturel. Quant aux artistes, ils le sont aussi mais par défaut de capital économique. Duchamps, le chauffeur, se place dans l'espace dominé-dominé. Le lecteur pourra se reporter à un excellent dossier d'analyse du film destiné à des lycéens français au titre suggestif de *Zéro de conduite*.

[22] Sa "rigidité" émotionnelle n'a que peu de rapports avec l'hyper-correction vestimentaire de Castella que nous avons soulignée. Tout chez elle est dans l'art de manier la litote et d'insinuer sans même qu'il soit besoin de verbaliser. Les regards suffisent et les prises de vues sont de ce fait souvent des gros plans sur les visages et les expressions qu'ils suggèrent et refoulent à la fois. Mais, pour lui, chez qui l'extraction populaire est le naturel toujours en phase de ressurgir inopinément, cette correction par l'habit est la contrainte qu'il impose à une nature vive, brouillonne et portée aux excès. Tout autant qu'à une nature charitable et bon enfant, qui sait faire amende honorable et voir en l'autre, autre chose et plus qu'un être de classe. Il saura s'abaisser jusqu'à demander à son Directeur, pourtant son inférieur hiérarchique, de reconsidérer sa démission et jusqu'à s'excuser auprès de lui de l'avoir mal jugé.

2. Subversion du modèle bourdieusien

On peut reprendre au point de départ l'analyse sociologique et apposer, en antithèse, un espace social autre et nié car plus subversif encore que celui présenté par l'analyse bourdieusienne en termes de classes, champs et habitus. C'est l'espace qui correspond précisément à un état postérieur du champ et qui est né vers le milieu des années 80 grâce à ce que l'on a appelé "le consensus de Washington".[23] Il n'est possible qu'en ajoutant à l'analyse dite "classique" une seconde en termes de néolibéralisme.[24] Depuis longtemps déjà, depuis la période des "Trente Glorieuses" (1945-1974) l'affaiblissement des classes sociales se fait sentir dans une société postindustrielle qui ne serait plus composée que d'une vaste classe moyenne plus ou moins indifférenciée dont les goûts et valeurs convergent. Cette vision d'un monde social homogène perdant ses structures de classes fixes produit parallèlement et nécessairement la déconstruction, au sens ici de déconfiture, de la critique artiste: on n'aurait plus d'un côté les intellectuels et les artistes et de l'autre les élites économiques car cet antagonisme se voit dépassé.

L'artiste supposé autrefois pur et désintéressé endosse de manière plus ou moins détournée la figure d'un "manager", d'un chef de projet dynamique sachant montrer des qualités de direction et fonctionner avec profit dans un système capitaliste triomphant depuis la chute de

---

[23] Ainsi nommé par l'économiste américain J. Willamson, il s'agit du corpus des principes économiques partagés par un nombre croissant de gouvernements et par les institutions de Washington, FMI et Banque Mondiale. Ce crédo néolibéral universalise les lois de la science économique en vigueur dans les économies les plus industrialisées, spécialement aux États-Unis: seule la loi du marché doit faire loi. Ceci permet d'abaisser le poids des interventions étatiques, de favoriser la seule initiative privée, de libéraliser l'environnement économique de ses entraves, d'abaisser les barrières tarifaires et d'opérer une déréglementation généralisée. On espère ainsi en finir avec l'interventionnisme, surtout en matière sociale, et remplacer les entreprises publiques par des programmes de privatisation.

[24] Par néolibéralisme, j'entends le triomphe de la logique économique et individualiste de la concurrence sur la logique sociale. Cette définition se base sur l'essai instructif de Bourdieu, "Le néo-libéralisme, utopie (en voie de réalisation) d'une exploitation sans limites" (*Contre-feux* 108-19). Pour expliciter ce titre qui peut apparaître comme jugement de valeur, on peut avancer que ce régime économique, mis en place au milieu des années 80, exerce notamment une violence structurelle sur les acteurs sociaux, violence basée sur la peur du chômage et la précarisation.

Reynaud 169

l'empire soviétique. Nous sommes loin de la vision — déjà idéolo-
gique — de l'artiste romantique tourmenté, singulier, aristocrate de
l'art pur, au génie incompris, opposant la gratuité à l'utilitarisme am-
biant. Ce manager de productions culturelles, tout en gardant sa qualité d'artiste, est devenu plus "réaliste " assez au moins pour initier des
affaires lucratives. Voilà ce qui arrive aux artistes du film, Antoine et
son ami Benoît qui combinant tour à tour idéalisme et pragmatisme (il
faut bien vivre après tout…) se sont parfaitement intégrés à cet espace
social que nous appellerons celui des "nouveaux managers". Dans
notre monde en réseau, les artistes sont conduits à développer des
activités de connexion avec des instances diverses, d'instaurer des
partenariats, notamment sur le plan financier, tant, aujourd'hui, les
productions culturelles peuvent être onéreuses. Dès lors qu'ils se
comportent comme des managers, ils doivent nécessairement incorporer les disciplines propres au management: calculer, quantifier,
soutirer des profits des projets, plaire au public,[25] "savoir abandonner
l'autonomie de l'artiste pour une vie plus équilibrée dans laquelle la
méritocratie a remplacé l'idéologie du don inné".[26]

Le statut précaire d'intermittent étant répandu chez les artistes
dès lors qu'ils vivent pour l'art mais pas nécessairement de l'art, il
devient donc urgent pour eux de s'engager dans une multitude de
projets, d'ailleurs plus ou moins compatibles entre eux, comme le re-
prochera Clara à Antoine et son ami qui, s'étant fait commissionner,
vont désormais travailler à une grande fresque murale pour embellir
l'usine de Castella. En soi, le projet n'a rien de ridicule et montre que

---

[25] Notons que cette vision du public auquel il faut savoir faire des concessions,
joue en sens opposé pour ce qui est du spectateur du film. Je souscris à l'analyse de
Sarah Leahy lorsqu'elle écrit: " However, in terms of the spectator, the film can be
said to flatter its target audience while playing on their prejudice and expectations: we
can assume that the film is intended for those who have at least heard of *Bérénice*"
(Newcastle University E-prints).

[26] On se réfère ici à ce qu'Ève Chiapello nomme "la logique du binôme" et
qu'elle définit ainsi: "Le binôme est la forme que prend la logique de l'amour quand
elle s'incarne au sein de l'entreprise dans la relation entre les deux représentants du
principe artistique et du principe économique. Chacun d'eux incarne une rationalité
irréductible à celle de l'autre. Le conflit entre les deux rationalités, dont la critique
artiste est un indicateur, est apparu d'autant plus fort que l'organisation a besoin des
deux logiques: de celle de l'art (dans sa conception issue du romantisme) pour
satisfaire à sa vocation innovante, de celle de la gestion pour assurer sa survie
économique" (161).

170   *FLS, Vol. XXXVII, 2010*

les goûts de tout individu évoluent et qu'ils peuvent même, avec le temps, devenir légitimes. Plus problématique cependant est l'instrumentalisation que les artistes semblent faire de Castella, lui soutirant leur moyen de subsistance tout en continuant à le dédaigner superbement. N'est-il pas surprenant de critiquer son partenaire d'affaires mais de continuer à traiter avec lui? En d'autres termes, ces artistes-managers dans ce nouvel état du champ, ne se seraient-ils pas fait "contaminer" par les valeurs du capitalisme qu'ils semblaient pourtant abhorrer?[27] Voici bien là un autre exemple de l'ironie dramatique du film et voilà l'intertexte du *Bourgeois Gentilhomme* réitéré quoiqu'inversé.[28]

Et que vont au juste échanger, vendre, marchandiser les artistes amis de Clara? L'authentique, certes, de l'œuvre d'art, mais lui faisant par là perdre son caractère authentique puisqu'ils replacent à l'intérieur de la sphère marchande ce qui lui était extérieur. On pourrait penser, en référence à Walter Benjamin que ce nouveau "produit" artistique a perdu son "aura". La pure valeur d'usage du bien devient bien marchande ayant une valeur d'échange qui est stipulée dans le contrat de vente. En outre, dans l'appréciation du tableau abstrait exposé par Antoine, qui montre l'attitude la plus révérencieuse par rapport à l'œuvre d'art? Certes pas les artistes, mais bien Castella qui remplace dans son salon *La Liseuse* de Fragonard par cette peinture achetée pour laquelle il a eu un coup de cœur. Substitution doublement ironique qui sera d'une part le mobile tangible de sa séparation et d'autre part un clin d'œil ironique de la réalisatrice quant au choix

---

[27] Cette convergence de deux univers que tout opposait pose problème face à la posture critique. Laissons parler Luc Boltanski sur ce point: "elle [la posture critique] est à la fois plus nécessaire que jamais et largement inopérante. Elle est nécessaire parce qu'elle constitue, pour les intellectuels, le dernier marqueur capable de maintenir leur spécificité ou leur identité face aux hommes d'affaires et de pouvoir. Mais la critique développée par ces intellectuels ou ces artistes, vite saluée comme 'décapante', 'dérangeante' ou 'radicale' par les grands médias et par les adversaires qu'elle était censée scandaliser et qui, se révélant plutôt être des partenaires — voire des doubles —, s'empressent de reprendre la critique à leur compte, perd son point d'application et se condamne à un éternel changement ou à une vaine surenchère" (399).

[28] Sans inversion cette fois, l'intertexte se lit dans la scène où Castella apprend à prononcer l'anglais et celle où il lui déclare son amour. Notons que le dossier d'analyse de ce film (Bissière, ch. 3) détaille les parallèles à exploiter entre le film et l'œuvre de Molière.

Reynaud   *171*

d'un tableau d'autant plus "abstrait" ou lointain que cette jeune fille lisant ne renvoyait à rien dans l'imaginaire de ses deux propriétaires qui... ne lisent jamais![29]

Le lieu de neutralité relative est, dans cette nouvelle configuration du champ, le bistrot où l'on se sent bien, tenu par Manie,[30] personnage peu conventionnel qui brouille les repères d'une analyse sociologique simple par ses appartenances sociales multiples, elle qui sert de lien entre le monde de l'art en sa qualité d'amie des artistes et le monde des affaires, en tant que protectrice de Castella et la seule à lui montrer quelque affection et surtout à en comprendre la valeur humaine. Sa liaison avec Moreno, garde du corps de Castella, offre un élément d'hétérogénéité créatrice dans le film:[31] elle est attirée par cet homme de droite conservateur, réactionnaire même, bien qu'il représente l'idéologie de la méfiance qu'elle sait dépasser par une intégration harmonieuse au-delà des classes ou des jugements de valeur sur les individus. Son habitus est difficilement classable: féministe et passablement bohème, elle aspire à une relation plus traditionnelle et plus fixe mais ne veut pas être ancrée et prise au piège des corvées domestiques qui définissent, selon elle, le mariage. Légitime dans son activité de serveuse à temps partiel dans un bistro fréquenté chaque jour par des intellectuels, elle n'en pratique pas moins la vente illégale de drogues douces chez elle, pour "arrondir ses fins de mois" et

---

[29] Cette critique de leur inculture notoire est rachetée en ce qui concerne M. Castella par la répartie qu'il donne à Clara lorsqu'elle vient le mettre en garde à la fin du film contre les visées intéressées d'Antoine et qu'ils abordent l'achat du tableau: "Vous n'avez pas imaginé une minute que ça pouvait être... par goût" lui dit-il avant de le quitter. À partir de ce moment Clara comprendra qu'elle s'est fourvoyée dans son jugement et surtout son jugement de goût, et que ce patron représente beaucoup plus que ce à quoi elle a voulu le réduire.

[30] L'analyse du personnage Manie menée par S. Leahy est complémentaire à la mienne: "*Le Goût des autres* offers a *mise en scène* of this process [legitimating social differences] through the juxtaposition of multiple view points: different sequences privilege different characters as the central point of identification, forcing the spectator to consider multiple interpretations of particular actions" (Newcastle U. E-prints).

[31] Selon toute vraisemblance cette relation subversive est, à un niveau purement individuel, emblématique des rapports controversés entre les fractions de classe bourgeoise (que Moreno typifie) et artiste (que Manie incarne). Obligés de composer ensemble, à l'instar d'un couple physiquement bien assorti mais dont les goûts et choix idéologiques divergent irrémédiablement, ils vivent leur relation en porte-à-faux du début à fin, lorsque Moreno décide de prendre unilatéralement la fuite.

172   FLS, Vol. XXXVII, 2010

s'insurge contre le fait que son amant lui reproche avec véhémence son manque de respect pour la loi. Elle partage avec lui ce caractère nomade, lui sur le mode du garde du corps itinérant qui voyage de lieu en lieu au gré des missions qui lui sont confiées[32] par les compagnies d'assurances et elle, par sa grande ouverture d'esprit et la disponibilité avec laquelle elle entraide et conseille ses habitués. Ce bistro tient lieu d'espace qui rassemble et fait interagir des univers sociaux en apparence opposés: lieu de discussions sur l'art et le spectacle où l'être et le paraître des protagonistes est intimement lié, où, derrière une façade d'intellectualisme progressif perce une conclusion souvent cynique, à savoir que le monde de l'art baigne dans la mesquinerie et que les artistes, derrière une rhétorique soignée, ne sont certes pas les derniers à asséner des coups bas.[33] Ce film tragicomique se termine pourtant sur la note optimiste des artistes composant avec Castella pour réaliser la fresque, sans animosité apparente et toute honte bue, le tout accompagné de la bande sonore du "Je ne regrette rien",[34] prouvant qu'un nouveau départ est toujours possible à qui parvient à dépasser les cadres sociaux contraignants et artificiels et concevoir de nouveaux projets.[35]

---

[32] Rappelons que c'est un ex-flic devenu garde du corps parce que désabusé par la corruption de son corps de métier, la police.

[33] La scène du repas au bistro est significative à cet égard. C'est une scène où la violence symbolique s'impose comme arbitraire. Elle apparaît comme destinée à certains à l'exclusion d'autres. Les amis de Clara discutent de pièces de théâtre peu connues pour exclure Castella de leur conversation et se moquer de son ignorance.

[34] La bande sonore qui avait auparavant servi à déchaîner les foudres des artistes contre l'inculture musicale de Castella concernait l'aria de l'opéra de Verdi, *Rigoletto*. Castella n'avait en effet reconnu dans ce refrain que la chanson populaire d'Henri Salvador *Juanita Banana!* Il est intéressant de noter que la célèbre chanson d'E. Piaf, si elle réconcilie les sensibilités musicales et permet à tous les spectateurs de se reconnaître par-delà le clivage des classes, a néanmoins fait passer du registre de l'opéra à celui de la chanson populaire. Est-ce à dire que, pour n'aliéner personne, il faille ramener l'art à son plus petit commun dénominateur et donc que l'élitisme artiste puisse se justifier pour sauver ce qui est qualitativement supérieur? Pas dans le film. C'est la fanfare où joue Deschamps, le chauffeur, qui entraîne les foules, galvanise les énergies et procure cette note optimiste des lendemains qui chantent à la fin du film. L'aria, dans sa majestueuse beauté, n'était parvenu qu'à diviser les classes entre les élus pouvant le reconnaître (et se reconnaître en lui) et les exclus de la culture musicale, indignes de cette reconnaissance.

[35] Manie par contre sera moins chanceuse et se retrouvera seule. En ce sens, ce film pourrait se lire comme un produit culturel ayant pour sujet le déterminisme social: Castella-Clara, c'est la réunion réussie des fractions de classes opposées. Manie, qui est hors normes et qui refuse les jeux sociaux, échoue. On ne peut rester en

En ce qui concerne notre niveau d'analyse macroéconomique, cela prouverait que le management peut être aussi une discipline de rationalisation des firmes (dont les entreprises culturelles ne sont pas les moindres aujourd'hui) mais sans que le but de maximisation du profit lui soit nécessairement associé, ou, ce qui revient au même, que le management peut servir aujourd'hui à des fins artistiques pour peu que l'on ait à faire à de petits patrons "visionnaires" et que les artistes qui travaillent à parachever leurs vues puissent dépasser leur mépris de classe et leur prétention infondée.[36] C'est déjà poser beaucoup de conditions!

La créativité n'émane plus uniquement de l'artiste incréé tel que Bourdieu en avait tracé le portrait génial, mais de tout novateur et producteur culturel qui anticipe les goûts et désirs du public dans une logique d'investissements culturels jaillissant au départ d'une intuition spontanée: l'art et l'argent ne sont plus des entités incompatibles mais des frères ennemis qu'il faut bien tenter de réconcilier. La logique du monde réticulaire dans lequel nous vivons a permis de redéfinir ce qui fait l'objet du "marchandisable": les activités littéraires et artistiques ne peuvent plus vivre en marge du capitalisme ni en opposition avec lui et l'œuvre d'art sans prix représente désormais une vue de l'esprit. Le film pose en filigrane la question de l'intérêt et du désintéressement avec, en toile de fond, l'idée que les relations d'affaires sont légitimement intéressées que les artistes se leurrent ou non à ce sujet, qu'ils en aient conscience ou non. Il y a certes des illusions bien fondées, et celle de l'œuvre d'art désintéressée en est une, mais elle a manifestement fait son temps. L'ascétisme n'est plus à l'ordre du jour, et le mépris de l'argent est passé de mode, y compris pour les artistes. Sauf peut-être, et c'est tant mieux, pour Clara, qui semble parfois vivre dans un autre monde, dans un monde suranné où le commerce ne règne pas en maître et où elle a, paradoxalement, entrainé le dirigeant progressiste amoureux d'elle et prêt à tous les sacrifices. Étant

---

dehors du système social, et le non-conventionnalisme, par manque de positionnement, se paye en définitive très cher.

[36] Ce mouvement de convergence n'est certes pas nouveau en Amérique du Nord, où les fondations privées font des dons aux artistes. Pour les Français, cet équilibre qui devient possible entre l'art et l'argent est révolutionnaire en soi et il aura fallu attendre la conjoncture historique des années 90 pour le voir se répandre vite et à grande échelle.

donné que les catégories sociales sont brouillées, que, pour réussir, l'artiste doit savoir être réaliste et le néo-manager idéaliste, la critique artiste ne peut plus honnêtement et sans mauvaise foi revendiquer ce qui restait encore pertinent jusqu'à la veille de 68: les intellectuels d'une part et les élites économiques de l'autre ne sont plus constitutivement opposés. Dans un monde fonctionnant dans une logique de réseaux, une telle opposition a perdu de sa pertinence et, là où elle fonctionne encore, elle s'amenuise rapidement. L'optimisme enjoué de la fin du film revient à donner une version, cette fois positive, du comportement qui consiste à faire de nécessité vertu:

> Le monde de l'art se montre de moins en moins capable de vivre sans gestion tant les enjeux économiques qui lui sont liés sont devenus aujourd'hui importants. Le manager est ainsi en passe de devenir le meilleur allié de l'artiste après avoir été considéré comme son bourreau. (Chiapello 211).

Tel sera le fin mot de cette étude sur une réconciliation nécessaire, sinon tout à fait admise, et heuristique si, et seulement si elle préserve, à ses côtés, la possibilité d'un îlot de pureté artistique dès lors que certaines créations peu rentables sont incapables de survivre sans une intervention qui puissent les protéger par-delà le simple jeu du marché.

Une remarque annexe: certes Jaoui s'est inspirée des théories de Bourdieu et elle les a superbement adaptées au cinéma. Ce succès dissimule pourtant un paradoxe. Agnès Jaoui, qui est juive d'origine tunisienne, nous décrit une France de classe où la diversité culturelle est étrangement absente. Laissons s'exprimer ici Sarah Leahy: "And yet, the notion of otherness raised by the film's title is explored only in a very narrow way: all the characters are white, (more or less) middle-class and are almost all from Rouen" (Newcastle U. E-prints) et renvoyons le lecteur aux pertinentes analyses de son article (117-29).

Reynaud

Ouvrages cités

Accardo, Alain. *Introduction à une sociologie critique. Lire Pierre Bourdieu.* Marseille: Agone, 2006.

Benjamin, Walter. "L'œuvre d'art à l'ère de sa reproductibilité technique". *Essais 2, 1935-1940.* Paris: Dennoël/Gonthier, 1983. 87-126.

Bissière, Michèle. *Séquences. Intermediate French Through Film.* Boston: Thomson Heinle, 2008.

Boltanski, Luc, et Ève Chiapello. *Le nouvel esprit du capitalisme.* Paris: Gallimard, 1999.

Bourdieu, Pierre. *Ce que parler veut dire. L'économie des échanges linguistiques.* Paris: Fayard, 1982.

_____. *Contre-feux. Propos pour servir à la résistance contre l'invasion néolibérale.* Paris: Raisons d'agir, 1998.

_____. *La distinction.* Paris: Éditions de Minuit, 1979.

_____. *Les règles de l'art. Genèse et structure du champ littéraire.* Paris: Seuil, 1992.

_____. *Raisons pratiques. Sur la théorie de l'action.* Paris: Seuil, 1994.

_____, et Loïc Wacquant. *Réponses. Pour une anthropologie réflexive.* Paris: Seuil, 1992.

Chiapello, Ève. *Artistes versus Managers: Le management culturel face à la critique artiste.* Paris: Métailié, 1998.

Faillefer, Anne, et Erwan Le Nader. "Zéro de conduite". *La séance du mois. Nov. 2006.*

<http://www.agence-cinema-education.fr/zdc-goutdesautres.pdf>

Leahy, Sarah. "A (middle-) Class Act: Taste and Otherness in *Le Goût des Autres* (Jaoui, 2000)". *France at the Flicks. Trends in Contemporary French Popular Cinema.* Ed. Darren Waldron and Isabelle Vanderschelden. Cambridge Scholarly Press, 2007. 117-29.

Newcastle University E-prints: <http://rogue.ncl.ac.uk/deposit_details.php?deposit_id=4474>

Nathalie Wourm

Birkbeck, University of London

Non-readings, Misreadings, Unreadings: Deleuze and Cadiot on *Robinson Crusoe* and Capitalism

> Did Gilles Deleuze ever read Defoe's *Robinson Crusoe*? His criticism of it, made in the light of Michel Tournier's version of the story, *Vendredi ou les limbes du Pacifique*, would suggest not. Deleuze uses an often inaccurate comparison to put forward his idea of what is wrong with Robinson psychologically — that he is the archetypal capitalist. By contrast, Olivier Cadiot has read both Defoe and Deleuze. In *Futur, ancien, fugitif* he presents a schizophrenic Robinson, an anticapitalist archetype, of which Deleuze would have been proud. Non-readings, misreadings, and unreadings mesh together in the production of Cadiot's masterpiece of anticapitalist literature.

Gilles Deleuze did not like *Robinson Crusoe*. That much is plain. In his essay "Causes et raisons des îles désertes," written in the 1950s, he argues that "it is difficult to imagine a more boring novel, it is sad to still see some children reading it."[1] He even opines that "any sane reader would dream to finally see [Friday] eat Robinson" (*L'Île déserte* 15). But why is Deleuze's dislike so intense? And what does it have to do with adaptation and appropriation? I shall look at the relationship between Deleuze and Defoe, and the influence of this relationship on two modern French versions of the Robinson story: Michel Tournier's *Vendredi ou les limbes du Pacifique*, published in

---

[1] All quotations from *L'Île déserte* are translated by me.

1967, and Olivier Cadiot's *Futur, ancien, fugitif,* published in 1993. I aim to show how the processes — by which something of *Robinson Crusoe* is transmitted to Cadiot through Deleuze and Tournier (independently of the direct transmission from Defoe) — reveal something of how literary borrowing and the incurrence of literary debt is as unstable, frequently incomprehensible, and sometimes as systemically doubtful as the real world of lending and borrowing has often, and very recently, been shown to be.

First of all, a look at the main points of Deleuze's objection. He argues that

> Robinson's vision of the world resides exclusively in property, never have we seen such a moralising proprietor. The mythical re-creation of the world based on the deserted island has been replaced by the re-composition of the bourgeois daily life based on capital. (15)

Seeing a capitalist message in Defoe's novel has a longstanding heritage, stemming at first from the presentation by the classical political economists of Crusoe as *homo oeconomicus*, an embodiment of the principle that the behaviour and psychology of free market capitalism is a natural state of being, reaching its apogee in the argument Marx frames in *Capital* in response to this position. Having chastised even David Ricardo — Marx's favourite classical economist — for his weakness in the face of this myth, Marx reassesses Robinson on the island to show a) the priority of use-value over exchange-value and b) the fundamental relationship between labour time and cost, in capitalist calculation.

> Robinson soon learns by experience [explains Marx] and having rescued a watch, ledger, and pen and ink from the wreck, commences, like a true-born Briton, to keep a set of books. His stock-book contains a list of the objects of utility that belong to him, of the operations necessary for their production; and lastly, of the labour time that definite quantities of those objects have, on average, cost him. (88-89).

There is no surprise to find that Deleuze, a noted anticapitalist radical and an influence on the modern anticapitalist movement (e.g. Tormey 160), has read Marx on Crusoe. Indeed, it seems he has read him very closely, inasmuch as the principle substance of his characterization of Robinson's capitalistic behaviour is effectively a précis of Marx, and

Wourm 179

appears directly appropriated from him: "Everything comes from the boat, nothing is invented, everything is laboriously applied to the island. Time is only the time necessary for capital to yield its benefit after labour" (15).

So is Deleuze's Robinson simply a reading of Marx's reading? Of course not. Nothing is ever "simply" something with Deleuze. Marx's interpretation stands aside in both form and purpose in being strictly a piece of technical analysis. Although it provides the substance of Deleuze's characterization, it does not provide the content of his deeply personal objection. If there is a pre-echo of Deleuze's position in the Crusoes of the economists, it is a negative image in John Stuart Mill's comment that "Robinson Crusoe continued to delight me through all my boyhood" (9). Capitalism is one standard plank of Deleuze's objection that there is no imagination in Crusoe's life on the island (15-16). As the archetypal capitalist, Robinson Crusoe has a view of the world that corresponds to what Deleuze and Félix Guattari would describe in *Mille Plateaux* as arborescent, that of a man with a tree planted in his head (24). Here is someone who finds himself on a deserted island, a potential paradise, with the possibility of creating a new life for himself, a new type of humanity, something mythical, something of a dream, far from the pressures of society as we know it.

Yet he spends all his energy and invention reproducing the economic structure that he is familiar with, based on two linear paradigms of the European mind: hierarchy and chronology. His mind is systemic, applied to create order and a sense of beginning and ending, a purpose. This is why it can be described as arborescent or tree-like, growing upwards with a clear sense of direction. Crusoe could have led a random, happy-go-lucky life on his island, a chaotic, irrational, anarchic existence. He could have re-created the world on his own terms. This would have been an imaginative existence, abounding in exciting possibilities. In Deleuze-Guattarian terms, it would have been a rhizomatic way of life, something resembling the shape of a tangled network of roots, a rhizome, proliferating randomly, and full of creative potential. Deleuze describes how he would have liked Defoe's Robinson to have been subversive, to have taken another route, to have offered a deviation from the capitalist humanity that is ours. He would have wanted him to be much closer to the schizophrenic mind, a psychotic, endorsing all manners of imaginary worlds, and liberating himself from the shackles of structured thought. Instead, Robinson recreates an old word of capitalism, Protestantism ("This novel represents the best illustration of the thesis which asserts the link between capitalism and Protestantism"), and Puritanism (Deleuze implicitly raising the question of sexuality by stating: "Robinson's companion is not Eve, but Friday") (*L'Île déserte* 15). This objection is echoed by Michel Tournier. In his autobiography, *The Wind Spirit*, he views Defoe's Robinson as "purely retrospective, confined to describing the restoration of a lost civilization with the means at hand," and sees Crusoe as "one of the basic constituents of the Western soul [...]. His myth is surely one of the most topical and vital that we possess. Perhaps it would be more accurate to say that it possesses us" (191, 183). By contrast, Tournier considers that in his own Robinson, "the very roots of [Robinson's] life are being laid bare, and he must then create from nothing a new world" (*The Wind Spirit* 190-91). Tournier recognized the influence of many thinkers on his work — Bachelard, Sartre, Levi-Strauss (*The Wind Spirit* 123-75) — but this description seems to answer directly to Deleuze's requirements. And this is probably not accidental. Although Deleuze's essay remained unpublished until 2002, he and Tournier became friends during their *lycée* years (*The Wind Spirit* 127). Some critics have identified the possibility of direct influence (e.g. Hallward 93).

It is conceivable, however, that Tournier was revising history in his autobiography published in 1977, because Deleuze returned to the Robinson theme in *Logique du sens*, published in 1969, in which he expands his thoughts in an essay about Tournier's *Vendredi ou les limbes du Pacifique* (*Logique du sens* 350-72). Deleuze is evidently charmed by Tournier's Robinson, who gradually diverges from the economic structuration which makes our humanity, and undergoes a process of "dehumanization" or destructuration. The role of sexuality now comes to the fore, probably under the influence of Tournier's Freudianism, in a type of cosmic sexuality, something which Robinson himself describes as "soft jubilation" (*Friday* 180). In this, a transcendental form of sexual transport is achieved through physical intercourse with the rays of the sun god. Ultimately, Tournier's Friday chooses to leave the island when a ship finally finds the two men, while Tournier's Robinson chooses to stay, thus making good his rupture with the human world as we know it. This essay stems from

Wourm   181

the transitional period of Deleuze's work, when the impact of Guattari's ideas was beginning to be visible in it, particularly with respect to the idea of the schizophrenic. Deleuze is keen to describe *this* Robinson as a schizophrenic who achieves complete liberation from the capitalist paradigm, which is structuring our humanity, and invents himself anew, when our humanity deserts him. The loss of the other within him is the loss of our humanity as well as his. After years of solitude, he is no more able to apprehend our otherness, and consequently becomes one with the elements. This, Deleuze writes, is typical of psychotic behaviour, where "super-human filiation" is seen as a way of overcoming the absence of real others in the psychotic's mind (*Logique du sens* 366). Deleuze even compares the productive frenzy into which Robinson enters, to the way a schizophrenic builds a table, as described by Henri Michaux:

> As it stood, it was a table of additions, much like certain schizophrenics' drawings, described as "overstuffed," and if finished it was only in so far as there was no way of adding anything more to it, the table having become more and more an accumulation, less and less a table... It was not intended for any specific purpose, for anything one expects of a table. Heavy, cumbersome, it was virtually immovable. A dehumanized table, nothing cozy about it, nothing "middle-class," nothing rustic, nothing countrified, not a kitchen table or a work table. A table which lent itself to no function, self-protective, denying itself to service and communication alike. There was something stunned about it, something petrified. Perhaps it suggested a stalled engine.[2]

What is not clear is whether the opposition of Tournier's Robinson to Defoe's on these grounds is actually supported. For instance, Robinson discovers a deep cave within which a small cavity can just about hold him when he assumes a foetal position (*Friday* 90-95). This becomes a safe retreat for him, and a place of regression, where the limits between his own body and the earth become blurred. The obvious interpretation here is Freudian and Jungian, but Deleuze regards this "return to the Earth and cosmic genealogy," this "principle of burying oneself" in the interior of the earth, as characteristic of the

---

[2] Deleuze and Guattari, *Anti-Oedipus: Capitalism and Schizophrenia*, 6-7, for translation. From Michaux's *Les Grandes Épreuves de l'Esprit*. See *Logique du Sens*, 365, footnote.

schizophrenic mind (*Logique du sens* 365), omitting that Defoe's Robinson also has a safe retreat deep inside a cave, where he has to creep on his hands and knees in order to reach what he views as a "place of security," and where he indulges in childlike fantasies about ancient cave-dwelling giants:

> [A]nd going into this low Place, I was oblig'd to creep upon all Fours, *as I have said*, almost ten Yards [...]. When I was got through the Strait, I found the Roof rose higher up, I believe near twenty Foot [...]. I fancy'd my self now like one of the ancient Giants, which are said to live in Caves, and Holes, in the Rocks, where none could come at them. (Defoe 139-40).

Similarly, Deleuze considers Tournier's Robinson to display signs of psychosis when he builds a boat to flee the island, and then cannot move it to the water:

> It did not much surprise him to find that he was quite incapable of dragging the hull, which must weigh over half a ton, down the gently sloping grass and over the sand to the sea. [...] Since he could not drag the *Escape* to the sea, he must bring the sea to her. [...] The task was one that he could scarcely hope to complete single-handed in all that remained of his natural life. (*Friday* 33-34).

This "schizophrenic production of objects which are unfit for consumption," Deleuze writes, is defining (*Logique du sens* 365). There again, though, this exact episode is one which Tournier borrows from Defoe: "But all my Devices to get it into the Water fail'd me; tho' they cost me infinite Labour too. It lay about one hundred Yards from the Water, and not more: But the first Inconvenience was, it was up Hill towards the Creek" the original Robinson explains (100). Remarks like these suggest that Deleuze may never have read the original *Robinson Crusoe*, or that his memory of it is vague — perhaps he read it as a child. He offers, then, a comparison between a non-reading of Defoe and a consequent misreading of Tournier, deployed in the service of his emerging philosophy of capitalism and schizophrenia.[3]

Tournier's Robinson can be understood (at least in part) in terms of its departures from Defoe. And those departures can be understood

---

[3] Walter Redfern argues that Deleuze "wilfully minimises the novel's heavy stress on regression" (199).

Wourm 183

(at least in part) in terms of a broad agreement between Tournier and Deleuze about what is wrong with Robinson psychologically — that he suffers from the peculiar psychosis which the modern western world has labelled sanity. We can even be fairly confident that this agreement has a basis in the personal relationship of the philosopher and the novelist (although as the convincing evidence arises from texts written after the fact, we cannot be entirely sure that there is no revision of history going on). What we must doubt is whether Tournier's Robinson is the Robinson Deleuze presents him as. It is not as though the reader is forced by confrontation with the former to make the revision of thought which the latter is taken to imply. Look, for example, at a notable English critic of Defoe, Ian Watt, who interprets *Vendredi* prevailingly in terms of Robinson's preference for individual solitude "to avoid the sordid littleness of his fellow human beings back home" (274), a view which rather makes Tournier's book sound more like Gulliver than Deleuze — and thereby more like Defoe.

However, Cadiot's *Futur, ancien, fugitif* is an appropriation of the Crusoe myth which *does* present a schizophrenic Robinson. Moreover, Robinson's schizophrenia is not accidental, but invokes Deleuze: Cadiot was coauthor (with Pierre Alferi) of "La Mécanique Lyrique," published in 1995, a radical literary manifesto, which imported deconstructionist ideas of both a Deleuzian and a Derridean type directly into literary activity. The young generation of writers inspired by it, such as Anne-James Chaton, Christophe Fiat, Jérôme Game, Christophe Hanna, and Eric Sadin, have frequently used these ideas (and often a concomitant anticapitalism) in their work. Cadiot's novel does not obviously invite reading in terms of an explicit departure from Defoe, and it seems unlikely that it could be read within the parameters of the original in the way Watt reads *Vendredi*. If there is a parameter for its reading in terms of literary history, it is the complex of Tournier's and Deleuze's ideas outlined above. What is most interesting, then, is that Cadiot's work precisely *is* directly engaged with Defoe's.

The novel is the story of a man called Robinson, who is shipwrecked on an island. It restores the first person perspective of Defoe's original, away from the third person mode of *Vendredi*. His experiences and concerns are identical to those of the original Robinson: he has to survive, feed himself, shelter himself, protect himself from danger, and find a way of building a boat from a tree trunk, in order to flee: "Listen it's really very simple" he writes:

> 1. I arrive on this island and purely for my own comfort I begin to talk out loud in order not to lose the power of speech. 2. I consult old documents, letters, etc. to try to reclassify my memories. 3. At the same time — and it's not easy — I try to do the work necessary for survival — food, shelter, defence and distractions — and it's no vacation if you consider the difficult position in which I find myself. 4. I make as precise a record of it all as possible. (59)[4]

The original Robinson likes to make numbered lists of goods, thoughts, plans, and he likes to make timetables. In typical fashion, he recounts:

> I had three Encouragements. 1. A smooth calm Sea, 2. The Tide rising and setting in to the Shore, 3. What little Wind there was blew towards the Land; and thus, having found two or three broken Oars belonging to the Boat, and besides the Tools which were in the Chest, I found two Saws, an Axe, and a Hammer. (Defoe, 42)

Ordering and classifying is a favourite activity of his, and it is for him a way of re-creating on his island the structure of the society he has lost. But Crusoe's various rationalising endeavours become ridiculous when re-interpreted by someone lacking the very sense of hierarchical, ordered rationality that this kind of classification presupposes. Cadiot's book is a parody of the type of rationalisation of society which is the extreme capitalist approach of Crusoe. Cadiot's Robinson is a man with a rhizome, rather than a tree, in his head. The schizophrenic plays the role of the outsider who does not understand the world he is faced with, much in the tradition of the two Persians in Montesquieu's *Lettres Persanes*, or of the Martian in the Martian school of poetry. He spends his time classifying dreams, memories, crises, packets of letters, birdsongs, trees. These define the titles of many of the book sections: "Walk n° 428," "First Crisis," "Memories I, Memories II, Memories III, Memories IV," "Letters, Packet I, Packet II, Packet III, Packet IV." He classifies his nightmares into: "1. The most frequent [...] 2. Rather frequent [...] 3. Frequent [...] 4. Rather rare [...] 5. Rare [...] 6. Very rare" (Cadiot 53). Cadiot parodies

---

[4] Quotations are from the published translation, *Future, former, fugitive.*

Wourm 185

Crusoe's minute attention to detail regarding what he needs and what he finds to meet his needs. Robinson the schizophrenic creates a list of items "recovered from the edge of the beach," which is ridiculous because of the sheer arbitrariness and convenience of it:

> 1. A box containing nails screws saws and all the tools necessary for carpentry. 2. A box containing tar ready for melting. 3. A box containing extra sails ropes and fishing gear. 4. A narrower box containing carbines. 5. A box containing some very beat up books including: a. A New Description of the Sir John Soame's Museum. b. Merwurdige Bemerkungen uber einen autobiographisch beschriebenen Fall von extreme Paranoia. c. The A.B.C. of Optics. d. Yellow blue Deep Blue Light Yellow, the complete poems of Mrs.***. 6. A metal box containing a portable press ink rollers magnifying glass and all the materials necessary for printing. 7. A wooden box containing a smaller metal box containing a series of letters classified by date and person. (Cadiot 50-51)

The accidental process by which the original Robinson finds faith, the chance result of a search for remaining tobacco, is re-imagined without even the rational basis of a serendipitous discovery. The original Robinson presents himself as having no "divine Knowledge," being "wicked and prophane to the last Degree" (Defoe 70). However, a third into the book, he describes how, quite accidentally, he became a Christian:

> I open'd the Chest, and found what I look'd for, *viz.* the Tobacco; and as the few Books, I had sav'd, lay there too, I took out one of the Bibles which I mention'd before, and which to this Time I had not found Leisure, or so much as Inclination to look into; I say, I took it out, and brought both that and the Tobacco with me to the Table. (Defoe 74-75).

Crusoe then explains the various ways in which he attempts to ingest the tobacco, first by chewing it, then by steeping it for an hour in some rum, and finally by burning it to inhale the smoke. Then, he comes back to the Bible:

> In the Interval of this Operation, I took up the Bible and began to read, but my Head was too much disturb'd with the Tobacco to bear reading, at least that Time; only having opened the Book casually, the first Words that occurr'd to me were these, *Call on me in the Day of Trouble, and I will de-*

> *liver, and thou shalt glorify me* [...]. The Words made a great Impression upon me, and I mused upon them very often. (Defoe 75)

It is the comical aspect of Crusoe's haphazard encounter with religion — a life-changing event for him — while fully engrossed in a trivial activity relating to tobacco, which the schizophrenic mimics, and Cadiot parodies in "Why I Became a Saint":

> In the evening I had to continue mapping the island — precursor to the three-dimensional model — using cross-hatchings spaced in inverse relation to the slope equal to a quarter of the distance between two consecutive curves [...]. As I was drawing, I realized that I was becoming more and more contemplative. And that's why today I am a saint — right before that I wasn't a saint — today *Just like that I'm a saint.* (Cadiot 96).

Crusoe's obsession with order, with the rationalization of time and space, becomes absurd when seen through the eyes of the schizophrenic. While Cadiot's parody is very funny, it also has the more serious function of weakening, or at least disturbing slightly, the all-encompassing foundations of our way of thought. For all the comedic aspect of this parody, we begin to learn that the schizophrenic Robinson has not found himself in some desert paradise. He is an outcast, banished to a deserted island, or, to speak more bluntly, sectioned and locked up in an institution by a repressive system, which does not allow for divergent structures of the mind. Inside the walls which cut him away from the rest of society, he is still being haunted by the oppressive and repressive voice of the society that he has left. The jumble of voices and memories from which he was hoping to free himself does not leave him, voices which are undermining and cruel, forced and formal: "[G]et that into your little bird brain. It's distressing to have a head like that, you'll be decapitated one day, my friend, in the name of good taste. Your mother — poor woman — has told me how worried she is about you" (62). They demand the very sense of order which he struggles for but can only fail to find: "You'll see that things go better if you manage to get organized / Organization my dear! / That's what makes the difference! [...] Note that in your case it's a total loss / all for the good cause / it's lost! [...] Listen instead of just mumbling any old thing" (51-52). And so he dreams of escape from his island as did Crusoe, and he, too, builds an immovable boat. One made of matchsticks.

Wourm 187

For much of the book, it is not clear whether we are dealing with the original Crusoe, struggling mentally with the reality of a life without others, or whether we are being given access to the workings of the mind of an institutionalised schizophrenic, who believes himself to *be* Robinson Crusoe. Are we witnessing the progressive disintegration of Crusoe's coherent self, and is this a book about Robinson's mental survival in a situation of complete solitude, of complete alienation from society? Or is this the story of a psychotic in his "interior 'island'"? This latter reading would be a reversal of roles, which Deleuze considers in his essay on Tournier's Robinson when he writes: "Can we not say that this progressive but irreversible dissolution of structure, is what the perverse reaches through other means, in his interior 'island' "? (*Logique du sens* 359). (Of course, "perverse" here must not be taken in its moralistic sense, but as referring to someone whose humanity takes another route from the usual socially accepted one). Do we have a schizophrenic transforming himself into Robinson, or Robinson transforming himself into a schizophrenic, thus fulfilling the aesthetic paradigm discussed by Deleuze in *Logique du sens*?

Clearly, the uncertainty produced by the writer here, the blurring of the status of his character, is philosophically relevant. On the one hand, we have Robinson, the archetypal capitalist, discovering a new type of humanity, far from the pressures of society as we know it, and structuring his mind differently, or "de-structuring" his mind altogether. On the other hand, we have an unknown individual, alienating himself from the structures of capitalist society and "de-structuring" his mind altogether. And this is where his identification with Crusoe comes in. Defoe's Robinson Crusoe is being re-invented by Cadiot as myth, but as anticapitalist myth this time. Ambiguity starts with the chapter titles (The Shipwreck, The Island, The Return, and Zero Sum) which create the assumption in our minds that this is going to be a rewriting on the well-known Crusoe theme. The main character and narrator is called Robinson, which inevitably reinforces this assumption. The first few pages resemble a type of interior monologue, intersected by random remembered pieces of discourse from a remote past, and flashbacks. In the second section of "The Shipwreck," entitled "Why I Always Make Mistakes," the narrator mentions having reticently accepted an invitation to a place (which remains enigmatic to the reader), "before making decisions," as he says, "of which we will later see the tragic consequences" (17). Echoes of the original Crusoe style of narration cannot fail to be noticed here: "But as it was always my Fate to choose for the worse, so I did here," Crusoe reflects in his characteristic style.

Or again, "This was but a Taste of the Misery I was to go thro', as will appear in the Sequel of this Story" (Defoe 15, 17). The enigmatic place is presented to Cadiot's character as "the site of an edifying life" (Cadiot 17), in which he will recover his health, re-create himself, i.e., as he understands it, acquire a new identity. Towards the end of the chapter, the narrator makes a note to himself in brackets: "[A]dd here: Why I hear voices" (19). He also explains how his departure was meant to liberate him from a jumble of accumulated words and memories. This departure is described by him in terms of a crossing, after which he finds himself alone on an island. There are two ways of understanding the section. Either this is a parallel to the original Robinson story, where the rebellious young man rejects the pathway suggested to him by his father, in order to lead a risky life at sea; or the section describes the narrator's admission in a mental institution, which is the moment when his link with society is being severed, hence the association in his mind with the island of Robinson Crusoe. On the one hand, we could have Robinson reminiscing about unpleasant events of his past, beginning to hear voices and to display other symptoms of psychosis. On the other hand, we could have a psychotic trying to make sense of his experience. It gradually becomes clear to the reader progressing through the book, that this "either/or" dynamic is beside the point, and that both readings are concomitant; they function together in counterpoint to create another kind of reality.

This Robinson, too, is dehumanized, not by the "soft jubilation" of new possibilities, but by the very psychoanalytic process which Deleuze and Guattari set out to undermine. He is himself an object of study by a psychiatrist working on his case — "The Robinson File" — and is regarded as a lost cause, someone who will never be able to make sense of the system (Cadiot 134). In a structural inversion of *Vendredi*, in which a third-person narrative is punctuated by extracts from Robinson's log books, the first-person structure of Cadiot's novel gives way to the psychiatrist's notes. Given the obvious psychoanalytic element in Tournier, it makes Tournier's text seem like the report of an analyst in comparison. And the fact that this type of text is

Wourm 189

marginalized in Cadiot's work, along with the fact that it is unsuccessful in terms of its desired impact on Robinson, holds a vein of schizophrenic hope of the kind Deleuze would presumably have endorsed.

It is ironic that to appreciate Cadiot's parody — which serves to exemplify Deleuze's philosophy — the French philosopher would have needed to go back to the original Defoe, to refresh whatever, perhaps childhood, memory of the text he had. Cadiot's Robinson could be seen as an unreading of the accumulated mis-, non-, and re-readings through which the sense of Robinson passed in the hands of Deleuze and Tournier. On one level, we can see Cadiot's work as a return to Defoe's text, a new re-reading. But this view ignores the extent to which Deleuze and Tournier are required to make sense of what Cadiot is doing. In what sounds like financial market manoeuvring of the most dubious legality, Cadiot borrows from both Defoe and Deleuze, and yet it is they who are in *his* debt: Defoe, while parodied, is at least restored as an exacting model of what is being parodied; Deleuze, while *unread*, finds his stance validated, albeit in a somewhat attenuated form. The question, then, remaining to be asked — but which I make no attempt to answer here — is whether *Futur, ancien, fugitif* is a suitable book for children.

Works Cited

Alferi, Pierre, and Olivier Cadiot. "La Mécanique Lyrique." *Revue de littérature générale*. Ed. Alferi and Cadiot. Paris: P.O.L, 1995.

Cadiot, Olivier. *Futur, Ancien, Fugitif*. Paris: P.O.L., 1993.

_____. *Future, Former, Fugitive*. Trans. Cole Swensen. New York: Roof Books, 2003.

Defoe, Daniel. *Robinson Crusoe*. 1719. New York: W. W. Norton, 1975.

Deleuze, Gilles. *L'Île déserte et autres textes*. Ed. David Lapoujade. Paris: Minuit, 2002.

_____. *Logique du Sens*. Paris: Minuit, 1969.

Deleuze, Gilles, and Félix Guattari. *Anti-Oedipus: Capitalism and Schizophrenia*. 1972. Trans. Robert Hurley, Mark Seem, and Helen R. Lane. London: The Athlone Press Ltd., 1984.

_____. *Mille Plateaux*. Paris: Minuit, 1980.

Hallward, Peter. *Out of this World: Deleuze and the Philosophy of Creation.* London and New York: Verso, 2006.

Marx, Karl. *Capital.* 1867, 1885, and 1894. Trans. Aveling and Moore. Chicago: Charles H. Kerr and Co., 1921.

Mill, John Stuart. *Autobiography.* London: Longmans, Green, Reader, and Dyer, 1873.

Redfern, Walter. "Introduction to Michel Tournier, 'Gilles Deleuze.' " *Deleuze and Religion.* Ed. Mary Bryden. London and New York: Routledge, 2001.

Tormey, Simon. *Anti-Capitalism.* Oxford: Oneworld Publications, 2004.

Tournier, Michel. *Friday or The Other Island.* Trans. Norman Denny. Harmondsworth: Penguin Books, 1974. Trans. of *Vendredi ou les Limbes du Pacifique.* Paris: Gallimard, 1967.

_____. *The Wind Spirit: an Autobiography.* Trans. Arthur Goldhammer. London: Methuen, 1991. Trans. of *Le vent Paraclet.* Paris: Gallimard, 1977. Orig.

Watt, Ian. *Myths of Modern Individualism.* Cambridge and New York: Cambridge University Press, 1996.

Corinne François-Denève

Université de Versailles-Saint-Quentin

L'homme qui racontait des histoires:
Paul Pavlowitch[1]

Après avoir été, ou ne pas avoir été Émile Ajar, Paul Pavlowitch a tenté d'être un "imposteur littéraire" "vrai", à savoir un écrivain à part entière. Son dernier ouvrage en date, *Tom, roman*, propose une variation, à la fictionnalité affichée, sur une série de romans de Patricia Highsmith dont le héros, Tom Ripley, est un imposteur professionnel. *Tom, roman*, est un objet littéraire non identifié, qui tient tout à la fois de l'essai, de la biographie (d'un personnage fictif), de la généalogie farcesque, du pamphlet, et du règlement de comptes. En parlant de l'affaire Gianfranco Sanguinetti, ou de Clifford Irving, Pavlowitch évoque aussi par la bande sa propre affaire d'imposture. Le livre, et son paratexte, déroulent donc une série de réflexions sur le thème de l'imitation (*Tom* comme réécriture des livres de Highsmith), sur l'angoisse de l'influence (écrire un livre sur un personnage déjà inventé) et évidemment sur le thème du faux.

Mais que vient donc faire Paul Pavlowitch dans un volume consacré au plagiat, à la copie, à l'adaptation? Rien du tout, diront ses détracteurs: il n'a jamais plagié, jamais rien copié, jamais rien adapté, il n'a de fait jamais rien fait, et c'est précisément ce qu'on lui reproche. Certes, mais d'un autre côté Paul Pavlowitch a aussi tout à faire dans un ouvrage qui parle de supercherie et de désir prométhéen de "voler le feu" ou de "jouer avec le feu". Paul Pavlowitch est en effet le petit-neveu de Romain Gary, et cet "homme de paille" que Gary élut lorsqu'il eut besoin d'un corps, d'une forme humaine pour incarner le double littéraire, fictif, qu'il s'était créé, Émile Ajar, auteur de *La Vie*

---

[1] Le titre de cet article est emprunté, pour les raisons que l'on verra plus loin, au livre de Patricia Highsmith, *L'Homme qui racontait des histoires* (*The Story-Teller*).

devant soi, et récipiendaire, fait exceptionnel, d'un "deuxième" Prix Goncourt. Paul Pavlowitch est donc cet acteur improvisé, ou ce personnage de roman, balancé sur la scène littéraire par un Gary démiurge. Pour que l'histoire soit encore plus belle, on sait que, dans les langues slaves, "Gary" veut dire "brasier", et que "Ajar" appartient au même champ sémantique du feu. Avec Ajar, Gary a donc voulu voler le feu céleste, et s'y est sans doute brûlé — et que dire de Paul Pavlowitch, condamné à son incarnation, et tentant depuis d'en sortir et d'exister, à tout le moins littérairement, en tant que Paul Pavlowitch.

De fait, il est faux de dire que Paul Pavlowitch n'a jamais rien écrit: si l'on excepte *L'Homme que l'on croyait*, paru en 1981, lié à l'affaire "Ajar", Paul Pavlowitch a en effet écrit en son nom propre, un certain nombre de romans: *La Peau de l'ours*, publié en 1986, qualifié par la quatrième de couverture de "premier roman" de "l'homme qu'on croyait Ajar", *Céline, Victor,* et *Un autre monde*, trilogie paysanne publiée entre 2000 et 2004, et *Tom*, roman paru en 2005. Il n'est sans doute pas inintéressant de constater que les deux romans qui entourent cette trilogie paysanne, réaliste et charnelle, sont deux ouvrages qui pourraient se présenter comme des biographies fictives de personnages plus ou moins fictifs, et qu'ils brassent en tout cas les thèmes de l'imposture et du rapport tendu avec le "réel".

La Peau de l'ours, le premier roman, donc qui ne figure même pas dans la liste des ouvrages de Paul Pavlowitch recensés à la BNF[2], est une reconstruction fantasmatique par le narrateur, Alex Nikouline, de la vie d'un peintre, faussaire, escroc, magouilleur de génie, curieusement appelé Paul, et mystérieusement assassiné. Le titre du roman, *La Peau de l'ours*, est évidemment tiré d'un proverbe français bien connu, ici tronqué: "il ne faut pas vendre la peau de l'ours avant de l'avoir tué". Ce proverbe réactive l'idée de la défiance, mais aussi une idée de commerce ("vendre", on sait que la querelle Ajar-Pavlowitch avait aussi des motivations financières) à moins qu'il ne réactive aussi la thématique slave ("l'ours"). Et l'on pourrait aussi y voir peut-être une métaphore de l'auteur, de l'autorité, qui préoccupe tant Paul Pavlowitch: on sait que "l'ours", en typographie, est le "petit pavé qui

---

[2] Le lecteur français devra voyager jusqu'à la BU de Limoges, ou investir dans un bouquiniste, pour trouver le premier ouvrage de "Paul Pavlowitch".

François-Denève **193**

recense les noms et adresses de l'imprimeur" et le nom des collabora-teurs ayant participé à la fabrication de l'imprimé":[3] il ne faudrait donc pas croire ce que dit l'ours! Quant à *Tom,* il s'agit d'un objet lit-téraire non identifié, qui tient du collage, du "sampling", et qui se veut une biographie fictive d'un personnage fictif, à savoir le Tom Ripley de Patricia Highsmith.

Auteur(s) en quête de personnage(s)

Selon Jean-François Jeandillou, le spécialiste français de la ques-tion, l'"affaire Émile Ajar-Romain Gary" ne peut être rangée dans la catégorie "mystification", au motif que les romans signés "Émile Ajar" ont fini par être intégrés dans l'œuvre complète de Romain Gary. De fait, chez Mercure de France, c'est sous le nom de "Romain Gary" que l'on trouve désormais les "romans d'Émile Ajar", sorte de cycle, donc, variante de *La Comédie Humaine*, qui comporte d'ail-leurs, en guise d'ouverture, le *Vie et Mort d'Émile Ajar* de Romain Gary. "Émile Ajar", explique Jeandillou, n'est donc qu'un "masque hétéronymique" de Gary, par ailleurs grand spécialiste de la pseudo-nymie (171). Comme pour ses autres ouvrages publiés sous nom d'emprunt, il s'agissait pour Gary de défier les étiquettes (163), de se moquer d'une critique qui le jugeait fini, et, surtout, d'être un autre, las qu'il était de lui-même (Gary, *Vie et mort* viii). Mais Gary n'a pas seulement inventé Ajar, il l'a aussi fait incarner. Jeandillou parle de trois "anthroponymes différents" — Ajar, Gary, Pavlowitch — plus précisément d'un orthonyme, Pavlowitch, caché sous un pseudonyme, Ajar (99-101). Paul Pavlowitch a dès le début tout fait pour s'appro-prier Ajar: ainsi, dans l'article "La Maison Ajar", du *Monde,* acte de naissance d'"Émile Ajar", Paul Pavlowitch changeait l'étymologie de son nom de plume en le faisant remonter à l'anglais "ajar", la porte à demi ouverte — sans doute parce qu'il était en quête d'air frais, ou d'une éventuelle sortie.

Le "jeu de rôles", on le sait, a donné lieu à des situations co-casses. Que penser en effet de ces déguisements, de ces photos d'iden-tité floues, ou en passe-montagne, comme dans la grande tradition

---

[3] Voir sur ce point le dictionnaire de l'argot et des typographes: <http://www.synec-doc.be/librairie/typo/>.

terroriste, de ces rendez-vous manqués en Suisse, numéro de téléphone mal noté oblige, puis à Copenhague? Mais Gary ne jouait pas seulement avec la critique, l'institution littéraire, il devait aussi affronter son acteur récalcitrant, décidé à devenir auteur. Dans *Vie et mort d'Émile Ajar*, Gary affirme en tout cas

> [qu'] il y eut des moments comiques. Notamment, lorsque Paul Pavlowitch exigea de moi les manuscrits, pour ne pas être à ma merci, et moi, lorsque je ne lui donnai que les premiers brouillons, et encore après les avoir photocopiés, pour ne pas être à la sienne. La scène où Jean Seberg emballait lesdits manuscrits, que je portais au coffre au fur et à mesure, était digne de Courteline. (xv)

Gary a inventé en tout cas une biographie à son écrivain fictif (Émile Ajar, ancien étudiant en médecine, en délicatesse avec la justice pour un avortement illégal, immigré au Brésil) avant que Paul Pavlowitch ne vienne ajouter des données de son cru, tirées de sa propre biographie, et ainsi conférer une autre identité bien encombrante à cet écrivain "fictif" (Émile Ajar, d'origine russe et yougoslave, qui a passé son enfance à Nice, et a fait des études de médecine à Toulouse...). "Émile Ajar" prend son envol, et Gary devient, dans tous les sens du terme, coupable du crime d'emprunter le nom d'un écrivain connu pour signer ses livres... À l'inverse, Gary a pu dire que Paul Pavlowitch avait choisi le pseudonyme d'Émile Ajar pour écrire ses livres pour ne pas avoir l'ombre portée de l'illustre autre écrivain de la famille. L'incarnation d'Ajar par Pavlowitch provenait par ailleurs du légitime désir de Gary de mettre un terme à tous ces faux Ajar qui appelaient Gallimard pour révéler leur prétendue "véritable" identité: Pavlowitch, lors de son premier appel à la Grande Maison, ne sut d'ailleurs pas se montrer assez convaincant... (Pavlowitch, *L'homme* 84-85). Lorsque Gary se lassa de l'écriture Ajar, ce fut Paul Pavlowitch qui en fut le plus ennuyé, au point d'envisager de se mettre à écrire *lui-même* sous ce pseudonyme... (Anissimov 594).

Le dernier roman d'"Émile Ajar", *Pseudo*, brasse jusqu'au vertige les identités auctoriales, fictives ou réelles: *Pseudo*, écrit par Gary, signé par Ajar, se présente comme le monologue intérieur de "Paul Pavlowitch", interné, et surtout en proie à une haine froide contre son oncle "Tonton Macoute" — Gary, bien sûr, qui refusa noblement de lire le manuscrit que Gallimard, par prudence, voulait lui

François-Denève 195

soumettre (Catonné 103). Il n'en avait d'ailleurs pas besoin; Gary écrivait _Pseudo_ et Paul Pavlowitch, un peu dépassé par les évènements, recopiait les feuillets, devenant le (re)lecteur, le scribe, le copiste de sa propre histoire.

Avec Ajar, Gary a donc flirté avec la mystification, et ses limites. Polyonyme notoire, il a d'ailleurs parfaitement résumé cette situation insolite dans cette confession écrite remise à une journaliste: "j'affirme que je ne suis pas Émile Ajar et que je n'ai collaboré en aucune façon aux ouvrages de cet auteur. Romain Gary", confession il est vrai accompagnée de ce P.S.: "si ce n'était pas vrai, j'agirais exactement de la même manière" (Anissimov 561). "Romain Gary" étant en soi un personnage de fiction, et l'une des plus belles réussites de l'auteur, il est vrai qu'on voit mal pourquoi on irait lui demander des comptes sur le réel.[4]

Dans cette affaire, qui donc fut mystifié? Michel Cournot, l'avocat de Gary? Le fait que Pavlowitch connaisse assez mal sa propre œuvre ne lui mit pas la puce à l'oreille (Pavlowitch, _L'Homme..._ 93). Simone Gallimard? Elle semblait le souhaiter ardemment, comme certaines personnes qui préfèrent qu'on leur mente, bien. Les lecteurs d'Ajar-Gary? Ils lurent des livres qu'ils aimèrent ou détestèrent. Le jury du Goncourt? Il ne décerna pas le Prix au même _auteur._ S'il y eut mystification, ce fut bien celle que _subit_ Gary, coupable d'en avoir initié une, et surtout celle de Paul Pavlowitch, coupable de s'en être rendu complice. Des années après "l'affaire", alors qu'il a tenté sa propre démystification psychanalytique en révélant le "secret" contre les volontés de Gary, dans _L'Homme que l'on croyait_ — tuant ainsi le père, brisant sa promesse — Pavlowitch ne finit pas de payer le prix de ce jeu dangereux.

Dans _L'Homme que l'on croyait,_ réponse à _Pseudo,_ Pavlowitch se décrit comme une victime du charisme slave de son oncle, son obligé, surtout, mais aussi comme "standardiste à 'S.O.S. dépannages' et 'documentaliste dans un lycée parisien' " (Pavlowitch, _L'Homme_ 33). Voilà qui fait de Pavlowitch la personne idéale pour "dépanner" son oncle en "documentant" ses livres. Pavlowitch, à dessein ou inconsciemment, semble toutefois occulter une partie de ses aspirations.

---

[4] La biographie de Miriam Anissimov accorde une large place aux "noms" de Gary. Voir son annexe I: "le nom du père. Une stratégie de survie" (655-58).

FLS, Vol. XXXVII, 2010

Homme passionné de littérature selon Catonné, grand connaisseur de livres et bon liseur selon Schoolcraft, Pavlowitch a oublié de dire qu'il a été aussi correcteur chez Gallimard, rédacteur d'articles d'encyclo-pédie, *presque* écrivain lui-même, donc... mais écrivain caché, *"in the closet"*, diraient les Anglo-Saxons.

Pavlowitch a dû voir inconsciemment dans le fait d'incarner Ajar une possibilité de devenir non un homme de paille, mais un homme de plume. De fait, Pavlowitch a dû à son masque d'"Émile Ajar", le fait d'avoir été engagé comme directeur littéraire au Mercure de France. Mais le premier livre signé "Paul Pavlowicth" ne parlait que de "l'af-faire" et le fameux passage de Pavlowitch à *Apostrophes,* en juillet 1981, ne se serait pas fait sans Ajar, et donc sans Gary. Si Gary est l'homme qui a perdu son ombre, selon Schoolcraft, Pavlowitch est bien cet homme qui ne peut se débarrasser de l'ombre que lui fait "tonton macoute", comme il le dit dans *L'Homme que l'on croyait:* "secrétaire de Romain — c'était donc arrivé —, j'étais au plus près de la création littéraire, sans écrire" (Pavlowitch, *L'Homme* 194-95).

Pour avoir été un faux écrivain, et avoir dérobé le feu céleste (Gary, Ajar, la brûlure, le brasier, encore...). Pavlowitch semble con-damné ainsi à ne jamais devenir un écrivain *reconnu* — la "reconnais-sance" mettant un terme à la mystification en la couronnant. Il est celui qui a mystifié, a été mystifié, parle de mystification, ne peut parler que de cela. Il ne sait s'il est un auteur ou un personnage, comme le démiurge Gary le souhaitait, lui qui évoquait: "ce rêve de roman total, personnage et auteur" (Gary, *Vie et Mort* viii).

Paul Ripley

Personnage? auteur? roman? mystification? Le curieux ouvrage du cru 2004 de Pavlowitch, *Tom,* ne fait que relancer ces lancinantes interrogations: Pavlowitch s'est en effet penché sur un *personnage,* est-il utile de dire "fictif", Thomas Ripley, héros de cinq romans de Patricia Highsmith, *The Talented Mr. Ripley* (1955), *Ripley Under Ground* (1970), *Ripley's Game* (1974), *The Boy Who Followed Ripley* (1980) et *Ripley Under Water* (1991), parfois rassemblés sous le plai-sant titre de *The Ripliad.*

Fictif, Ripley? Il est vrai que Tom a connu quelques incarnations cinématographiques, dans *Plein Soleil* de René Clément, en 1960,

François-Denève 197

L'Ami Américain de Wim Wenders en 1980 ou *Le Talentueux Monsieur Ripley* d'Anthony Minghella en 1999 — Pavlowitch parle d'ailleurs de ce film, pour exprimer son insatisfaction devant la composition de Matt Damon. Fictif? Pour être "fictif" un personnage doit avoir une certaine épaisseur; or Ripley est un homme sans qualités, un être falot, sans personnalité, franchement déplaisant, transparent jusqu'au malaise.

Aucun "effet de réel" dans ce personnage. Le temps n'a pas de prise sur lui: Ripley devrait être un quinquagénaire tranquille dans le dernier roman, mais il semble pour toujours figé dans sa maigre dégaine d'Américain débrouillard. Il est doté d'une femme évanescente et aérienne, Héloïse, avec laquelle il n'a pas d'enfants et peu de relations charnelles. Ripley est invincible, invincible au temps, et invincible à tout: il *s'en sort toujours*, en dépit de ce que veulent faire croire les adaptations cinématographiques d'une Amérique bien pensante. Ripley est donc le *personnage* idéal, modeste et sans relief, qui passe au travers des usurpations les plus impossibles et des impostures les plus incroyables. Sur sa carte de visite est écrit "personnage de roman", et aussi, cela va avec, "imposteur, usurpateur, mystificateur, magicien". On comprend ce qui a pu séduire Pavlowitch dans un tel "personnage". Car Ripley ne meurt pas, contrairement à Highsmith, morte en 1995, contrairement à Ajar, "assassiné" en 1981, en plus à titre posthume, par Gary, dans *Vie et Mort d'Émile Ajar*, contrairement à Gary, assassiné par lui-même, et contrairement à Paul Pavlowitch — le plus tard possible, comme il se doit.

À la lecture des ouvrages de Highsmith, on comprend ce qui a pu fasciner Pavlowitch dans *The Ripliad*. De façon anecdotique, Tom ressemble beaucoup au père de l'auteur, un temps comptable, comme Tom, un temps employé à Paris de l'American Express, que Tom utilise comme poste restante sous ses diverses identités. Tom est au fait des arcanes des impôts américains, et on se souvient qu'une des réticences de Gary à dévoiler la véritable identité d'Ajar était la peur de voir les impôts français lui tomber dessus... C'est d'ailleurs par une querelle de droits d'auteur que commence *L'Homme que l'on croyait*, et semble justifier pour Pavlowitch la révélation de la supercherie (Pavlowitch, *L'Homme* 11). Enfin, on pourra se rappeler que dans *Pseudo,* Gary déguise Annie, la femme de Pavlowitch, sous le prénom d'Alyette, ou d'Héloïse, prénom de la femme de Tom...

Bien plus, Tom aime les contrefaçons, les signatures improbables (selon Miriam Anissimov, toutes les signatures d'Ajar étaient dissemblables, comme celles de Dickie imitées par Tom [520]), les copies et les faux, les impostures et les usurpations d'identité. Dans *L'Homme que l'on croyait,* Paul Pavlowitch raconte d'ailleurs qu'il a dû se faire faire des faux papiers au nom d'Ajar chez un marchand de couleurs rue de Rennes (Pavlowitch, *L'Homme* 87), ce qui lie aussi Paul à Tom, grand amateur de peinture. Dans *Tom,* Pavlowitch fait semblant de croire que des Derwatt sont suspendus au Centre Pompidou, et il évoque Van Meegeren, grand faussaire en Vermeer. Tom, en effet, à l'imitation de Dickie, de Derwatt, de Bernard, se rêve peintre, comme Pavlowitch a pu se rêver écrivain. Tom, chez lui, provocateur, expose même en face à face, un "vrai" Derwatt, et un "faux" Derwatt, ou un vrai Tufts (Highsmith, *Sur les pas* 880). Les discussions savantes par Murchison sur le style de Derwatt rappellent d'ailleurs les querelles d'experts sur les "ajarismes" ou les "garysmes" de *La Vie devant soi,* ou d'ouvrages d'ailleurs parfois antérieurs de Gary: pour *L'Horloge,* en effet, Murchison affirme que le violet, à base de cobalt, a été abandonné par Derwatt, quelques années avant la composition supposée de ce tableau, au profit d'un mélange de rouge cadmium et de bleu outremer...

Homme sans qualité, donc, Tom acquiert une stature, une épaisseur en se glissant dans la peau d'un autre — Dickie, d'abord, puis Derwatt. Ces diverses incarnations ne peuvent bien sûr que faire penser à l'incarnation par Pavlowitch d'Ajar. Tom a donc ressuscité Derwatt, qu'il a envoyé dans un village du Mexique (Highsmith, *Ripley et les ombres* 453), comme Ajar avait été d'abord exilé au Brésil par Gary. Devant l'insistance de Murchison à rencontrer Derwatt, on croirait entendre Gary: "là, ça poserait effectivement un problème, se dit Tom, pour la bonne raison que Derwatt n'existait pas" (Highsmith, *Ripley et les ombres* 445). Tom a donc une grande idée: "si je jouais le rôle de [...] notre ami disparu... en tout cas pendant quelques heures? [...] [L]es vêtements, ce n'est rien. L'important, c'est le visage" (Highsmith, *Ripley et les ombres* 450). Tom va donc se déguiser: il enlève les bagues de Dickie, qui le déguisaient déjà en quelqu'un d'autre, ajoute une fausse barbe et des lunettes, prend le soin de faire sa conférence dans une pièce mal éclairée (Highsmith, *Ripley et les ombres* 459): on n'est pas loin de la photo floue, cliché de vacances

François-Denève 199

d'un Pavlowitch hirsute et bronzé... Dans *L'Homme que l'on croyait,* Pavlowitch rappelle d'ailleurs que Gary aimait à se grimer (Pavlowitch, *L'Homme* 109), et que, dans un message signé "Ducon", il lui avait conseillé: "il faudra te maquiller, te déguiser; je passerai faire ça à Joigny avec du matériel de grimage" (Pavlowitch, *L'Homme* 109). La même anecdote se retrouve dans *Tom,* à la note 45 de la page 192:

> dans l'affaire dite du "Deuxième Goncourt", Gary l'auteur possédait lui aussi, une mallette personnelle de maquillage. Souvent outrageusement grimé; couvert de cuir noir ou d'oripeaux mexicains, R. Gary déambulait dans les rues de Paris, mais dans son cas, c'était plutôt pour frapper l'imagination. Il aimait décontenancer, et changer d'apparence.

Et puis, il y a, évidemment, ces suicidés, de la société, ou de l'art, qui ne peuvent que faire penser à Gary, à son suicide, et au "suicide" d'Ajar, commandité par Gary avant le sien.

Pavlowitch a donc pu se reconnaître dans Tom, au point de lui consacrer un ouvrage. Le ton est donné dès la quatrième de couverture, qui aligne, comme c'est l'usage, un résumé, un extrait, une présentation du livre, et une brève biographie de l'auteur, nantie d'une photo, nette, et sans passe-montagne. Le résumé de l'ouvrage est en soi un programme d'intention, en ce sens qu'il fait de Ripley un "faussaire, voleur, chef de bande, [qui] toujours suivra son désir plutôt que l'ordre du monde". La présentation du roman joue quant à elle curieusement sur la notoriété de Pavlowitch:

> Qui est donc Thomas Ripley? Aventurier, imposteur, criminel multirécidiviste? Simplement un homme que l'on croyait lorsqu'il inventait sa vie en empruntant celle des autres. Hommage du romancier ou subtile autodérision de Paul Pavlowitch à l'égard de cet autre lui-même: Émile Ajar, prix Goncourt 1975 et auteur des romans à succès de son oncle Romain Gary? Pavlowitch ne pouvait qu'aimer Ripley avec qui il partage une aversion totale pour le principe de réalité et une prédilection pour la musique de Mendelssohn.

À la différence de Tom, pourrait-on ajouter, Paul est un homme que l'on a cessé de croire. Sur la quatrième de couverture de *Tom,* toujours, la biographie de Pavlowitch est d'une sobriété étonnante: "Paul Pavlowitch vit dans le Sud de la France et a récemment publié aux Éditions Fayard la trilogie: *Victor, Céline* et *Un autre monde*".

Tom, présenté comme un roman, tient en tout cas de l'objet litté-raire non identifié. Dans "L'avertissement", Pavlowitch revient sur le lien qui le lie à Tom: Tom, qui a pu tuer, alors que Paul en aurait sou-vent eu envie. C'est ensuite une épigraphe: "*'jouer son rôle', en fran-çais, cela rendait un son si gai si innocent, selon Tom*" (Paris, 1970). Voilà donc le thème de l'imposture et du masque posé, sauf que la ci-tation n'est pas identifiée: on peut juste supposer qu'elle vient de *Rip-ley Under Ground*, paru en 1970, dans lequel justement Tom s'incarne en Derwatt.

Tom tient de l'essai littéraire et de la biographie à l'américaine, c'est-à-dire explicative et historicisante. Toutefois cette biographie concerne un personnage fictif (qui n'est donc ni né, ni mort), et n'est en rien objective. L'*a priori* est patent: selon Pavlowitch, Tom a été mal jugé, et il s'agit de le réhabiliter. On a mésestimé la part de rêve, de merveilleux que recèle Tom, faussement pris pour un personnage "réaliste" de romans policiers. Tom s'inscrit en fait dans la grande tra-dition des héros américains oniriques et mythiques, des Tom Pouce, Tom Sawyer ou des Rip van Winkle.

Tom se donne également une apparence scientifique, en se pré-sentant comme un "hommage à Thomas Phelps Ripley (1929-1991), *avec notes, sources et un bref appendice*". *Tom* multiplie les para-textes savants et trace la généalogie d'un personnage fictif grâce à des personnages "réels". Voilà tante Dottie fille de Rory Hooligan, voilà Tom un lointain parent de George Ripley, traditionaliste américain de la fin du XIXe siècle, peut-être à relier avec les "Ripley's Believe It or Not", série de *comics* pour enfants, qui jouent d'ailleurs sur l'énormité des mystifications racontées... Et Pavlowitch de mentionner à l'appui de ses dires une publication savante, "*Studies in English*, vol. 12, page 666 et suivantes, Princeton University, 1989" (Pavlowitch, *Tom* 184). C'est tout juste si Pavlowitch ne mentionne pas "The Ripley", parasite du *Dreamcatcher* de Stephen King, ou Ellen Ripley, l'héroïne des films Alien, qui auraient pourtant eu leur place dans la série...

Mais *Tom* est en même temps un ouvrage que l'on ne pourrait qualifier d'objectif, tant y fourmillent les formules à l'emporte-pièce, qui rappellent d'ailleurs curieusement les assassinats (littéraires) en règle de Romain Gary: sont par exemple visés Pompidou: "on doit à G. Pompidou, outre les deux hommes guillotinés, une anthologie de la poésie française, la voie express sur berge et le Centre Artistique, qui

François-Denève 201

porte son nom, lequel musée abrite dans ses réserves de nombreux Derwatt, parmi les plus beaux" (Pavlowitch, *Tom* 192, note 40; il est vrai que la référence à ce peintre fictif annihile la portée polémique de la charge); Giscard et Robbe-Grillet ("question distinction, Giscard, président recalé au Centre National d'Auvergne, sera coopté par l'Académie Française, l'année où celle-ci s'adjoint Robbe-Grillet Alain, géomètre par éducation et cinéaste pompier, pornographe *soft* de vocation" (Pavlowitch, *Tom* 196, note 60), ou encore Wim Wenders ("le cadre, voilà de qui intéresser Wenders, artiste qui cadre admirablement la vacuité" (Pavlowitch, *Tom* 197, note 69).

Tom prend alors la forme d'un pamphlet, d'une restitution subjective de l'époque des années 70, marquée, selon Pavlowitch, par le règne de l'hypocrisie, du faux, de la mystification. Sont évoquées en vrac les affaires: l'affaire Gary, bien sûr, mais aussi l'affaire Gianfranco Sanguinetti, et l'affaire C. Irving/H. Hughes (Pavlowitch, *Tom* 189, note 29; 190-91, note 37). Pavlowitch ne juge pas utile de revenir sur son affaire, il renvoie à sa bibliographie. Pourtant, *Tom* est aussi un règlement de comptes de Pavlowitch envers Gary qui, rageusement, traîtreusement, s'exerce dans les notes: traité de cas psychiatrique dans *Pseudo*, le petit-neveu indigne ravale son grand-oncle au rang d'entremets pour dames, en parlant de "Romain Gary, l'auteur franco-russe de romans d'amour", d'ailleurs souvent constipé... (Pavlowitch, *Tom* 185). Mais l'affaire Gary est remise en perspective, et prend place au côté d'autres "affaires" de même ampleur, et est donc, ainsi, neutralisée, démythifiée. Pavlowitch indique que l'affaire Gianfranco Sanguinetti fut aussi nommée celle du "Nouveau Machiavel", et que l'affaire "C. Irving/H. Hughes" fut, elle, connue sous le nom de "the Hoax". Loin de rentrer dans le détail de ces affaires, Pavlowitch en tire une morale générale: ces "affaires" ont finalement donné naissance à une "multitude d'ouvrages". "Ces histoires véridiques" n'ont pour fonction que de donner un "bonheur de lecture" (Pavlowitch, *Tom* 191). Peu importe la vérité, donc, pourvu qu'on ait le livre.

Pavlowitch suppose connues les affaires dont il parle. On rappellera simplement que Gianfranco Sanguinetti est l'auteur de *On Terrorism and the State* (1969) et qu'il a été soupçonné d'avoir écrit *Is the Reichstag Burning?*, la même année. L'affaire "Irving/Hughes" est quant à elle une véritable "mystification" littéraire: en 1971, Clifford Irving, un journaliste américain, fit en effet croire que Howard

Hughes, alors reclus et silencieux, lui avait dicté *The Autobiography of Howard Hughes*. La supercherie ayant été révélée, Irving passa quelque temps en prison, écrivit... *Hoax (Arnaque)*, et également un essai sur le faussaire Elmyr de Hory. Orson Welles, en 1975, réalisa *F for Fake (F pour Faux)*, un documentaire délibérément contrefait mettant en scène une fausse interview par Irving de Hory... Enfin, si les lecteurs ne sont pas encore perdus, on retrouve également quelques citations de "Colin Decayeux" (Pavlowitch, *Tom* 183, note 2, sur les "enfants perdus", et *passim*), "Colin Decayeux", compagnon de François Villon, étant bien sûr un des alias de Guy Debord...

Où donc est Tom, dans *Tom*? Partout et nulle part. Dans la bibliographie figurent les "ouvrages de madame Patricia Highsmith" (aucune bibliographie scientifique ne mentionnerait ce "madame"), ceux de Clifford Irving, de Gianfranco Sanguinetti, mais aussi *L'Homme que l'on croyait*, et *Vie et Mort d'Émile Ajar*. D'ailleurs, les notes ne renvoient que par accident aux ouvrages de Highsmith. Il faut dire que Pavlowitch n'a pas besoin d'indiquer les références des citations: Pavlowitch semble recopier Highsmith, sans s'en cacher.

Où donc alors est le "roman", annoncé sur la couverture? Partout et nulle part. *Tom* est une mystification: un roman qui parle plus de Paul que de Tom, un roman-copie, assumé comme tel, qui ne vit que par la respiration de ses notes, dans lequel "Paul" s'explique, éructe sur le plagiat, et surtout, se dit victime d'un temps où la mystification était une façon de vivre, où vivre était une mystification.

Pavlowitch, dans *L'Homme que l'on croyait,* détaillait sa punition, qu'il appelait sa vocation: "ma vraie vocation, celle que je garderai jusqu'à la fin, était et reste la lecture. Je suis lecteur" (Pavlowitch, *L'Homme* 53). *Tom* en est une parfaite illustration. Et Pavlowitch de clore son "dernier bilan, ultimes précisions et sources" par un énigmatique: "grande spécialiste de la préservation des espèces rares, la littérature peut être remerciée" (Pavlowitch, *Tom* 175). Autre chose: depuis *Tom*, paru donc il y a quatre ans, Paul Pavlowitch n'a rien publié. "Il n'y a pas de commencement. J'ai été engendré, chacun son tour, et depuis, c'est l'appartenance" (Gary, *Pseudo* 498).

François-Denève   *203*

Ouvrages cités et consultés

Anissimov, Miriam. *Romain Gary le caméléon*. Paris: Denoël, 2004.

Catonné, Jean-Marie. *Gary-Émile Ajar*. Paris: Belfond, 1990.

Gary, Romain. *Pseudo*. 1976. *Les Œuvres complètes d'Émile Ajar*. Paris: Mercure de France, 1991.

_____.*Vie et Mort d'Émile Ajar*. 1981. *Les Œuvres complètes d'Émile Ajar*. Paris: Mercure de France, 1991.

Highsmith, Patricia. *The Boy Who Followed Ripley*. Londres: Heinemann, 1980. *Sur les pas de Ripley*. Trad. Alain Delahaye, 1980. *Œuvres*. Paris: Laffont, 1991. Bouquins.

_____. *L'Homme qui racontait des histoires*. Trad. Renée Rosenthal, 1966. Paris: LGF, 1994.

_____. *Ripley's Game*. New York: Doubleday, 1974. *Ripley s'amuse*. Trad. Janine Herisson, 1974. *Œuvres*. Paris: Laffont, 1991. Bouquins.

_____. *Ripley Under Ground*. Londres: Heinemann, 1970. *Ripley et les Ombres*. Trad. Élisabeth Gille, 1970. *Œuvres*. Paris: Laffont, 1991. Bouquins.

_____. *Ripley Under Water*. Londres: Bloomsbury, 1991. *Ripley entre deux eaux*. Trad. Pierre Ménard. Paris: Calmann-Lévy, 1991.

_____. *The Story-Teller*. Londres: Heinemann, 1965.

_____. *The Talented Mr. Ripley*. New York: Coward McCann, 1955. *Monsieur Ripley*. Trad. Jean Rosenthal, 1956. *Œuvres*. Paris: Laffont, 1991. Bouquins.

Jeandillou, Jean-François. *Esthétique de la mystification: tactique et stratégie littéraires*. Paris: Éditions de Minuit, 1994.

Pavlowitch, Paul. *Un autre monde*. Paris: Fayard, 2004.

_____. *Céline*. Paris: Fayard, 2002.

_____. "Entretien d'Émile Ajar avec Yvonne Baby". *Le Monde* 10 octobre 1975.

_____. *L'Homme que l'on croyait*. Paris: Fayard, 1981.

_____. *La peau de l'ours*. Paris: Mazarine, 1986.

_____. *Tom, roman*. Paris: Ramsay, 2005.

_____. *Victor*. Paris: Fayard, 2000.

Rivière, François. *Un long et merveilleux suicide. Regards sur Patricia Highsmith*. Paris: Calmann-Lévy, 2003.

Schoolcraft, Ralph. *Romain Gary, The Man Who Sold His Shadow*. Philadelphia: University of Pennsylvania Press, 2002.

FLS, Volume XXXVII, 2010

Stealing the Fire

Alexander Hertich

Bradley University

Erratum... Errata... Erasum...: The Selection of Sources for Raymond Queneau's *Le Chiendent*

> There has been considerable debate over potential links between Queneau's *Le Chiendent* and Descartes's *Discours de la Méthode*, fueled primarily by Queneau's own contradictory accounts. In 1937, he described how a translation of the *Discours* into modern French became his first novel. Then, his 1969 article, "Errata," refuted this explanation. Although Queneau purports to be telling us the truth in "Errata," if one examines the notes and drafts for the article, a different, less clear-cut answer arises. These manipulations reveal many important themes of Queneau's *œuvre*: questions of literary heritage, potential literature, and the place of the author.

I do not wish to ruin the ending of Agatha Christie's *The A.B.C. Murders*, but the murderer is not Alexander Bonaparte Cust, as our ostensibly reliable narrator, Captain Arthur Hastings, O.B.E., has led us to believe throughout much of the novel. Similarly, Raymond Queneau's explanation in his article, "Errata," of the inspiration for his first novel, *Le Chiendent,* is also specious. In "Errata," Queneau discusses the subjective nature of truth in testimony, quoting Christie's famed detective, Hercule Poirot: "But telling everything you know always implies *selection* [...]. [P]eople select what they think is important. But quite frequently they think wrong!" (Christie 147; Queneau, *Voyage* 221).

For decades, debate has burned regarding the possible links between *Le Chiendent* and René Descartes's *Discours de la Méthode*, in

206 FLS, Vol. XXXVII, 2010

part because no single document completely delineates the novel's origins, as Henri Godard observes (*Œuvres complètes II* 1442-43). The controversy is fueled primarily by Queneau's own contradictory accounts, with some critics, such as Jean-Marie Catonné, questioning the importance of Descartes's philosophical treatise in Queneau's novel — "C'est un roman. Pas un momento universitaire," he argues (151) — while I have shown important similarities between the two texts on the levels of both language and narrative structure (Hertich 72-79). Although Queneau purports to be telling us the entire truth in "Errata," he, too, appears to be making a selection; for if one examines the evidence — in this case, the notes and drafts for the article — a different, less clear-cut answer emerges. In an attempt to better understand *Le Chiendent* and its genesis, I will examine Queneau's own selections and obfuscations regarding his sources, inspirations, and intertexts, for, like the use of intertext in Queneau's works in general, his manipulations reveal many important themes of his *œuvre*: questions of literary heritage, potential literature, and the place of the author.

In the article "Écrit en 1937," Queneau recounts — four years after *Le Chiendent* was published — the various circumstances which ultimately led to his first novel. Unpublished until the appearance in 1950 of *Bâtons, chiffres et lettres*, this essay details Queneau's interest in language and what he specifically labeled "le néo-français." Eminently aware of the antiquated nature of "literary French," which he considered to be a "véritable langue morte" (Debon 27), Queneau took a didactic tack:

> Il me parut aussi que la première façon d'affirmer cette nouvelle langue serait non pas de romancer quelque événement populaire (car on pourrait se méprendre sur les intentions), mais bien, à l'exemple des hommes du XVIe qui utilisèrent les langues modernes au lieu du latin pour traiter de théologie ou de philosophie, de rédiger en français parlé quelque dissertation philosophique; et, comme j'avais emporté avec moi *Le Discours de la Méthode*, de le traduire dans ce français parlé. C'est avec cette idée en tête que je me mis à écrire "quelque chose" qui devint un roman devant plus tard s'intituler *Le Chiendent* [...]. (*Bâtons, chiffres et lettres* 18)[1]

---

[1] In "Conversation avec Georges Ribemont-Dessaignes," a text in the same collection as "Écrit en 1937" and recorded in March of 1950, Queneau recounts a very similar version: "Et quand j'ai commencé à écrire ce qui devait devenir *Le Chiendent*,

Now, due to Queneau's specific contextualizing of the novel, the conscientious reader is predisposed to analyze the work following specific directions indicated by the author. It is through these linguistic, philosophical, and ultimately intertextual doorways indicated by the author that nearly all critics pass, whatever their final destination may be.

Then, thirty-two years later in "Errata,"[2] piquantly described by André Blavier as a "texte de position essentiel, une chiquenaude déroutante sous prétexte ultérieur et d'équivoque contrition" (297), Queneau refutes this previously related lineage. This refutation is important, not only because Queneau alters his story, but also because of the nearly mythical stature that his trip to Greece had assumed, given the various texts that allude to it. In fact, it was Jean Blot's article, "Chroniques: Raymond Queneau" (*Nouvelle revue française*, février 1969), in which the author discussed the desire of a young man to "transcrire en français parlé, équivalent au démotique, le katharevousa du *Discours de la Méthode*" that served as the catalyst for Queneau's recantation (qtd. in *Voyage* 219). Moreover, Queneau, in his semi-autobiographical novel *Odile* (1937), offers a fictionalized version of this voyage. The novel's protagonist, Roland Travy, exasperated with his life in Paris, decides to leave for Greece. After several months of self-doubt and exploration, he begins to better understand himself: "[...] maintenant j'avais en moi quelque chose comme une sorte d'espoir, germe qui loin de Paris ne pourrissait pas" (*Œuvres complètes II* 612). He is ready to return to Paris, but he has changed: "J'emportais avec moi la promesse d'une signification: une œuvre commencée dans l'île" (614).

Stark differences become immediately apparent when one compares the two accounts. In "Errata" Queneau abjures and then explains:

> J'avais l'intention de "travailler" et je commençai la traduction de... Attention.

---

c'est le titre de ce premier roman, je voulais simplement faire un petit essai de traduction du *Discours de la Méthode* en français moderne. Bientôt je me suis aperçu que j'étais tombé dans le bain romanesque" (*Bâtons, chiffres et lettres* 41).

[2] Originally published in *La Nouvelle revue française*, avril 1969, and later included in *Le Voyage en Grèce* (Paris: Gallimard, 1973; 219-22).

> J'avais emporté avec moi quatre livres: le *Discours de la Méthode* de René Descartes, le *Traité du Désespoir* de Kierkegaard (qui venait de paraître), *Sanctuary* de Faulkner (encore inconnu et non traduit) et *An Experiment with Time* de Dunne. C'est ce dernier livre que, sur le conseil de Jolas, j'avais l'intention de traduire. Je dus en faire une vingtaine de pages. C'est cette traduction-là abandonnée qui se transformera en les premières pages du *Chiendent* où l'on retrouve l'"observateur" dont Dunne fait usage pour expliquer les rêves prémonitoires, l'empruntant à la théorie de relativité. Sans doute, avais-je en tête l'intérêt que présenterait une traduction en français contemporain du *Discours*, mais je n'entrepris jamais réellement ce travail qui resta toujours à l'état de projet. (*Voyage* 220-21)

Here Queneau appears to be admitting his previous mistake and telling us the truth; this is the *true* story of *Le Chiendent*. Thus, even these secondary texts, essays written by Queneau himself whose purpose appears to be elucidative, are problematic and polyvalent. Like writers such as Alain Robbe-Grillet — who after nearly forty years of disavowing any relationship between his works and his personal life, wrote the infamous line, "Je n'ai jamais parlé d'autre chose que de moi" (*Le Miroir qui revient* 10) — Queneau undermines his previous accounts, which formed, in part for many readers, the *raison d'être* of his text.

However, this new explanation is less definite if one studies the various drafts of "Errata." In *Classeur 15bis*, housed at Centre de Documentation Raymond Queneau in Verviers, Belgium, one finds four distinct versions of the text: one fragmentary handwritten draft with notes, two handwritten manuscript drafts, and a typed version with corrections. The progression of these four texts tells an extremely interesting tale. While many of the themes remain unmodified from his notes to the published version — for example, Queneau's opinion that interviews are frequently imprecise and his avowal that it was not on the boat to Greece that he spoke with several Greeks, as he recounts in *Bâtons, chiffres et lettres* (17), but rather after arriving in Greece — Queneau's account of the conception of *Le Chiendent*, his certainty about the events of 1932, as well as the importance and role of the various texts that he was reading at the time, changes slightly with each successive version. After comparing the first draft of the article with the final published version, one is tempted to join Queneau's self-criticism, but for completely different reasons. Quoting Queneau quoting Agatha Christie (and it should be noted that I could not find this exact quotation in the English-language original): "Vous vous éloignez de la verité" (*Voyage* 220).

In the first manuscript pages, which include six pages of notes and several extended paragraphs, some of which follow one another logically and some of which appear to be isolated ideas, Queneau seems to be trying to determine the links between *Le Chiendent* and the *Discours de la Méthode*. After two pages of notes and dates he writes: "Je crains que les choses ne se soient passées différemment: j'ai commencé à écrire *Le Chiendent* et *ensuite* je me suis dit: tiens, je devrais traduire le *Discours de la Méthode* en français moderne" (*Classeur 15bis* CDRQ). This statement is rather shocking, given the fact that it contradicts both of Queneau's published accounts.

Then, on page five, he admits that he had started a translation of J. W. Dunne's *An Experiment with Time*, which evolved into *Le Chiendent*. He also proclaims that he never started a translation of Descartes's *Discours*. These are the same story elements that we find in "Errata" (*Voyage* 220-21). Yet in this primitive version he adds, "Sans doute y ai-je pensé [of the *Discours de la Méthode*] et les allusions à Descartes doivent se retrouver dans *Le Chiendent*" (*Classeur 15bis* CDRQ). Ah, says the reader, the philosophical work *does* have a direct link with Queneau's novel. But then several lines later Queneau again obfuscates the situation, declaring: "Que je me sois mis à écrire un roman *Le Chiendent* est resté pour moi toujours un mystère. Ça a vraiment été le coup de foudre, l'inspiration." This idea contrasts starkly with a phrase, frequently intoned by Queneau scholars and OuLiPo members, "il faut affirmer que *le poète n'est jamais 'inspiré'* [...]" (*Voyage* 126). These notes for "Errata," while subtly shading the story, unquestionably leave the reader perplexed. Given the contradictory accounts within a few pages, Queneau himself seems unsure of the precise circumstances that led to his first novel.

However, as one reads through the successive drafts for the article, this uncertainty slowly dissipates. In the first full draft of the article some nuances remain, but most indecision has been crossed out. After setting the scene of his arrival in Greece, he writes: "et je commençai la traduction de [...]" (*Classeur 15bis* CDRQ), a phrase that remains in the final version. Yet unlike the published version, which reads "la traduction de... Attention" (*Voyage* 220), in this first full draft after "de" is an illegible word, followed by "*Discours de la Méthode*," all of which has been crossed out. If he is certain that he did not translate Descartes's *Discours*, why would he write it? Is this a symptomatic action, a Freudian slip of the pen that unearths evidence that Queneau wishes to repress? As Hercule Poirot exclaims to his group of witnesses in *The A.B.C. Murders*: "I make the assumption that one — or possibly *all* of you — *knows something that they do not know they know*" (Christie 155).

The article continues in a vein similar to that found in the published article, listing the four books he had taken with him to Greece and the role of the "observer" from Dunne's *An Experiment with Time* as the starting point of the novel. He then observes: "*Le Discours* vint apporter sa contribution au *Chiendent* comme *Sanctuary* (pour la construction) et le *Traité du Désespoir* (pour la philosophie)" (*Classeur 15bis* CDRQ). The second handwritten draft also contains this declaration. But here it is crossed out and does not appear in any subsequent versions of the article. Looking at these gradual modifications, one understands, contrary to Queneau's two "official" versions of the novel's genesis, that *Le Chiendent* did not stem from one specific text. While some works — such as the *Discours*, Dunne's *An Experiment in Time*, or Plato's *Parmenides* — are primary sources for *Le Chiendent*, specifically influencing extended sections of the text, others — such as Madame Cloche's "sac en tapisserie," which refers to the tapestry that Penelope wove while waiting for Odysseus's return (and which also constitutes one of several direct and indirect allusions to Joyce's *Ulysses*) [*Œuvres complètes II* 22, 60, 61, 146)],[3] or the "lampe mazda" borrowed from Breton's *Nadja* (18), to highlight but two examples — are only mentioned in passing. The novel is the sum of a variety of influences, "une caisse de résonnance de toute la littérature française" (Queval 59), just as we find in Queneau's other works such as *Les Enfants du limon*, *Zazie dans le métro*, or *Les Fleurs bleues*.

After studying the various drafts of "Errata," it becomes obvious that Queneau, too, is making a selection, although he does not admit

---

[3] In an interview with Georges Charbonnier, Queneau said: "À ce moment-là [when he first started writing novels] j'étais très influencé par Joyce [...]" (*Entretiens avec Georges Charbonnier* 50).

to this in the published version. In fact, he systematically suppresses any explanations that do not fit into his revised understanding of the conception of *Le Chiendent*. This action is reminiscent of Queneau's early theories on textual structures. While Queneau believed "qu'une œuvre littéraire devait avoir une structure et une forme [...]" (*Entretiens avec Georges Charbonnier* 47), the reader should not perceive the structure: "À ce moment-là je pensais qu'en effet c'était comme [...] des échafaudages qu'on enlève, c'est exactement ça, qu'on enlève une fois que la construction est terminée" (49-50). Although necessary, a text's internal workings should not be noticed. As Derrida remarked, "un texte n'est un texte que s'il cache au premier regard, au premier venu, la loi de sa composition et la règle de son jeu" (*La Dissémination* 71). This understanding of structure, intertext, and allusion closely follows the Hegelian concept of *Aufhebung*, for Queneau is concurrently creating and destroying. We also find here an echo of the two sides of Queneau's personality — *le chêne et le chien* — which he describes in an early "roman en vers" of the same name, where one side wishes to preserve and the other cannot stop itself from obliterating (*Œuvres complètes I* 3-36).

Concluding the first full draft, Queneau writes: "C'est pourquoi faisant le même récit qu'il y a vingt ans, je ne ferais plus maintenant la même selection" (*Classeur 15bis* CDRQ), but this moment of subjective understanding is crossed out. In later versions Queneau speaks simply of a "*rectification*" of his previous account in *Bâtons, chiffres et lettres*, not a selection (*Voyage* 221). This distinction is important, for in the published text, Queneau appears to be positioning the article as the authoritative version; he wishes to "raffiner sur [s]on témoignage" (220), to tell us the truth. Yet in the first full draft he seems to understand more clearly the concept of the "fragilité du témoignage," which he finds in Christie's novel (219), and which appears as the starting point of his article. All versions of the genesis of *Le Chiendent* are a selection, as the various permutations of "Errata" have shown. To borrow a well-known phrase from Julia Kristeva, "tout texte se construit comme mosaïque de citations" (85); the notion of a singular, absolute version, where 1 = 1, is untenable.

Given these various explanations and rectifications, an answer to the question, "What was Queneau's inspiration for *Le Chiendent*?" will be at best provisional and limited. But perhaps, to quote Christie's

Poirot, "we are in the peculiar position of *not knowing what questions to ask*" (49). Stepping back and examining his use of and relationship with intertexts more generally, however, we might be able to draw some conclusions about Queneau's works. In "Errata" Queneau seems to be attempting to posit himself as the authority on the matter. One should keep in mind the etymology of author, or *auctor* in Latin, which originally has several distinct, yet related meanings. Both a writer *and* an authority, the *auctor* is someone who can correctly comprehend, assess, and disseminate information about a given situation. Yet the intertextual, polyphonic, and circular structures that recur throughout Queneau's works indicate that the author has a much larger role.

In *Le Plagiat par anticipation,* Pierre Bayard writes:

> Un grand écrivain ne se contente pas d'interférer avec tel ou tel de ses prédécesseurs qui se révèle alors avoir influé sur lui. Il modifie aussi après coup, en les perturbant par sa logique singulière, l'ensemble des lignes de force de l'histoire littéraire antérieure [...] comme devant irrésistiblement conduire à sa présence. (66)

This possibility is amplified when one examines Queneau's later work and relationship with the OuLiPo. Jacques Roubaud observes: "l'oulipo est un roman; c'est un roman *non écrit* de Queneau. C'est un roman selon le pôle quenellien de l'oulipo, à contraintes invisibles" (Contat 83). An entire literary movement, with its members, works, and perspectives, is but part of a vast novel that is ever expanding, even past the "author's" death.

However, as numerous members of the OuLiPo themselves have asked, are "potential" works possible? As several members argued, Queneau's *Cent mille milliards de poèmes*, which is frequently cited as a prime example of an oulipian text, is *not* a work of potential literature because the author anticipated every possibility. Answering the query as to what constitutes a "potential work," François le Lionnais opined that to constitute a potential work, the author must include something that allows the reader to explore (Bens 109-10). What all of these observations highlight in the context of a work, regardless of the final answer, is the importance of the *author*.

Hertich *213*

Hercule Poirot, echoing Descartes, notes: "[...] I never permit myself to get false impressions from anything anyone tells me. I form my own judgments" (Christie 208-09). Intertext, in whatever form it may appear in a work — reproduction, replication, borrowing, allusion, quotation or outright theft — while recalling other works, is a method for an author to inscribe himself in the text. There is an unavoidable fusion of producer and product. While Queneau's ever-mutating versions may make absolute answers difficult — there can be no shocking revelation that "the real murderer is X" — they do reveal the depth of Queneau's work as well as the ambiguity and subjectivity that lie at the center of any analysis. Just as it seems that the author cannot be completely removed from his work, so Queneau's texts cannot be separated from their inspirations. They are both dependent and independent. In this paradigm, questions of adaptation and appropriation do not have a beginning and an end. As Jean-Luc Hennig proclaims in *Apologie du plagiat*: "copier [...] c'est être les livres qu'on copie" (71).

Works Cited

Bayard, Pierre. *Le Plagiat par anticipation.* Paris: Minuit, 2009.

Bens, Jacques. *OuLiPo 1960-1963.* Paris: Christian Bourgeois, 1980.

Blavier, André. *Lettres croisées 1949-1976.* Bruxelles: Labor, 1988.

Catonné, Jean-Marie. *Queneau.* Paris: Pierre Belfond, 1992.

Christie, Agatha. *The A.B.C. Murders.* New York: Dodd, Mead & Co., 1936.

Contat, Michel, ed. "Jacques Roubaud, l'auteur oulipien." *L'Auteur et le manuscrit.* Paris: PUF, 1991.

Debon, Claude. *Doukiplèdonktan? Études sur Raymond Queneau.* Paris: Presses de la Sorbonne nouvelle, 1998.

Derrida, Jacques. *La Dissémination.* Paris: Seuil, 1972.

Hennig, Jean-Luc. *Apologie du plagiat.* L'infini. Paris: Gallimard, 1997.

Hertich, Alexander. "Philosophes et / ou voyous: The Case of Queneau and Descartes." *Dalhousie French Studies* 79 (Summer 2007): 71-81.

Kristeva, Julia. *Séméiôtiké. Recherches pour une sémanalyse.* Points. Paris: Seuil 1969.

Queneau, Raymond. *Bâtons, chiffres et lettres.* Folio essais. Paris: Gallimard, 1965.

_____. Drafts and notes for "Errata." *Classeur 15bis*. Centre de Documentation Raymond Queneau. Verviers, Belgium.

_____. *Entretiens avec Georges Charbonnier*. Paris: Gallimard, 1962.

_____. *Œuvres complètes I*. Ed. Claude Debon. Pléiade. Paris: Gallimard 1989.

_____. *Œuvres complètes II*. Ed. Henri Godard. Pléiade. Paris: Gallimard, 2002.

_____. *Le Voyage en Grèce*. Paris: Gallimard, 1973.

Queval, Jean. "De quelques aspects peu connus du génie de Jean Queval." *Amis de Valentin Brû* 18 (December 1980): 58-63.

Robbe-Grillet, Alain. *Le Miroir qui revient*. Paris: Minuit, 1984.

Peter Sorrell

Rutgers University

"Cette nouvelle réalité": at the *Mouviez* with Raymond Queneau

> This article examines Raymond Queneau's treatment of the American actress, Alice Faye, in the novel, *Les Temps mêlés* (1941), as well as in the autobiographical text, "Alice Faye au Marigny" (1939). By comparing these textual representations in a scene from the Faye film, *On the Avenue* (1937), it emerges that the cinema represents a highly significant part of the pluralistic, transitional fictional worlds of Queneau, one which is related to the role of Queneau's reader.

In a recent article, Christopher Shorely claimed that Raymond Queneau's representations of social life remain convincing even at their most fantastic because, rather than presenting a complete portrait of a fictional world, they evoke the incomplete lived worlds of fictional characters (30). One of Queneau's most spectacular tools in bringing these fragmentary fictional worlds to life is the cinema. "The movie house is more than a new novelistic place, much more than a decor. It is a privileged, fundamental scene for the Quenellian novel," writes Jean-Pierre Martin ("Spectacle" 267). What makes Queneau's engagement with the movies so unique is the mix of the High and the Low, the intermingling of Culture with burgeoning popular culture (which was not always equally appreciated by other authors of Queneau's generation — nor ours, for that matter). In this way, disparate worldbuilding elements such as Gnosticism, Hegel, and actress Alice Faye are transmuted by the author into a layered narrative structure marked by a constant proliferation of worlds. The wide scope of these worlds gives, in the words of Martin, a lower-case "l" back to "Literature" ("Roman" 291-300). Moreover, Queneau was born eight years and one week to the day (February 21, 1903) after the Lumière brothers patented the *cinématographe* (February 13, 1895). What better place, then, to examine the elaboration of the unique fictional worlds associated with the author's novels than at the fictional movie theater, where they are already springing into life on the fictional space of a fictional movie screen?

Two novels in particular foreground the role of what Queneau's characters often refer to as the "mouviez": *Loin de Rueil* (published in 1944) and *Les Temps mêlés* (published in 1941). In *Saint Glinglin* (published in 1948), Queneau reworked parts of both *Les Temps mêlés* and his second novel, *Gueule de Pierre* (1934). I am, of course, glossing over Queneau's participation on film juries, his work on screenplays (such as Alain Resnais's *Le Chant du styrène*), and his occasional turn as an actor (for example, as Clemenceau (!) in Claude Chabrol's 1963 film *Landru*), all of which are admirably described in Michel Lecureur's 2002 biography, *Raymond Queneau*. In this essay, I will focus on *Les Temps mêlés* (before its incorporation into *Saint Glinglin*, although I will make reference to this other work), in which Paul Kougard, smitten with the movie star, Cécile Haye, draws her out of the big screen and into his small town, the appropriately named "Ville Natale." In this way, the cinema mediates the character's interactions with multiple metadiegetic fictional worlds. I will argue that spectatorship as presented in *Les Temps mêlés* informs the broader ontological shifts in character and reader characteristic of Queneau's work, shifts involving an ongoing cycle of appearance and disappearance (Lecompte 59-74; Longre, "Métamorphoses" 121-125; Longre, *Scènes*; Martin, "Passant" 137-149; Sorrell, "Découvertes"; Sorrell, "Becoming"; Velguth 107-120). Paul's experience at the movies reveals the intentional fault lines of Queneau's fictional worlds, which are constantly shifting under character and reader.

I will also take into consideration an earlier autobiographical text, "Alice Faye au Marigny" (1939), written two years before the publication of *Les Temps mêlés*, in which Queneau longs for the American actress Alice Faye herself, celebrated for her sultry yet no-nonsense roles in 20th Century Fox musical comedies from 1934-1945. This unpublished text seems to have been the genesis for the plotline of Paul's

Sorrell 217

relationship with the shapely blonde actress in the novel. We can gain a more nuanced understanding of Queneau's particular brand of "fictioning" by taking a closer look at this text, available in an appendix of the Pléiade edition of the novel, in which the author, hungover, confesses his love for Faye (and women's undergarments!).

In both *Les Temps mêlés* and "Alice Faye au Marigny," the intentional structures of the moviewatching experience that have been remarked upon by, among others, Christian Metz, Edgar Morin, and Vivian Sobchak, come to the fore (Metz 31, 54, 56, 62-63, 65, 68-69, 72, 86, 88-89; Morin, *Homme* 80, 101; Morin, *Stars* 33, 87; Sobchak 9, 15, 134). The shared interaction between spectator and screen attains a greater importance than either spectator or screen on their own. Both fictional character Paul and real-world author Queneau forcibly manipulate their interaction with the movies by refusing to sit still. Here, Queneau finds a public restroom in which to masturbate, and Paul always insists on leaving before the end of the movie. In each case, the spectator acts in such a way as to link the fictional worlds of cinema more closely to the real world. In this way, the passive perception of the seated spectator has become an act of expression even before he leaves the theater. The spectator's activity belies the monolithic power supposedly exercised by the projected film. By becoming part of another world, character-spectator, author, and reader engage in what Morin calls "projection-identification," making themselves fictional while ensuring that the resulting fictions still bear the stamp of the real (Morin, *Homme* 93). Thus does the power of affect reach beyond the silver screen on many levels.

Examining one of the Alice Faye films that figure in these texts sheds some light on Queneau's depictions of what Shorley calls the "mobile and contingent nature of experience" (30). The musical number, "Let's Go Slumming," from Roy Del Ruth's 1937 film *On the Avenue*, corresponds to a similar scene breathlessly described by Paul in *Les Temps mêlés* and by Queneau himself — who claimed to have seen the movie six times — in "Alice Faye au Marigny." If we take into account the various versions of the movie star character's name in the unpublished drafts of *Les Temps mêlés* — according to the archives, Queneau hesitated among the names "Cécile Haye," "Alice Haye," and even "Alice Faye" — I think that we may speak about the character Cécile Haye and the actress Alice Faye in the same breath.

In *Saint Glinglin*, published seven years later, "Cécile Haye" has become "Alice Phaye," the different spelling of which — the "ph" instead of an "f" — has prompted rather wild speculation among critics (David 121-36; Pestureau, "Amours" 34; Queneau, CDRQ folder 113H; Queneau, *Glinglin* 137). I am not as concerned, though, with seeking out the real world referents of Queneau's fiction as I am with juxtaposing the novel, the autobiographical text, and the film in order to demonstrate the slippery nature of Queneau's rapidly multiplying fictional worlds, worlds whose structure is predicated upon an ever-present state of transition. I hope to establish that Queneau's literary experimentation goes far beyond the humor and language games for which he is best known.

Following Jean-Pierre Longre's work on Queneau and theater, in which he proposes the existence of an active "reader-spectator," I contend that Queneau's writing about the cinema highlights the shared structures of the aesthetic experience (*Scènes* 184). Through participation, the reader moves beyond the text, just as the spectator interacts with the worlds onscreen. Text and screen reach back by requiring this interaction, as in Lacan's well-known diagram of the interconnected triangles of the gaze.

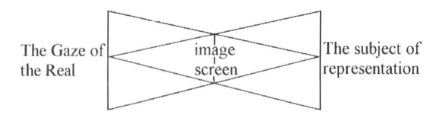

Lacan's diagram illustrates how the gaze determines the subject from the exterior as well as the interior, demonstrating, in our case, the underlying intentional, back-and-forth nature of the movie-watching situation (121). Presence (image) and absence (referent) meet onscreen, a logical endpoint for the Quenellian character caught up in a ceaseless process of (be)coming and going. It is important to recall that Queneau's character-spectator sees the fictional world onscreen in a different way from the reader, who makes a leap of faith from words

Sorrell 219

to fictional screen by means of what Pierre Bayard has called "intermediate worlds" (104-07). The multiple nature of Queneau's fictional worlds places particular emphasis on this aspect of fictional lived worlds, while the reader can only conjecture about their content. Yet, as we will see, when fictional boundaries are fictionally crossed, fictional worlds pay the consequences, as does the reader, who is their co-creator.

In *Loin de Rueil*, the character Des Cigales succinctly sums up this game of shifting subjectivities when he states:

> When I see a film like the one we just saw, I transport myself onscreen by a somewhat magical and in any case transcendental act, and I discover myself regaining consciousness of myself as one of the heroes of the story told to us by means of flat but moving images. (Queneau, *Rueil* 41)

For Des Cigales, becoming is a "magical" act that is democratic at the same time, available to any spectator ("transcendental"). At the movies, Queneau's fictional character-spectators and real readers awake to virtual realities (or fictions) across a reversible intentional field that, by transcending the materiality of the screen or the text, redefines the ontological status of character and reader.

In the novel, *Les Temps mêlés*, Paul is drawn in by the "radical distraction" provided by movies. Since Paul is particularly enamored of women onscreen — "Les Femmes," with a capital "F" — the movies form the abstract context for his future real relationship with the movie star (Queneau, *Temps* 1026). Paul, like his namesake, has seen the light, directly comparing actresses and "Stars, like them, incredibly distant, like them, shown by a ray of light..." (1026). Demonstrating the necessity of obstacles in the creation of desire, Paul shuns the movies offered in his own language offered by the "Natal Palace" theater (1024), instead preferring the foreign-language offerings of the "Twentieth Century" (1026; *On the Avenue* was a Twentieth Century-Fox Film Corporation production.) Queneau's studies of Gnostic thought under Henri Puech at the École Pratique des Hautes Études from 1933-39 have been well documented, and Paul's lament about the base nature of earthly life in the country and the perfection of the artifice found in the city certainly strike a certain Gnostic chord

(Puech). Treating going to these seemingly exotic movies like receiving the sacrament, Paul believes that the power of his affect reaches the star beyond the screen. He seizes the hybrid being of the movie star, who is half real (actress) and half fictional (character), and brings her down to earth:

> That the star did not know me, did that stop my thought from reaching her? How can you suppose that the force of a feeling does not attain its goal, no matter where it is? And didn't the ideal rapport that I was creating have as much force and value as any rapport established by the spirit between two things separated in space? The violence of imagination established a link between us that she could not escape [...]. (1030)

Paul's imagination, driven by desire, crosses impossible boundaries in order to create a link with the actress, whose professional identity depends on a similar elasticity. The restrictions of the viewing experience only serve to intensify imaginary interaction: in Paul's words, "distance" becomes a "link." Paul's participation in the movies is just as "radical" as the distraction that they provide; his link with Cécile is so strong that, according to him: "Among all the attributes whose interferences composed her personality, you had to count — and among the most important ones, even if unknown by her — my love" (1030). Haye's sudden appearance in Paul's world shows us that he is not just "projecting," as we might say in our day and age; in his own words, he is "broken by the blows that this new reality had just dealt me" (1027). The dimensions of this "new reality" will spread even further when Cécile Haye comes to town in the flesh.

In the autobiographical text, "Alice Faye au Marigny," Queneau, writing in the first person, also argues vehemently for the reciprocal links between subject and object of aesthetic experience:

> And what does my love for Alice Faye have to do with all the ideas of these men on the reality of the imagination and all the rest. My love is real, and I am real as well, and she is also real. And the homage that I pay to her is also real. [...]. The links that I have created between us, separated as we are by the curving kilometers which lie between Paris and the coast of the Pacific Ocean, these links hold up [*tiennent*]. They are braided with threads of gold, a gold that is not worth the realities of this world. And if over there this woman does not know me — no I have not written to her asking for a

Sorrell 221

> signed photograph — however there must still be something in her life like a caress that comes from me. Thoughts do not go long without echoes and love always attains its goal. ("Alice" 1426)

According to Jean-Philippe Coen (*Œuvres* 1745), this reference to "all the ideas of these men on the reality of the imagination and all the rest" concerns Sartre's 1936 text, *L'Imagination*, read by Queneau in 1937, in which the author underlines the duality of the image, endowed with both psychic and seemingly external reality: (Sartre, *Imagination* 5, 138). In *L'Imaginaire*, Sartre further explores the ways in which the work of art uses the supports of reality — in this case, language — in order objectively to signify a subjective world (Sartre, *Imaginaire* 105, 128, 357). This poetic passage, written under the sign of intentionality, demonstrates the intermingling of consciousnesses across unbounded fictional worlds that gain more concrete form in the novel *Les Temps mêlés*. Once again, the reference to the "gold that is not worth the realities of this world" reveals the profoundly Gnostic nature of Paul's thought, something that will have a direct effect on his own cycle of appearance and disappearance.

And what of the film, *On the Avenue*, so reminiscent of a certain era of moviegoing still characterized by the Great Depression and escapist fantasy? In *Les Temps mêlés*, Paul describes the plot of the film, in which Faye's character, Mona Merrick, a Broadway star, repairs the breech between her love interest, her director and co-star, Gary (played by Dick Powell), and a millionairess, Mimi Caraway (played by Madeleine Carroll). Yet Paul, disgusted at the end of the film, in which Faye loses the battle for Gary's affections, always leaves before the final scene, declaring, "These are things that I take seriously," and he certainly does, going to see the movie every night for a week (and leaving each night before the ending) (1028). What Paul takes even more seriously is how Haye's tight-fitting leather skirt barely restrains her "slowly quivering firm and vibrant hemisphere," thus allowing him better view of her legs (1028). Captivated, Paul sighs, "I would have kept going to see this film forever" (1028). In "Alice Faye au Marigny," Queneau also admits that the principal attraction of this outfit is the glimpse it affords of the actress's legs (1426). Infatuated with the actress, Queneau himself even admits to buying cinema magazines (1425)!

The cinematic counterpart of the scene described in *Les Temps mêlés* and "Alice Faye au Marigny" is easily recognizable. In *On the Avenue*, Alice Faye, dancing in a tight black leather skirt and high heels (ostensibly a prostitute), sings the song, "Let's Go Slumming." Of course, the lyrics — "Let's go slumming... on Park Avenue" — are ironic, pointing up the benefits of reverse-slumming among the rich for the "masses." Furthermore, the whole number is cause for mockery because Mimi, angry at Gary's lampooning of her wealthy family, has hired three comics (the Ritz brothers) to sabotage the production. Thus questions of boundary-crossing and spectatorship are already present within the film. What is astonishing is the sheer amount of erotic energy with which Queneau as real spectator and Paul as fictional spectator invest Faye's performance. One might assume that the libidinal flow of such energy would be diverted by the subsequent appearance of the large, hairy man mimicking Mona's song and dance, but there is no mention of the following act in either of Queneau's texts. Perhaps the fact that Queneau was thirty-four years old when he saw the movie — and Faye a mere twenty-two — has something to do with this oversight! In any case, Laura Mulvey's well-known association of the gaze of the camera with an objectifying and dissecting male gaze is worth mentioning here. However, we must keep in mind, even if we have a chance to view the clip, ("Slumming") that Queneau's spectator is fictional, as is the gaze of the fictional camera, even if it seems to correspond fairly well with *On the Avenue*. By thus doubling the distance between fictional spectator and fictional film and by then allowing for interaction on the part of the reader, Queneau multiplies possible subject positions that would be restricted by the steady gaze of the camera in the real world. There is no real world in Queneau's fiction, only a plurality of ever-changing worlds, and reading too much into Queneau's depiction of women takes away from the far more significant dynamic of appearance and disappearance that seems to govern these worlds.

The kind of parodic boundary-crossing epitomized by the Ritz Brothers' parody of Faye's song and dance was even more evident during an earlier number that involved a man infatuated with a model he has seen on the cover of a tabloid, *The Police Gazette* (1845-1982!). The process by which this man seeks out the model and asks her for a picture in which she is wearing stockings takes on radical ontological implications in Queneau's fictional world when the spectator Paul miraculously meets movie star Cécile Haye the day after attentively examining her image on a movie poster and dreaming about stockings. Tellingly enough, the *Police Gazette* model is insulted by the demand, whereas Cécile Haye is already quite in love with Paul.

Moreover, as Marie-Claude Cherqui has remarked, the author's portrayal of Alice Faye as a sex symbol is in itself provocative ("Corps"; "*Limelight*" 241-46; "Intertextualité"; "Images" 31-55; "Mort" 109-26; "Scénariste"; *Mouviez*; "Curnough" 57-85; *Écrivain*). Cherqui also discusses "Alice Faye au Marigny," in this case, the eroticized portrayal of a rather tame scene from Sidney Lanfield's 1935 musical comedy, *The King of Burlesque*. In this scene, Faye, dressed as a burlesque dancer, walks about listlessly in nothing like the manner we just witnessed. Yet this performance gives the author occasion to "render homage" to the actress — i.e. to masturbate (1427). Faye's biographer points out that Faye, like Betty Grable, even when she was supposed to portray a vamp, often played the good girl, eschewing the "exoticism" of a Hedy Lamar or the "mystery" of a Greta Garbo (Elder 141) and yet still capable of their own brand of innocent sauciness. Elder explains:

> A nation stumbling out of a worldwide depression and standing on the brink of a world war responded to these 'bland' actresses, who seemed to epitomize hard work and fair play, yet retained a sexy, lighthearted appeal. Americans took them to their hearts, named their babies after them, and made them the box office successes they were. (141-42)

And, judging from the sentiments expressed by a former serviceman in an obituary at the time of Faye's death — he reminisced about wondering "if Alice would ever know how I felt about her" — this was how she was perceived by her public as well (Elder 5). None of this is to say that Queneau's fictional treatment of the star was "wrong" — spectator and reader response are highly idiosyncratic events — after all, like the fictional character Paul, the serviceman had pondered the possibility of an intentional link between subject and object of aesthetic experience. And, as Gilbert Pestureau has pointed out, "the imagination of a cosmopolitan Frenchman" transmogrified the American actress into an object of decidedly French literature ("Star"). Rather, putting the novel, autobiographical text, and film into a dialogue highlights the intensely labile nature of Queneau's fictional worlds.

Movement between what Nina Bastin has called the smaller "subworlds" making up these larger fictional worlds involves a re-evaluation of the status of the image (106-11). In the autobiographical "Alice Faye au Marigny," Queneau discovers that a "stranger" has defaced a poster advertising one of Faye's films by scratching out the actress' crotch with his fingernail (1425). However, in *Les Temps mêlés*, this act takes on greater philosophical significance. Paul takes possession of the image on the movie poster by means of an act that straddles the figurative and the literal: "I peeled her image from the paper in order better to place it in myself. I gorged myself on it. I detached this beauty, which was already liberated from a real presence, in order to inoculate myself with it, to feed off of it, to be consumed by it" (1029). By altering a static representation, Paul opens the door to metaleptic movement among different types of worlds — and to possibilities beyond the figurative and the literal. In a modern twist on his Biblical namesake, Paul's conversion occurs in the light of a lamp that illuminates a poster for Cécile's next film, which resembles Alice Faye's *In Old Chicago*, about the Great Chicago fire of 1871. Queneau's Paul experiences a moment of transformation linked to light: the light from the lamp, the fire depicted on the poster, the light from the movie screen, the light from the stars. Paul undergoes a thoroughly modern equivalent of Paul's transfiguring moment, finally opting to leave this earthy text-world. In fact, Elaine Pagels calls into question the traditional "antignostic" interpretation of Paul's letters, raising the possibility that Paul the apostle was more influenced by Gnostic thought than previously assumed. Paul's thought may be imbued with religious and philosophical overtones, but the consequences of his actions are, in his fictional world, very real. Wondering which new movies of Cécile Haye will come to the Ville Natale and "live the life of phantoms in his soul," Paul declares, "Woman taken as an irreal image and model of realities thus leads to a living conception of so-called abstraction" (1033).

He has no idea how right he is. On the very next page of the novel, Cécile Haye makes her appearance in the Ville Natale (1034).

Sorrell 225

The two fall in love, and, like characters in a movie, spout the requisite banalities, which are here tinged with the same intentional undertones as Paul's earlier lament. Paul declares himself to be "just one of the great crowd of your imaginary lovers" driven mad by the actress's bathing suits (1065). Cécile confesses that she, too, felt a pull from beyond the screen: "when I slowly clothed myself in this delicate and fragile article of clothing, I thought of he who would one day tell me what you are telling me now" (1066). The intentional interaction enabled by the moviewatching experience has opened a door between two worlds. Paul's faith in images has been rewarded; as he tells Cécile: "I could believe only in this image, and now you are here, inexplicably" (1066). Both spectator and star have undergone this transition, as Cécile informs Paul, "You neither, you are no longer an image, an anonymous image of my worshippers, you are real and present, you are there, I love you" (1066). Soon after this veritable transubstantiation, Paul and Cécile, spectator and star no longer, disappear from the plot of the novel! Paul's final declaration — and the last line of the novel — hails from the domain of fairy tales: "I love you. And we will have a lot of children" (1091).

In *Saint Glinglin*, this becomes "shitloads of kids," demonstrating even further the fall from grace of the once unattainable — or sublime, to put it in Lacanian-Zizekian terms — object of desire (265). "The sublime object is an object which cannot be approached too closely: if we get too near it, it loses its sublime features and becomes a vulgar ordinary object" writes Zizek (17). In fact, this return to banality is even clearer in Queneau's preparatory notes for *Saint Glinglin*, where Alice takes up her movie career again before it turns to an "Exhibition de striptease," with Alice becoming Hélène, Paul's sister. The double message is clear: Alice cannot stay in the *Ville Natale* without becoming one of the family and Alice cannot stay away from the cinema. And Paul understood all along what happens once ethereal beauty made itself available in reality. At the end of his lament about Alice Faye and underwear, he admits, "I need beauty — not carnal beauty, which is related to animal instincts — but beauty conceived of as a statue" (1033). No longer able to pine for the abstraction of Haye as star, the logic of the text dictates that the two characters must disappear. Of course, in the earlier novel, *Gueule de Pierre*, Pierre, Paul's older brother, chased their father into the "Petrifying Source," which turned him into a statue, so the metaphor is not at all innocent. As a solitary spectator, Paul is content to muse about images and abstractions, but he is also more than happy to accept Haye as a concrete part of his world when she does come to town.

In a trajectory that readers of Queneau's other novels will recognize, Paul and Cécile gain being only to lose it — they (be) come only to go. In an interesting real world parallel, Faye herself turned her back on a thriving movie career only eight years after *On the Avenue* was released, effectively disappearing from the world of cinema at the very height of her popularity as a star! In 1947, Queneau wrote an unpublished play about Greta Garbo — yet another actress who renounced the silver screen at the height of her fame — appearing in the flesh to a lovelorn fan (*L'Ombre de Greta Garbo*). In this play, Jérôme, cuckolded by his wife, dreams of achieving stardom alongside the famous actress. He writes a screenplay, which he will direct, produce, and star in with Garbo: "Your love on the screen as in life will be me," he tells Garbo (Queneau, CDRQ, folder 94 bis), just as Paul declares to Haye in *Les Temps mêlés*, "I am one of the common class, one of the numerous crowd of your imaginary lovers" (1065). Jérôme, like Paul, collapses the distinction between the world off-screen and the world on-screen in order to fill a lack in his own life. Garbo, like Haye, is caught between two realms and at the disposition "unknown people reduced to spiritual begging" (Longre, "Théâtralité" 502). Such is the lot not only of the starlet but also of these fictional characters who beg and plead their way out of the plots in which they are trapped (Longre, *Scènes* 74). At the end of this brief unfinished play, Jérôme remains stuck in his world and Garbo in hers; boundary-crossings are not as fruitful as they are in *Les Temps mêlés*. Thus for Longre, Queneau's theater — as opposed to Queneau's movie theater — is a place of unfulfilled aspirations marked by "the theater of dream that slips into the novelistic fabric itself" (Longre, "Rêves" 223). Queneau may dream of the theater, in his journals and several plays, but it is his novelistic world itself that is theatrical: a theater of dreams in which his characters live through dream and spectacle, in particular the cinema.

The double movement across the barrier of the movie screen in *Les Temps mêlés* demonstrates the power of boundary-crossing in Queneau's fictional worlds as a quasi-religious process of transub-

Sorrell 227

stantiation. As we have intimated, though, such acts do carry consequences. Obviously, in the autobiographical text, "Alice Faye au Marigny," Queneau does not witness any such concrete acts of ontological boundary-crossing. The text does end, though, on what the author labels a "voyeuristic" note. In an act reminiscent of the "philosophers" at the amusement park in his 1942 novel *Pierrot mon ami*, who ogle unsuspecting women from below, here, Queneau and a group of men watch a young "babe" with blonde hair, balancing on a seesaw, and showing off her thighs and garters in the process. The author who presents himself as nothing more than a simple spectator allows his characters much freer access among worlds.

Nowhere is the unique status of Queneau's plethora of vacillating peripheral fictional worlds more vividly in evidence than when characters go to the movies. The rapidly moving and, for Queneau, nascent world of cinema differentiates these engagements from other literary representations of cinema or painting. In the works of authors of a slightly later generation, such as Claude Simon (1913-2005) or Alain Robbe-Grillet (1922-2008), such representations often call into question the notion of representation in an either/or fashion that proves antithetical to the labile interaction of Queneau's characters with the movies, where the goal is not to question the worldbuilding capabilities of fiction but rather to enhance them to an almost impossible degree.

The cinema, like dreaming, sustains a pleasure on the borders of everyday life, what Metz refers to as a "'hole' in the social fabric, a gap which opens on something that is a little bit crazy, a little less approved than what one does the rest of the time" (91). Because they are deeply ingrained in the experience of everyday imaginary life, Queneau's movies open onto other worlds in a way that often encapsulates the experience of the reader of his novels.

Works Cited

"Alice Faye — Slumming on Park Avenue." YouTube. 19 April 2009. <http://www.youtube.com/watch?v=4P1G9N4vOsc&feature=PlayList& p=222EEDEDE4F81837&playnext=1&index=2>.

Bastin, Nina. *Queneau's Fictional Worlds*. New York: Peter Lang, 2002.

Bayard, Pierre. *Who Killed Roger Ackroyd? The Mystery Behind the Agatha Christie Mystery*. Trans. Carol Cosman. 1998. New York: The New Press, 2000.

Cherqui, Marie-Claude. "Avec le temps... ou Les Récifs de la rigolade: À propos de *Limelight* de Charlie Chaplin." *Les Temps Mêlés* 150.65-68 (1996): 231-46.

_____. "Dans le noir et en lumière: le corps au cinéma." *Raymond Queneau et le corps*. Éditions Calliopées, forthcoming 2009/10.

_____. "Images de Queneau II: nouvel essai de filmographie." *Amis de Valentin Brû* (1994): 31-55.

_____. "La Mort en ce Jardin: *l'ivrogne dans la jungle*." *Amis de Valentin Brû* 40-41-42 (2005): 109-26.

_____. "Du problème de l'intertextualité dans l'œuvre scénariste de Raymond Queneau et du problème de l'adaptation d'une œuvre littéraire en particulier." Mémoire de DEA. Université de Paris III, 1992.

_____. "Queneau scénariste." MA thesis. Université de Paris III, 1990.

_____, ed. *Queneau's Mouviez, Amis de Valentin Brû* 43-44 (2006).

_____. "La *Ramon Curnough Company* présente une séance au Rueil Palace." *Amis de Valentin Brû* 48-49 (2007): 57-85.

_____. *Raymond Queneau, écrivain de cinema*. Diss. Université de Paris III, 2009.

David, Pierre. "Encycloquenie: amour de cinéma (Mémoire de défayances)." *Raymond Queneau encyclopédiste?* Paris: Éditions du Limon, 1990. 121-36.

Elder, Jane Lenz. *Alice Faye: A Life Beyond the Silver Screen*. Jackson: University of Mississippi Press, 2002.

Lacan, Jacques. *Le Séminaire, Livre XI: Les Quatre Concepts fondamentaux de la psychanalyse*. Paris: Seuil, 1973.

Lecompte, Nelly. "La notion d'irréalité des personnages chez Queneau: le personnage comme illusion passagère qui dure l'espace d'un roman." *Le Personnage dans l'œuvre de Raymond Queneau*. Éd. Daniel Delbreil. Paris: Presses de la Sorbonne Nouvelle, 2000. 59-74.

Lecureur, Michel. *Raymond Queneau*. Paris: Les Belles Lettres/Archimbaud, 2002.

Longre, Jean-Pierre. "Métamorphoses et effacements (le personnage théâtral)." *Le Personnage dans l'œuvre de Raymond Queneau*. Éd. Daniel Delbreil. Paris: Presses de la Sorbonne Nouvelle, 2000. 121-35.

———. *Raymond Queneau en scènes*. Limoges: PULIM, 2005.

———. "Rêves de théâtre, théâtre de rêve." *Raymond Queneau et les spectacles*. Éd. Daniel Delbreil. *AVB* 28-31/*Formules* 8 (2003-04). 220-226.

———. "Théâtre et théâtralité dans l'œuvre de Raymond Queneau." Diss. Université de Paris III, 1998.

Martin, Jean-Pierre. "Le petit pas du passant qui passe." *Le Personnage dans l'œuvre de Raymond Queneau*. Éd. Daniel Delbreil. Paris: Presses de la Sorbonne Nouvelle, 2000. 137-49.

———. "Le roman à voix basse." *Poétique* 24 (1994): 291-300.

———. "Le spectacle est dans la salle." *Raymond Queneau et les spectacles*. Éd. Daniel Delbreil. *AVB* 28-31/*Formules* 8 (2003-04). 263-69.

Metz, Christian. *Le signifiant imaginaire: psychanalyse et cinema*. 1975. Paris: Christian Bourgois, 2002.

Morin, Edgar. *L'Homme imaginaire*. Paris: Minuit, 1956.

———. *Les Stars*. Paris: Seuil, 1972.

Mulvey, Laura. "Visual Pleasure and Narrative Cinema." *Screen* 16.3 (1975): 6-18.

Pagels, Elaine. *The Gnostic Paul: Gnostic Exegesis of the Pauline Letters*. 1975. Harrisburg: Trinity Press International, 1992.

Pestureau, Gilbert. "Les amours cinémagiques de Queneau." *Les Amis de Valentin Brû* 8 (1997): 27-39.

———. "La star chez Raymond Queneau." *Le Personnage dans l'œuvre de Raymond Queneau*. Éd. Daniel Delbreil. Paris: Presses de la Sorbonne Nouvelle, 2000. 255-68.

Puech, Henri-Charles. *En quête de la Gnose I: La Gnose et le temps et autres essais*. Paris: Gallimard, 1978.

Queneau, Raymond. "Alice Faye au Marigny." In *Œuvres complètes II. Romans I*. Éd. Henri Godard.

———. Centre de Documentation Raymond Queneau (CDRQ). Verviers, Belgium. Folders 94 bis and 113H.

———. *Loin de Rueil*. Paris: Gallimard, 1941.

———. *Saint Glinglin*. Paris: Gallimard, 1948.

———. *Les Temps mêlés*. In *Œuvres complètes II. Romans I*. Éd. Henri Godard. 1941. Paris: Bibliothèque de la Pléiade, 2002.

Sartre, Jean-Paul. *L'Imagination*. Paris: PUF, 1936.

_____. *L'Imaginaire*. Paris: Gallimard, 1940.

Shorley, Christopher. "Le Chiendent (1933)." *Australian Journal of French Studies* 40.1-2 (2003): 20-39.

Sobchak, Vivian. *The Address of the Eye: a Phenomenology of the Film Experience*. Princeton: Princeton University Press, 1992.

Sorrell, Peter. "(Be) Coming and Going in Raymond Queneau's *Le Chiendent*"/"Va-et-(de)vient dans *Le Chiendent* de Raymond Queneau" (author's translation). *Transgressions Sémiotiques* (Presses Universitaires de Rennes, forthcoming 2009/10).

_____. "De Découvertes en découvertes: le corps chez Queneau." *Raymond Queneau et le corps*. Éditions Calliopées, forthcoming 2009/10.

Velguth, Madeleine. "Quelques personnages opaques de Raymond Queneau." *Le Personnage dans l'œuvre de Raymond Queneau*. Éd. Daniel Delbreil. Paris: Presses de la Sorbonne Nouvelle, 2000. 107-20.

Zizek, Slavoj. *The Sublime Object of Ideology*. New York: Verso, 1989.

Printed in the United States
By Bookmasters